Kings Way Christian H.S.
3606 NE 78th St.
Vancouver, WA 98665

STEPHEN
A Soldier of the Cross

by

Florence Morse Kingsley

Author of
Titus: A Comrade of the Cross

John 8:31

Lamplighter Publishing
Waverly, PA 18471
1-888-246-7735

Stephen: A Soldier of the Cross.

Copyright © 2001 by Mark Hamby
All rights reserved.
First Printing, August, 2001; Second Printing, October 2002; Third Printing, December 2003.

Published by Lamplighter Publishing; a division of Cornerstone Family Ministries, Inc.

No part of this edited publication may be reproduced, stored in a retrieval system, or transmitted in any form or by any means — electronic, mechanical, photocopy, recording, or otherwise — without prior permission of the copyright owner.

The Lamplighter Rare Collector's Series is a series of family Christian literature from the 17th, 18th, 19th, & 20th centuries. Each edition is printed in an attractive hard-bound collector's format. For more information, write: Lamplighter Publishing, P.O. Box 777, Waverly, PA 18471 or call 1-888-A-GOSPEL.

Author: F.M. Kingsley
Original Printing: 1896

Printed by Jostens in the United States of America
Permalin, gold M842

ISBN 1-58474-032-9

Preface

There are those who have asked me to write this book. There may be others who shall question me because I have written it. "Assuredly," these will cry out, "it is justly forbidden to ascribe words and deeds of one's own devising to them which have been set forever apart in the pages of the Book of books. The pen of inspiration has written of Stephen all that God wills us to know of him, therefore let us be content."

It is true that the story of Stephen is little known; scarcely for a single day does the light shine clearly upon him, and that day the last of his mortal life. A tale is told of ancient alchemists, how that they possessed the power of resurrecting from the ashes of a perished flower a dim ghost of the flower itself. In like manner, may not one gather the fragrant dust of this vanished life from out of the writings and legends of past ages, and from it build anew some faint image of its forgotten beauty?

Surely in these days, when the imagination hurries to and fro on the earth, delving amid all that is low and evil and noisome for some new panacea wherewith to deaden, if only for a moment, the feverish pain in the hearts of men, it were a good thing to lift up the eyes of the soul to the contemplation of those days when the memory of the living Jesus was yet fresh in the hearts of His followers; when His voice still echoed in their ears; when the glory of the cloud which had received Him out of their sight lingered with transfiguring splendor on all the commonplace happenings of their daily lives; when the words, "Lo, I am with you alway, even unto the end," meant a living presence all comforting, all powerful.

We are wont to look longingly back through the dark mists of the ages and sigh, "Oh, that I had known Him as they knew Him! But in these hard, grey days there is no glory that shines, no voice that speaks, no ecstatic vision of the Son of Man standing at the right hand of power."

Yet had we lived in those days the life which many of us live to-day, going to church and to prayer because such attendance is a Christian duty; giving of our abundance to the poor because our neighbors will marvel if we withhold; and for the rest, living as those before the flood, and since also—eating and drinking, and making such poor merriment as we are able in a life which was given us for another purpose—had we lived thus in those far-off days, would the flames of Pentecost have descended upon us? Could the crucified One have said unto us, "Lo, I am with you alway, even unto the end?" Would we not rather have cried out in terror and fled away from the light of those sad eyes into darkness, even as did Peter after that he had denied with curses.

There is an Apostolic Church in the world to-day. To-day Christ is on earth and walks with men. To-day the Spirit works mightily as of old; the blind see, the deaf hear, and the dead are raised up. But it is not alone in splendid temple, nor amid the solemn pomp of churchly magnificence that these things are being accomplished, but in the humble upper rooms where the good soldiers of the Salvation Army, and the workers in Rescue Missions, labor unceasingly for them that are lost.

In these places, and in the silence of repentant hearts also, one may yet touch the borders of that seamless robe; and lo, every one that touches is made whole.

-Florence Kingsley

INTRODUCTION.

The long-awaited sequel to Titus is finally here! However, if you are anticipating a continuation of the same style, you will be surprised. Not only is there a dramatic shift in style, but the author has skillfully combined several stories into one, building tensions that bring no relief until the dramatic climax is reached. This is truly a literary masterpiece. A just-barely surviving blind girl and her beloved brother find themselves the target of slave traders as they hide in the deserts of Egypt. After hearing reports of healings in Jerusalem, they flee for their lives in hope of a miracle, and find themselves in the midst of the greatest life-changing event in history. But will it be too late for the blind girl? Can a brother's love overcome the ruthlessness of thieves and robbers? Readers will find themselves engulfed in another of Florence Kingsley's intense dramas as it unfolds at the foot of the cross. As it is written, and so shall it be, that *"greater love hath no man than this, than a man lay down his life for his friends." John 15:13*

-Mark Hamby

Note: There are several expressions in this book that appear to be referring to God. "By Jove" is one such expression.
However, upon careful examination and research, it was found that this and other expressions are not referring to Jehovah God, but the gods of the heathen nations.

~ CONTENTS. ~

		PAGE
Preface		3

CHAPTER

I.	THE BLIND SINGER	9
II.	GOOD TIDINGS OUT OF THE DESERT	17
III.	AT THE PALACE OF THE HIGH PRIEST	25
IV.	IN PLACE OF JUDAS	32
V.	IN THE ABODE OF KINGS	39
VI.	THE LORD OF THE SOUTH-LAND	48
VII.	THE PHARISEE FROM TARSUS	56
VIII.	A BELIEVER IN THE NAZARENE	67
IX.	IN THE DESERT ENCAMPMENT	76
X.	THE WHITE DROMEDARY	85
XI.	AT THE GATE BEAUTIFUL	97
XII.	IN THE COUNCIL CHAMBER	106
XIII.	AT THE FEET OF THE APOSTLES	116
XIV.	A CUP OF COLD WATER	128
XV.	IN PURSUIT OF FUGITIVES	139
XVI.	A ROLL OF PARCHMENT	150
XVII.	IN THE PRISON HOUSE	160
XVIII.	"WHOSE WE ARE AND WHOM WE SERVE"	169
XIX.	IN THE SHADOW OF THE WALL	181
XX.	WITHOUT THE JAFFA GATE	195
XXI.	"NOT A SPARROW FALLETH"	209
XXII.	BY THE THORNY WAYS OF HIS SIN	218
XXIII.	IN THE SYNAGOGUE OF THE NAZARENES	227
XXIV.	THE WARNING	234
XXV.	THE WRATH OF MAN	245
XXVI.	UNTIL THE DAY BREAK	257
XXVII.	IN THE VALLEY OF THE SHADOW	265
XXVIII.	THE LIFTED VEIL	276
XXIX.	THE WATCHFUL LOVE.	285
XXX.	A FLASK OF CRYSTAL	293
XXXI.	A SCARLET THREAD	301
XXXII.	BEN HESED IN JERUSALEM	311
XXXIII.	THE MERCY OF ISRAEL	320
XXXIV.	AT THE THIRD HOUR	331
XXXV.	ON THE ROAD TO DAMASCUS	343
XXXVI.	THE AMULET	358

CHAPTER I.

THE BLIND SINGER.

"OUNTEOUS Nile! Father of all Living! Garlanded with lotus blooms, rosy as Horus!" As these words rang out over the rocky hillside in a clear sweet voice, two men who were climbing the steep declivity paused a moment and looked at each other.

"That is the voice," said one of them in a tone of deep satisfaction. "A voice of gold truly, if only breathed forth into royal ears."

"There are two of them," said his companion, wiping his hot face. "The other is a boy, a water carrier."

"Good! He also will bring a fair price. Valuable property both, and going to waste like water spilled in the desert. Why buy slaves for gold, when they grow wild in the desert?" And the speaker laughed under his breath.

"Thou art a favorite of the gods," said the other with a venomous gleam in his narrow black eyes. "In thy heaven-bestowed wisdom forget not that it was I who came upon the two nesting in a corner of yonder old tomb like a pair of swallows."

"Thou shalt have the boy."

"And who gave thee leave to say, friend?"

"Canst thou sell them then? Is it of thee that the princess will buy slaves? Half the price of the two shall be thine; if that pleaseth thee not, why then—"

> "Look at me! I am thy sister that loveth thee,
> Do not stay far from me, heavenly one!
> Come to thine abode with haste, with haste
> I see thee no more. I see thee no more—"

trilled the unseen singer.

"Ha! The song is Isis! The little one is religious," continued the speaker, who had stopped in the midst of his bargaining. "Come! What sayest thou?" he added persuasively. "Half the price—and it will be a good one—no one can do better in such a matter than—"

"No one better than Besa," interrupted the other rudely. "Be it so; but lie to me about the price and thou shalt regret it:"

The two had reached the top of the hill by this time.

"Hist! Do not let her see thee."

"Nay, rather, do not let her hear thee; she is blind."

"Ay! Stone blind; but what matters is when she carries a singing bird in her throat. Do they not blind the nightingale?"

Both men now advanced cautiously, their sandaled feet making little sound on the shelf-like plateau upon which yawned several recesses cut deep into the solid rock. In the door of one of these recesses sat, or rather crouched, the figure of a young girl. Her blue-black hair, gathered away from her forehead and plaited in several thick braids, revealed a thin face, delicately featured, the smooth brown cheeks faintly flushed with a warmth, which in the drooping mouth deepened to scarlet. Her eyes were large and black, but curiously expressionless, like the eyes of the great god Ptah in the temple below. For the rest, she was dressed in the shapeless blue linen robe of an Egyptian peasant woman, about her neck hung a string of shining coins, and upon the slender ankles tinkled hoops of wrought silver.

At the sound of the stealthy feet upon the rock, the blind girl bent her head anxiously.

"Is it you, Seth?" she said doubtfully.

"Nay, little one," said one of the men, advancing boldly, "it is only a wayfarer who heard a goddess chanting to herself in a nook of the mountain. Didst thou also hear it?"

The girl shrank back into the narrow recess, upon whose rocky walls were pictured gaudily in the long-since-ended career of its former occupant. She made no reply.

"This dismal spirit-haunted tomb is no place for thee," continued the speaker in honeyed tones, "for it is thou and no other who hast the voice of Isis herself. Thou shouldst sing in the abode of princes, and be crowned with perfumed garlands, and all this shall shortly happen if thou wilt but come with me. Listen!" he added imperatively in the Greek tongue, addressing his companion. "I will take the girl with me, her pretty face adds to her value by half, the blindness is no matter. But do thou wait for the boy and bring him to the city, to the place whereof thou knowest. To-morrow they shall both be sold."

He was standing as he spoke perilously near the edge of the rocky declivity up which he had just clambered, his black snaky eyes fixed upon the maiden, his hand already extended to grasp her, when with the lithe swiftness of a tigress she sprang to her feet, and with a sudden powerful push of her strong young arms sent the unfortunate man flying backward over the verge. Then with a loud scream she turned, and, eluding the outstretched arms of the other, fled away and disappeared in some hidden nook among the tombs. The man who remained behind stared after her a moment in silence, then he broke into a short sneering laugh.

"By the seven great gods! It appears that a nightingale is not easy to cage. And what then has become of our bargaining Besa? By Anubis! I care not if he be dead."

Peering over the edge of the precipice he presently descried a motionless mass of dingy red drapery, lodged against the side of a great boulder, and thither, grumbling morosely to himself, he slowly and deliberately made his way.

In the meantime the young girl was cowering breathlessly in a narrow crevice of the rocks, she listened intensely, her hands upon her heart, as though she feared that its loud beating might betray her hiding-place. But after a few moments the silence reassured her and she began to weep and moan softly to herself.

"O Isis, tender-hearted one, what is it that hath befallen me? O God of the Sun in thy shining chariot! why dost thou not smite such wickedness? What then if I have killed him. Nay, I care not! It is just."

"Anat! Anat!" shouted a voice. "Where art thou?"

"Ah! It is Seth," said the girl, rising to her feet. "Hist! Here am I."

"Why art thou here?" said the newcomer anxiously. "What hath happened?"

By way of answer the girl burst into a passion of sobbing, rocking herself to and fro and tearing at her black braids. The lad stared at her in amazement and fear, then hastily casting aside the skin water-bottle with its tinkling brass cups, which he carried upon his back, he knelt down by the convulsed little figure, and throwing one arm about it began to speak in low soothing tones.

"Anat, little sister, come tell me what hath happened. Thou must indeed, little one. I should not have left thee alone; thou hast been frightened, is it not so?"

Thus encouraged the blind girl finally managed to tell her story, albeit in disjointed, half intelligible words.

"He heard thee singing, little one," said her brother, knitting his black brows angrily, "and would have carried thee away like a bird."

"Yes," said the girl fiercely. "But that is not all, he said that to-morrow we should both be sold; yet it may be that he will not care for buying and selling on the morrow. I know not how I could have done it, but all of a sudden I felt a great strength come upon me. I pushed him over the ledge—I heard him fall—" and she caught her breath with a quick shudder.

"And thou didst well, little one!" said the boy. "It matters not what hath befallen him, the gods helped thee. But the other—there were two, saidst thou? He will return. We must get us away from here and at once."

"Where shall we go?" said Anat plaintively. "We are even as the birds that flee before the hunter, only to fall at last into his hand."

"Not so, little one; the pursued eaglets flee away into the desert. So also will we. I know of a secure resting-place, and thou shalt not again stay alone."

"Shall we go now?"

"Yes, now. When I shall have gathered together our possessions; but they be few, it will not take long."

The lad rose to his feet with a sigh, and looked out and away from their lofty eyrie. Far below them lay a floor of shining blue-green, the fertile plains of the Nile, shadowed here and there with groups of clustered palm trees. Through the midst of these plains rolled the sacred river, like a flood of gold. On either side of it rose the white walls and strange many-colored towers of the city of Memphis, all transfigured in the shining mist of the setting sun. And beyond trooped the grim procession of the pyramids, solemn sentinels on the borders of a desert which the Egyptians thought to be boundless, behind whose golden rim, they believed, lay the regions of the departed.

CHAPTER II

GOOD TIDINGS OUT OF THE DESERT.

hear some one coming."

"How can that be, Anat? I see no one."

"It matters not, there is some one; I can hear the tinkle of the harness bells, it is from the desert they come."

"A caravan thinkest thou, little one?" said Seth, looking with an indulgent smile at the flushed face with its strange widely opened dark eyes.

"Nay," said the girl after a pause, shaking her head decidedly; "there is but one—one on a swift dromedary."

"By Horus! thou art right, I see the man now, he is coming this way." And shaking his tinkling cups, the lad darted away to meet the traveler.

"Water! Fresh cool water, the gift of God to the thirsty!" he cried aloud. And the stranger, scorched by the withering breath of the desert, gladly dismounted and drank deep of the proffered cup.

"God grant thee peace, whoever thou art!" he said in a low deep voice, turning his piercing eyes upon the boy. "How doth it chance that thou art here in the desert? Surely not many come this way. Why art thou not rather plying thy trade in yonder city?" He felt in his wallet for a coin as he spoke.

The boy flushed deeply and hung his head without answering.

"It is a happy chance for me that thou hadst the desert traveler in thy thought," continued the stranger with a smile of singular sweetness, "for I could no longer abide the brackish water of the marsh, and was pushing ahead of the caravan with all possible speed for a draught from a certain cool fountain that I know not far from here."

"The fountain of Kera?" said the boy, looking up.

"Even so, and it is of that I have just drunken? Ay, I thought so, though it is many moons since I have tasted it." Stroking his long beard thoughtfully, the stranger continued, "I shall wait here now till the others come up, it will not be long. Who sits yonder in the shadow of the rock?"

"My sister," replied the lad briefly. "She is blind," he added, moved by a sudden impulse.

"Blind? Ah, the pity of it, the pity of it!" said the man, passing his hand swiftly across his eyes. "Would to God" —then he broke off suddenly and commanded his dromedary to lie down; the beast obeyed, moaning and shaking his head. "He also smells water, yet hath he drunken his fill yester eve. Be quiet, Neha! thou shalt again drink— And the little one is blind?"

"Yes, but she hath wonderful hearing," said Seth proudly. "She heard the tinkle of thy harness bells before I saw thee."

"Yes, yes! I know, no one better, it was once so with me, but seeing is also good. Thanks be to the Wonderful, the Prophet of Israel, I know that now!"

The lad looked at the man in puzzled silence. They had now approached the great rock, in the shadow where the blind girl was sitting.

"Greetings to thee, little one!" said the stranger, sitting down in the sand near the child and looking earnestly into her dark sightless eyes.

"Who is it that is speaking to me?"

"Do not fear, Anat, I am here," said Seth, quietly possessing himself of one of the slender brown hands.

"I am not afraid; the voice is good."

"Where dwellest thou?" continued the stranger.

"We are even as the wild goats of the desert," said the boy bitterly, "wandering among the rocks by day, and at night sleeping where the night overtakes us."

"Surely thou art not alone in the world," urged the stranger, "thy parents, where are they?"

"The Nile hath risen seven times now since they passed into the regions of the dead," said Anat, raising her drooping head. "Many passed with them by reason of a great sickness. I also was stricken, and afterward mine eyes were darkened, not suddenly, but slowly even as the evening deepens into the black night. It is always night now."

"Ah, yes!" said the stranger sighing, "a night wherein one hath strange dreams, and where fear standeth by the pillow of sleep, and walks always at the right hand in the waking hours."

"And thou alone carest for the little one?" he continued, fixing his keen eyes upon the boy.

"I alone," said the boy proudly. "We dwelt among yonder hills, and I plied my trade in the city below, but—" here he checked himself suddenly, and looked suspiciously at his questioner. "Wilt thou not break thy fast?" he said at length. "Thou art our guest."

The stranger bowed his head gravely, laying his hand upon his breast as he did so. He understood.

Then Seth made haste and fetched from a neighboring crevice in the rock dates and parched corn together with a gourd of water. Their guest ate of the food, the lad also and the maiden.

"I was blind," said the stranger at length rising, "and I was healed of my blindness by the great prophet of Israel. They call him Jesus."

"Where dwells he?"

"In Jerusalem, far away beyond the wilderness," and he pointed toward the desert from which he had just come.

"Dost thou return thither?"

"Not many days hence, when I shall have sold my goods and loaded my camels. I shall not forget thy hospitality; when I again pass this way fetch me water, my son, and hear what I shall say to thee. Maiden, I salute thee! Farewell." And he sprang upon his beast and was gone in a swift cloud of dust toward the slow-moving caravan, which crawled like a snake over the yellow wastes of the desert.

Seth did not run with his water-bottles and his tinkling cups to meet them, as was his wont. He sat silent in the shadow of the great rock, thinking.

Anat also was silent for a time, then she said timidly: "I would that I too might see the man of blessing, he who dwells beyond the wilderness and hath power to restore sight to the blind. There is no one in the land of Egypt who can do the like."

"We have no treasure to give him; would he not say to us, 'Where then is thy gold, or thy precious stones, or thy beasts of burden, before I shall do this thing for thee?' Thou knowest not the ways of magicians; I know, for I have heard, yet is there no magician in all Egypt who can cure blindness?"

Anat sighed. "I have my mother's necklace," she said at length, laying her hand upon the string of coins about her neck. "Some of them are of gold and very heavy."

Then she caught her breath with a half sob. "The men—yesterday—they would have sold us. I—yes, I would be a slave if only I might see!"

"I will be a slave, and thou shalt have thine eyes together with thy freedom," cried Seth, starting to his feet. "I will say to the man, give thou sight to these eyes and I am thy bondman from henceforth and forever. I will serve thee with my heart's blood."

"I also will serve him, for I will not leave thee, my brother; but how shall we pass the wilderness?"

"There are many caravans passing through," said the lad, looking with troubled eyes into the distance, "but the way is long and we have no beast."

"The stranger who ate of our bread, will he not take us to that far country?"

"It may be—" began Seth, then he stopped suddenly—Anat had grasped his arm convulsively, her face pallid to the lips.

"The voices!" she gasped. "I hear them, they will sell us into bondage! Let us hide, quick!"

Without a word the lad hurried her into a narrow cleft in the rocks not far distant. Here, tugging with all his strength at a broad stone which was half buried in the drifting sand, he at length succeeded in pulling it aside. The opening disclosed a flight of steps cut in the solid rock, winding down into impenetrable darkness. From the depths there ascended a stifling odor of resin and spices.

The girl drew back gasping, "Not here!" she said faintly. "I am afraid; I cannot go further, it is the breath of the dead."

The lad hesitated an instant; he too heard the sound of voices and the tinkling of harness bells. "Listen," he whispered, "I know not the voices, but thou knowest."

"Yes, yes! it is the voice; I will go anywhere to escape."

The tinkling sound and the slow steps of the beasts of burden became momently louder, together with the harsh tones of a human voice.

"'Tis a fool's errand, Besa; thou hast lost what little wit the gods gave thee in thy tumble of yesterday. By Sechet! I have not yet done laughing to think the way the little hell-witch served thee!"

"Who could know that the beggar understood Greek!"

"Pooh! that is nothing; no one better than the beggars, they whine for every man's gold in his own tongue. Ha, ha! 'Thou shouldst have perfumed garlands,' saidst thou with tongue as smooth as Sesamé oil; then I saw only a flying bundle of red cloth. Besa was gone. Ha, ha!"

"Why didst thou not seize her, fool?" snarled the other, grinding his teeth. "I will find her should I look a lifetime, if only to twist that little singing throat of hers."

"That shalt thou not do, friend; that singing throat is gold and it is mine. Come, we will go back; they are not here."

"What is this?" said Besa triumphantly, dismounting from his ass and holding up a brilliant bit of striped drapery; "this, or one like it, was on the girl's neck yesterday."

Amu, for so was the other man called, made no reply: he was looking fixedly into a narrow cleft of the rocks. Presently he too dismounted. "Some one has been here," he said, pointing to the fresh footmarks in the sand which had drifted deep into the opening.

CHAPTER III

AT THE PALACE OF THE HIGH PRIEST.

T is well that by the blessing of Jehovah thou hast recovered thy health, my son, for though we have accomplished the death of the blasphemer, there yet remains the rabble of his followers. With the trunk of the poisonous vine we must also thoroughly burn the branches lest they bud anew."

"Thou hast the tongue of wisdom," said Caiaphas in a tone of dull indifference, his eyes fixed vacantly on the range of blue hills at the verge of the horizon.

Annas glanced impatiently at the white worn face. "They are already spreading reports both in Jerusalem and in all Galilee that the man is alive again, that, forsooth, he has been seen of them. The temple resounds daily to the voice of their noisome praises and thanksgivings. I have counseled that they be thrust out," he continued frowning, "for what is it else than blasphemy—lies. It cannot be true!" And the speaker started to his feet, and began to pace up and down the terrace of the roof garden. "The Sanhedrim seems satisfied that nothing will come of it," he went on angrily. " 'Let be,' say they, 'the thing will die even as the man.' Pah! they are blind. Look you! here are the facts. The man's body disappears on the third day after the crucifixion, the Roman guards tell a drunken tale of earthquake and the appearance of an angel with a sword; lies, all lies! That I have managed—gold worketh wonders; they know now that they were drunken, and that his disciples stole the body away while they slept. So far, well. Then there is the matter of the rent veil before the Holy of Holies; a sore mischance, the fabric had been eaten of insects, there is no question of it, how else should it—"

"Who saw the thing done?" interrupted Caiaphas in a hollow tone.

"A half score of priests who were preparing the altar for the evening sacrifice. It was rent with a loud noise, say they, and the Holiest place revealed on a sudden. I have counseled that they hold their peace; it may be that they also are apostate, but I dare not take the steps that I would in the matter because of the people. Of one thing I am certain, the man is dead; in that have we triumphed. I saw him die, and he is as assuredly perished as are the wretched malefactors that groaned that day on either side of his cross."

The face of Caiaphas blanched to the livid color of death. "Say no more," he gasped huskily, "I am not well."

Annas stared at him for an instant with something like contempt. "I will call a servant," he said at length. "Thou shouldst drink wine to strengthen thy heart."

"The man is strangely wrought upon by this thing," he thought within himself as he strode away. "He is like to a rope of sand; I must not look to him for help. Who is there then of stout heart and good courage? Issachar—Johanan—Alexander? they all be like wax which the sun hath melted. Stay! there is the young Saul of Tarsus, a Pharisee of the Pharisees, and zealous for the upbuilding of Israel; I will even dispatch a swift messenger for him. He will be an instrument of wrath in mine hand against the enemies of the Lord Jehovah."

As the sound of his footsteps died away, the sick man raised his head. "Begone!" he said with an irritable gesture to the servant who stood awaiting his pleasure. "Call my wife."

Even as he spoke, the heavy curtains which hung over the doorway near at hand, parted, and the figure of a woman emerged onto the terrace.

"Where hast thou been?" said the invalid, fixing his sunken eyes angrily upon her. "Dost thou not know that I cannot abide that clumsy hind, Barak. Where is my cordial?"

"Here, my lord," said Anna soothingly, pouring a few drops of some bright-colored liquid into a cup. Her slender hand trembled so violently as she did this that a portion of the contents was spilled, and lay a crimson pool between them on the white marble of the pavement.

The sick man shrank back among his pillows, his eyes starting from his head. "Ay! there it is again!" he muttered, huskily. "Blood, blood—the blood of the Nazarene! I shall always see it. Look!" he shrieked, "it is crawling towards me!"

The woman sprang forward, her face colorless, "It is nothing!" she said, breathlessly, "nothing, my lord! See! it is gone. Come, drink the cordial, after that thou shalt rest; thou art weary."

Caiaphas looked into the cup. "It is blood," he said, shudderingly, "yet must I drink it; God is just!" Then he lay back among his pillows once more, his eyes closed. After a time a faint color crept into his livid face.

The woman watched him patiently for a full hour, more than once her pale lips moving as if in prayer. From her dark eyes there seemed to stream forth a visible radiance of love which brooded in silent blessing over the helpless form at her side.

At length the sick man stirred a little, his eyes unclosed. "Has it been told thee what hath befallen our son?" he said, slowly and clearly.

The woman bowed her head. "It hath been told me," she whispered brokenly, "that his life was ended even as—"

"He was crucified," said Caiaphas, still in the same slow, clear tone, "even as was the Nazarene. God is just. Blood for blood, it is the law, and hath been from the beginning."

"God is also love," said Anna, looking fearfully into her husband's face.

He returned the look with one of full intelligence. "Do not fear," he said, gently, "it is best that the matter hath been spoken between us; it were like an open grave else. The madness hath passed from my brain now, and I see—" He paused, and so terrible a look came over his face that his wife cried out faintly.

"God is love," she repeated in a low voice, wringing her hands; "He will forgive. How couldst thou know that the Nazarene was the Anointed One? Yet, even he said, 'Father, forgive them, for they know not what they do!' as they drove the nails into his hands."

"Woman!" said Caiaphas, with something of his old high-priestly authority, "hold thy peace, and forget that thou hast spoken blasphemy. Didst think then that I—I—the High Priest, was ready to confess that the Nazarene was the Messiah of Israel! I am ready to confess that he was an innocent man; and I am blood-guilty in that I brought about his death. God hath punished me by slaying my son, even as he punished David for his sin. After this once we will speak of the thing no more; it shall never again be named between us.

AT THE PALACE OF THE HIGH PRIEST. 27

Nor shall it be made known to any other. It were not meet that so shameful a thing be bruited about concerning the High Priest. Our flesh and blood is accursed."

The mother's face flushed hotly. "The lad was innocent!" she cried. "He was sinned against most foully, but he himself sinned not. He is in Paradise, for he hath the word of the Lord."

"What meanest thou? Who told thee concerning the thing?" said Caiaphas, raising himself up and fixing his burning eyes upon her face.

"I had it from a lad named Stephen, who was even a brother to him who was our son—Titus, he was called. As he hung upon the cross in agony, the Lord spake to him and said, 'This day shalt thou be with me in Paradise.'"

"Who is this Stephen?" said Caiaphas, in a low, terrible voice. "And whom dost thou call Lord?"

Anna trembled with terror, she tried to speak, but the words died upon her lips.

"Speak, woman!"

"Stephen is—the son of the Greek who took our child. The man hath been punished for his sin. He also perished with the Lord."

There was an awful silence. Then Caiaphas again spoke, and his voice was as the voice of a stranger in the ears of Anna. "This Stephen, the son of the malefactor, doth he still live?"

"He—lives; but, oh my husband, I beseech thee—do not harm him, so innocent, so heavenly a one!"

But through the words of her entreaty sounded the inexorable tones of the High Priest's voice.

"Blood for blood! The iniquities of the fathers shall be visited upon the children, even unto the third and fourth generations. It is the law."

CHAPTER IV.

IN PLACE OF JUDAS.

HAT and if while we wait for the fulfillment of the promise, the same men who have slain our Lord shall also turn their hand against us? We be few in number and there is naught to shield us from their fury. Thou didst see when we praised God in the temple even this day, how the chief priests and the elders cast upon us looks which were as sharp arrows in the hands of mighty men of valor. Shall the wolves which slew the Shepherd spare the flock?"

"Hadst thou faith even as a grain of mustard seed thou wouldst not doubt the word of the Lord, 'Ye shall be baptized with the Holy Spirit not many days hence; depart not from Jerusalem till that the promise is fulfilled to you!' And how sayest thou that there is naught to shield us. God, the Almighty One, even the Father of our Lord Jesus, whom we saw received up into heaven, he shall protect us from the wrath of the Jews.

"He hath suffered me to be tempted with doubts and fears more than most," said Thomas, glancing fearfully at a group of men in the garb of rabbis who were approaching them along the narrow street. "But do not thou despise me because of mine infirmities. The Lord said unto thee, 'Thou art Peter!' unto me he said, 'Be not faithless but believing.' It is not easy for me to believe, it is not easy for me to rejoice, when the Lord hath left us alone and unfriended.—Ah! sawest thou that look? The old man was Annas, the other was Issachar, the cruel; but in the eyes of the young man with them there burned a very fury of hate. He lusteth for our blood."

"I have not before seen his face," said Peter thoughtfully; then he turned himself about to look after the retreating figures. As he did so the young man of whom Thomas had spoken also turned, and again Peter felt the indignant fire of his gaze. "It matters not," he said after a pause, "what the heart of man shall devise, the will of the Almighty shall be done, on earth, as also in heaven," and he looked upward longingly, as if he hoped to pierce through the depths of the blue to that place whither his Lord had gone.

And having come now to the place where they were wont to gather together, they went in. It was the same house where they had made ready the Passover at the word of the Lord, on that awful night in which he was betrayed. And in the large upper room, made sacred by the memories of that last supper with their Lord, they found them which believed. It was to this place they found they had come after they had seen the cloud receive him out of their sight, the words of the angels yet ringing in their ears: "This Jesus which was received up from you into heaven, shall so come in like manner as ye beheld him going into heaven." And here day by day they gathered to wait for the mysterious Comforter, which was to come to them out of heaven, they knew not how. In the hearts of some of them burned the hope that the Comforter might be the Lord himself, and that at last they should see the promised kingdom of the Messiah.

"There be but eleven of us whom He chose for this ministry," said Peter, looking around on the little assembly, which numbered about one hundred and twenty persons. "It was needful that the scriptures should be fulfilled concerning Judas, who betrayed our Lord into the hands of them that slew him. But now he is dead, and hath gone to his own place, and it is written in the book of the Psalms, 'Let his habitation be made desolate, let no man dwell therein. His office let another take.' Of the men therefore which have companied with us while the Lord Jesus remained upon earth, from the day when he received baptism in the Jordan, unto that day in which he was taken up into heaven, of these must one become a witness of His resurrection."

"How then shall the will of God be known in the matter?" said John gravely. "We have not the spirit of discernment, for did we not trust even Judas who betrayed him? Albeit the Lord knew him from the beginning."

"Let God himself choose!" cried Peter. "It hath been the custom in Israel since the days of old to decide such matters by lot. So did God select his chosen priests from the family of Eleazar. So also doth he choose which one shall stand by the altar of incense in the temple."

Then wrote they upon tablets of wood, every one the name of the man he thought most holy and acceptable, and worthy to witness with the eleven to the resurrection of Jesus. And the tablets were cast into a basin; and it was found that Joseph Barsabas, called Justus, and Matthias were named. Then Peter called these two men to stand up before the company of the disciples, and he prayed aloud unto the Lord in these words:

IN PLACE OF JUDAS.

"Thou, Lord, which knowest the hearts of all men, show of these two the one whom thou hast chosen to take the place in this ministry and apostleship, from which Judas fell away that he might go to his own place."

Then cast they the tablets, whereon were written the names of Justus and Matthias, into the brazen cup; and Peter shook the cup, and the name of Matthias leapt out, and from henceforward he was numbered with the apostles.

As they went away from the upper room to their abiding places, Mary the mother of Jesus, and Salome, and Mary of Magdala together with John, the beloved disciple, they talked with one another of what had been done. Stephen also was with them.

"We are again twelve," said John with a sigh, for he bethought him of the days when there was yet another.

"The Lord was upon earth for forty days after that he arose from the dead," said Stephen thoughtfully, his eyes fixed upon a bright star which shone above the horizon like a golden lamp. "Why then did not he himself choose one to fill the place of Judas?"

John looked startled. "What dost thou mean?" he said quickly, turning to look at the young man in the half darkness.

"Could he not have chosen, had he wished it? Could he not yet choose, being set down at the right hand of God?"

"And dost thou think to question the doings of God's elect?" said John, a ring of authority in his mild tones.

"Nay, my son, chide not the lad," said Mary. "I myself doubted whether indeed the casting of lots be pleasing to God. God hath permitted men many things in the past because of their blindness."

"It is a practice of wicked men," cried Stephen. "I have seen thieves do the like to apportion their booty.

And did not the Roman soldiers also at the foot of his cross cast lots for the garments of the crucified one?"

"God knoweth that we meant it aright," said John humbly, his face full of trouble. "We have not yet the spirit of discernment, and are as those who stumble in the darkness."

"When the spirit of truth is come he will teach you all things," said Stephen softly.

"'And bring all things to your remembrance, whatsoever I have taught you.' Ay! those were his words. We have need of it, sore need; did we not forget on that day of dread that he had even told us, told us plainly, and many times, that so it must be? yet had we failed to understand. Nay! we would not understand."

The slight form of Mary trembled and her voice shook as she said, "Many years hath fear been a guest in my heart since the day Simeon said to me—when I presented my son a babe before the Lord, 'Behold, this child is set for the falling and rising up of many in Israel, and for a sign which is spoken against. Yea, and a sword shall pierce through thine own soul, that thoughts out of many hearts may be revealed.' The sword hath drunken deep of my heart's blood, yet will I trust him though he slay me."

"The worst hath happened for us all," said Stephen, clasping her hand. "He is alive! He is ascended! and yet is he with us, for he said, 'Lo, I am with you always, even unto the end of the world!'"

"It cannot be then that we have gone very far wrong," said John slowly. "It shall yet be according to his will. If Matthias be not the elect of God for the apostleship, yet shall he walk with us, and the pierced hand of the Master himself shall touch another which as yet we know not. There were thirteen in our fellowship while he was upon earth."

And having come to the place of their abode, they went in.

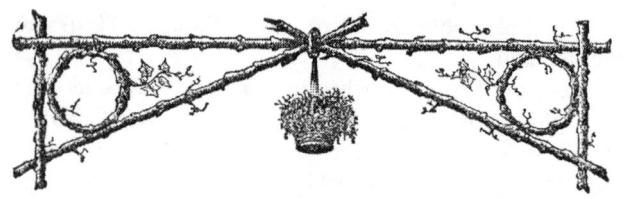

CHAPTER V.

IN THE ABODE OF KINGS.

AST thou a torch?"

"Nay, but it is impossible that they be here. Pah! I cannot abide the odor of mummies."

"Yet must thou pass centuries in their company, if indeed thou art fortunate enough to die in a civilized land." And the speaker's lips widened till they revealed a row of yellow teeth.

Amu bent over and gazed steadily for a moment into the black opening that yawned at his feet, then he looked up at his companion. Something in his sombre eyes caused the yellow row of teeth to disappear. "I am going home," he said suddenly.

"'Tis good! Go back, fetch me a torch, and I will explore for the singing bird. I am not minded to move from this place till I shall seize her."

"Hast thou water?"

"Nay, but thou hast a bottle at thy girdle; give it me. Even at this moment I thirst."

"By Sechet! it is empty. But stay, there is a fountain beyond the crest of yonder hill; go quench thy thirst. I will remain till thou shalt return."

Besa hesitated; he looked steadily into the lowering face of Amu. "Thou art in a strange humor to-day, friend," he said at length. "I have been patient with thee,

IN THE ABODE OF KINGS.   35

but I will bear no more. Give me thy flask; I will fill it at the fountain."

The face of Amu blanched to a sickly yellow hue. His eyes glowed with fury, but he said not a word; with a sudden quick movement, he seized the bridle of his mule, and leaping upon its back galloped away towards Memphis.

Besa looked after him quietly. "What may be the meaning of all this?" he said to himself. "Stay, let me consider for a moment. The man comes to me and says in effect this: 'Thou art a dealer in slaves; I can procure for thee two of good value, a lad and a maiden. The maiden hath a voice like to the sound of nightingales; yet cannot I bring them to the proper purchasers.' At the same time I, Besa, am commissioned to procure a singing slave for the princess, who pineth in a sickly melancholy. But what have I suffered in the matter thus far? I have been half killed by a fall, now am I parched with thirst, and the man lies to me concerning his water-bottle. I saw him fill it before we started, therefore I ventured to leave mine own, which I could not at the moment lay my hands upon. There is no fountain behind the brow of yonder hill. For what purpose hath the man lied? There is something here that I cannot see. I will for the present forego the matter, but there are two things to be set down for the future, and Besa is not the man to forget."

Then he advanced to the opening of the tomb, which showed black in its setting of yellow sand; kneeling down, he looked carefully at the stone stairway which led down into the depths. The sand was sifting in with each breath of the hot desert wind. "It has been opened but a short time," he remarked at length. "It will be a pious act for me to replace the stone; Anubis will reward me for it. One must not fail in duty to the sacred dead." Then he raised his voice, "Rest quietly, my children; there is nought to hurt thee in the abodes of the departed. Song and sunlight, laughter and air are needed no more by the slaves of Anubis. His slave shalt thou be unless thou presently come forth in answer to my cry."

The sound of his voice echoed in dismal reverberations through the hollow blackness within, but there was no sign that his words fell upon other ears than those sealed to eternal silence within their swathings of spiced linen. The heavy odor of death ascended in stupefying clouds into the face of the man as he knelt at the edge of the tomb. He drew back a little, and the malignant smile faded from his face.

"The stone shall be put back," he said doggedly, "for I believe by my life, that they be down there. They will live till I shall return with torches and men. If I secure them both, I shall be avenged also upon Amu."

Forthwith he bent over and laid hold upon the stone. It was heavy, and though the lad in his mad fear had succeeded in shoving it to one side, the man could with difficulty stir it a single inch. The sun beat down in fury upon his head, the hot wind sang in his ears with a strange sound of buzzing insects and humming wheels. He stepped down into the stairway, the better to grasp the stone for another mighty effort. Suddenly a wave as of fire swept before his eyes, his hands relaxed their hold, he reeled a little, and then fell, a nerveless heap, into the darkness.

To Seth and Anat, who were crouching behind a huge sarcophagus, the sound at first signified nothing but some fresh horror.

"I must cry out," urged Seth in a vehement whisper. "We shall perish in this place, for I cannot move the stone from beneath."

But Anat held him fast. "Better slavery to death than to such a man."

IN THE ABODE OF KINGS. 37

Seth watched the shaft of yellow light that pierced the thick darkness. "Presently," he thought shudderingly, "it will disappear." But the moments crept slowly by, and the sun still poured in, revealing the countless dancing atoms which had leapt up from the sleep of centuries beneath the feet of the fugitives.

"Anat," he whispered, "something has happened; I will go and see."

The blind girl held him fast for a moment longer. She bent her head. There was no sound save the sighing of the wind outside and the hissing murmur of the sand as it drifted onto the stairway of their prison. "Go," she said with a sigh of relief, "he has departed."

Seth rose cautiously to his feet and crept toward the opening; his eyes had grown accustomed to the darkness now, and he could see on either side the vast gaudily painted wooden cases in which dwelt the dead. Their great eyes stared at him as he hurried past. He stumbled presently over something which lay at the foot of the stone steps. Starting back with a cry he perceived that it was the body of a man. He had fallen upon his face in the sand and lay quite motionless. The lad stared at him for a moment in fascinated silence, then he bethought him that presently the man might recover his senses. Turning, he darted back into the darkness. "Come!" he said breathlessly in the ear of the blind girl.

Treading lightly that they might not awake the sleeper, the two crept up the stair, not without many a fearful backward glance at the quiet figure which still lay on its face, the monstrous staring eyes of the mummies looking on unmoved, and the stealthy wind already beginning to urge the uneasy desert to 'Come, cover this man that hath lain him down to sleep unasked in the abode of kings!' "

"Shall I put the stone in its place?" said Seth, when they had reached the upper air.

"Yes," said the girl, clenching her thin hands. "Let him bide there till the other shall seek him, and if that be never, then I care not. Would he not have left us to perish? But the gods stayed his hand."

The lad hesitated. "He hath no water."

"Fetch him water then and food also if thou wilt. Thou art soft-hearted; for myself I should leave him as he is. Dost thou not see that it is now that we must make good our escape? Once the man hath recovered himself we are lost. I can hear the bells of his beast, let us seize it and flee away into the desert that we may find the magician who can open the eyes of them that see not."

"We could not pass the wilderness, we should perish by the way."

Anat sat down in the sand. "Thou art a man," she said scornfully, "and therefore wise; I am as the dust under thy feet; I have no eyes to see with, yet shall I tell thee what shall come to pass. Go down now to our enemy whom the gods have smitten, raise him up and pour water into his mouth and upon his head, then when he shall come to himself say to him, 'Here now is thy beast, I will set thee upon it that thou mayest ride. As for this maid whom thou didst covet, behold she is thine; I also will run before thee.'" And the girl laughed aloud, and tossed her head so that all the gold and silver coins of her necklace clinked musically together.

Seth looked at her indignantly. "All women have the poison of asps under their tongues," he muttered. "It hath been told me, and it is even true, I have seen men beat their women for less; it purgeth them from folly."

The blind girl sprang to her feet. "Wilt thou beat me because I have proved that thou art the fool?" she cried, her voice choking with rage. "Yes, let it be so, I care not, but I had thought that thou wast not as others—that thou didst love me, blind, useless, helpless though I be," and she burst into a passion of weeping.

The lad was at her side in a moment. "I do love thee," he murmured penitently. "I have no other on earth, thou art my all. Come! it shall be as thou hast said, here is the beast, with such a pretty saddle, little one, all of crimson velvet, and hung with bells of silver. It is thine, the gods have given it thee. We will go away towards the first halting place, I am sure that I can find it."

Anat checked her sobs after a due space; she even allowed herself to be placed upon the back of the mule. "Have I the poison of asps under my tongue?" she said plaintively, but with a gleam of triumph.

"Not so, by Osiris, I was a brute to say such a thing. Rather hast thou a voice as sweet as the voice of fountains and as the voice of thrushes that sing by the river. But I shall place water where our enemy can drink when he awakens; and I will not close the stone altogether, I will leave a little space where the sun may enter into that noisome place. This shall be, shall it not, little sister?"

Anat tossed her head; she made no reply. Then Seth made haste and poured water into a cup and set it on the step where their enemy should see it when he awoke; he took also from his wallet a handful of parched corn and laid it beside the cup. Looking sidewise at the man, who still lay all along on his face just as he had been stricken, he fancied that he saw him stir a little, and the terror came back upon him so that he sprang up the steps two at a time, and with a mighty effort drew the great stone forward over the opening, forgetting in his fear to leave it open ever so little that the sun might look in.

After that the two fled away, their faces set towards the great and terrible wilderness, beyond which lay the land of their hope.

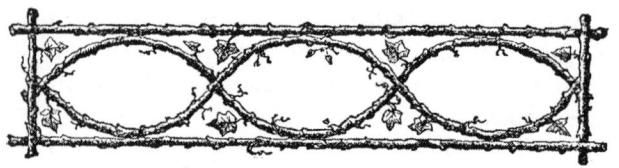

CHAPTER VI.

THE LORD OF THE SOUTH-LAND.

BU BEN HESED was a mighty man of war, he was also rich. Ten score of camels, swift dromedaries not a few, and horses, such that men paid great sums of gold to possess them; flocks of sheep and of goats; wives also and children in plenty; all of these things, together with the unquestioning obedience and devotion of his tribe, did this dweller in the desert call his own.

He was a tall man, and his beard descended upon his breast in waves of silvery whiteness. Yet were his eyes as keen as the eyes of a mountain eagle, and there was no one of all his tribe who could endure hunger and thirst as could Ben Hesed. Not that it was necessary for him to so endure, for was not he lord of all the land that lay betwixt the mountains on the south of the great wilderness of Shur, even unto the sea?

"To satisfy the appetite is not always good," he was wont to say to his sons. "This will the beasts do whenever they find provender. Man alone can say to himself, thou shalt fast because I have willed it. Hunger thus endured maketh man king over the beasts; thus is he set apart from them, and so do his thoughts soar above the earth even unto the region of the heavens, where dwelleth Ja, the maker of the stars and also of man."

THE LORD OF THE SOUTH-LAND.

On this day Ben Hesed sat alone in the door of his tent; the sun was sinking, a ball of scarlet behind the purple rim of the horizon; a group of camels, browsing on the scanty desert growths, showed black against its fiery glow, their shadows stretching long and gaunt across the sand. About the margin of a meagre pool close at hand a cluster of palm trees also meagre reared their heads, clasping their dusty fronds across the water as if to hide this sacred treasure of the desert from the fierce wooing of the sun.

The voices of the women, coming and going with their water-jars, and the laughter and cooing of half a score of naked brown babies, who lay contentedly kicking up their heels in the warm sand, came pleasantly to the ear of Abu Ben Hesed. He cared not the pool was meagre and the palm trees stunted, this only made them the more precious and wonderful, more truly the works of Jehovah, who had set them thus in the midst of this great and terrible wilderness, like jewels of price. He had looked upon fruitful lands and great rivers, upon cities also, where men dwelt by hundreds and by thousands, and his soul had grown sick within him at the sight.

"It was not because of their disobedience only," he said, "that Jehovah led the children of Israel for forty years in the desert, but also, because far from the lustful fat earth and teeming rivers and the abominations of stone and wood that men call cities, he might reveal to them himself."

In palm-shaded fountains, in the beauty of night and morning, and in the flowers which flourished in the arid soil of the desert, he beheld the love of God. In the deep valleys and solemn mountain crests where the seething primal rock in some remote and terrible time had gathered itself into mighty waves and fantastic pinnacles, only to stand still forever at the word of the Lord, he perceived his power, and in the blinding, scorching whirlwind of sand, before whose withering breath nothing mortal could stand, and in whose fiery garments the sun itself seemed smothered, he saw the wrath of Jehovah.

As Abu Ben Hesed mused thus within himself, he became aware after a time that a man was coming swiftly towards him out of the desert, his garments girt about him. He slackened not his pace till he came to the spot where Ben Hesed sat in the door of his tent, then he cast himself down before him and rent his garments with a loud cry of grief.

"Woe is me, my lord," he cried, when he could find his breath, "I am the bearer of evil tidings."

"Speak, my son," said Ben Hesed, who had recognized in the man one of his herdsmen. "What hath befallen?"

"Thine enemy who dwells in the south-land hath fallen upon the flocks this day and hath carried away of the herds a goodly number, of she-camels also and their foals, three, and of the horses, the stallion Dekar."

"And thou livest to tell me this," said Ben Hesed, his eyes burning with anger. "Why didst thou not defend the flocks?"

"Woe is me!" repeated the man, casting the dust upon his head. "I have not yet told the worst; we fought valiantly, and thy son Eri is slain, together with Kish, the herdsman. When this befell, we fled before the face of the enemy; the flocks also and the herds are scattered as the sand of the desert before the wind, and there is nought to hinder them from falling into the hand of the oppressor."

Then Abu Ben Hesed arose and rent his clothes and cast dust upon his head. "Jehovah hath caused me to be smitten," he said. "Nevertheless all his ways are right ways. I should have watched for mine enemy, for he hath grown lusty and flourishing of late. I will get me after him and smite him till he shall cry aloud for succor. Jehovah grant me my desire upon mine enemy! Alas for my son Eri! He hath been murderously cut down in the flower of his youth! From the bright morning of his days he hath been plunged suddenly into the night of death. But behold, his blood crieth to me for vengeance out of the desert. Let us make haste!"

The terrible news spread throughout the encampment, withering the peaceful evening joy, like the hot breath of a Sirocco. The women ceased their gay incessant chatter and broke into loud wailing, and the frightened children wept with fear at the sound.

"Alas! Alas!" cried the mother of the dead man. "Alas for my son! He was straight and comely as a palm tree, beautiful also, and pleasant in his speech. Woe! Woe! He will no more open his mouth with kindness, nor will his lips break forth with singing."

"Woe! Woe!" shrilled the other women, rocking to and fro, and casting the ashes from the dying fire upon their dishevelled heads.

"Morning and evening hath he led forth the flocks!" moaned the mother.

"He will lead them forth no more!" wailed her companions.

"Alas for the betrothed maiden! She is desolate, even as a widow without little ones hath she become!"

"Woe! Woe!"

Through all the clamor of the wailing sounded the clashing of weapons and the neighing of horses, as the men with set teeth and lowering brows made ready for the pursuit of their enemy. Within the hour they departed, a hundred strong, the swift hoofs of their horses casting up the dust of the desert behind them, as they vanished, a war-cloud big with storm, into the night.

Before dawn Abu Ben Hesed had seen his desire upon his enemy. They had discovered the marauders as they were making merry with their spoil, and had fallen upon them suddenly, so that they had no time to escape.

The eyes of Ben Hesed were terrible to look upon as he cut down the flying wretches.

"Let not one of them escape!" he cried aloud. "Slay and spare not!"

Afterward they gathered the spoil of the dead, together with their own stolen possessions and turned their faces once more toward the north. The heart of Ben Hesed was as lead within his bosom.

"After all," he thought, "what doth it profit to revenge oneself on an enemy? My son is not restored, nor is my herdsman. Yet it is the law, blood for blood, and the law is good." He raised his eyes wearily, and looked away toward the east, where the dawn was beginning with solemn pomp and splendor. Long rays of tremulous light flickered athwart the cold, clear blue of the heavens, the morning star burned pallid amidst the growing radiance, till at last it was swallowed up and lost in the oncoming flood of day. Abu Ben Hesed looked down at his clothing and at his hands which were red with the blood of his enemies. He loathed himself at that moment.

"I see something yonder which resembles a man," said his eldest son, who rode beside him. "Also a beast, lying down. What can it be, think you, my lord? Another of our enemies who hath perchance escaped us in the darkness?"

Abu Ben Hesed turned his eyes in the direction to which the man pointed. "It is death," he said quietly. "The vultures are already gathering to the feast."

"Nay, I have seen the figure move. Shall I go and see what the thing may be?"

THE LORD OF THE SOUTH-LAND.

"Go, my son; if the man be alive, slay him not, but bring him to me unhurt."

The son of Abu obeyed, drawing near the object and circling about it cautiously that he might view it from every side. Presently he dismounted and walked quite up to the thing, his horse following at his heels, and snuffing at the air suspiciously. Two or three great birds with bare flabby necks and red eyes, rose slowly from the ground at his approach and flapped heavily away, croaking dismally. They had been busy on the carcass of a mule, which lay dead upon the sand, its gay saddle of crimson velvet hung with silver bells, befouled and draggled. At a little distance, and quite motionless, was a heap of parti-colored drapery, from which protruded a slender brown foot.

"A child!" said Ben Abu. "Two of them," he added as he pulled aside the striped covering of cotton cloth which concealed their faces. "Dead from thirst," was his verdict after he had turned them over and had noted with a certain dimness of his keen vision, their swollen tongues and the goatskin water-bottle which lay beside the lad quite empty.

Then he stood up and blew a long blast on the ram's horn which he carried at his girdle.

CHAPTER VII.

THE PHARISEE FROM TARSUS.

H, that Jehovah would rend the heavens; that Israel might see his righteousness! My heart burneth within me as a live coal. I cannot sleep because of these things."

"God hath given thee this spirit, my son, because of the peril of his chosen. He shall greatly prosper the work of thine hand." Annas uttered these words in a low, smooth voice, drawing his long silvery beard through his delicate fingers and looking keenly from under his half-closed eyelids at the dark, eager face before him.

"If I could only help on the day of his coming!" said the young man, rising and pacing restlessly up and down the floor, his hands clasped behind him, his head sunken upon his breast.

As he walked thus, the eyes of the older man followed him with a peculiar satisfaction. They rested approvingly on the strong athletic figure, on the bent head crisped with dark curls, on the stern brow and fiery eyes, and the clear, strongly cut features.

"From my youth have I been struggling to keep the law with this one end in view!" continued the speaker. "If I, even I, might be he who shall by his holy living, by the exact fulfilling of the law of the Almighty, bring the Messiah! But the flesh is weak, I know not how I have offended. Of the two hundred and forty-eight commands and the three hundred and sixty-five prohibitions, I have not broken one knowingly for many days. But there has always been failure, a drop of unclean water, perchance, on the dish from which I have eaten, or my robe has touched one who is polluted and I knew it not, or I myself in all my zeal have omitted something. It must be all or nothing in the eyes of him who is God of gods, infinite, unsearchable, who knoweth all things. What is a man that he can please him who sitteth on the circle of the heavens?"

Annas smiled behind his hand. "The zeal of thine house hath eaten me up," he quoted piously. "Truly, my son, it giveth me heartfelt joy to perceive such holy aspirations in so young a man. Now do I know that God was with me when I was moved to send for Saul of Tarsus. As for me, I am an old man. I can no longer support all the rigor of the law, else would my flesh fail me. 'Behold to obey is better than sacrifice, and to hearken than the fat of rams,' as it is written in the law."

"It is that alone to which I press forward—obedience to the law. Thou knowest—why should I even speak of the matter to thee, my father, that if one person only can for a single day keep the whole law and not offend in one point, nay, if but one person could for once perfectly keep the Sabbath of the Lord our God, then—then the Messiah would come. Then would the Lord dwell once more among his people in visible form. Then would we tread our enemies under our feet, then would the Holy of Holies be filled with glory so that Jerusalem should shine as a bride prepared for her husband. Oh, Lord! when shall these things be? 'Why dost thou tarry? Why is thy holy city defiled by the Gentiles?' " The speaker paused and lifted his face as if to listen for some word from the unanswering heavens.

The deep tones of the old man broke the silence. "These things can never be until Jerusalem is purged of the followers of that blasphemer, who hath of late paid the just penalty of his crimes on the accursed tree. Take counsel with me, my son, and I will tell thee how thou shalt hasten this day of which thou hast spoken. 'With thine eyes shalt thou behold and see the reward of the wicked. The Lord will not cast off his people, neither will he forsake his inheritance.' He speaks to thee, my son, through the words of my mouth, listen therefore, 'Judgment shall return unto righteousness, and all the upright in heart shall follow it. But who will rise up for me against the evil doers; who will stand up for me against the workers of iniquity?' "

"I will stand against the workers of iniquity," answered the young man solemnly. "I will utterly crush them and cast them out, even as did Elijah in the day when he slew the prophets of Baal at the brook Kishon."

"Upon thee, my son, hath the mantle of the prophet fallen, and into thy hand will I commit this work. Only must thou submit thyself to my direction in the matter, for I know the ways of this people and of this city as thou dost not. Listen therefore while I shall speak to thee of what we must accomplish."

"Speak! for my spirit burns within me. I long to come up to the help of the Lord against the mighty."

"Thou hast well said the mighty, my son, for strange and terrible things have happened. Thou hast already heard how that suddenly out of the hill country of Galilee there arose a man called Jesus of Nazareth. He was a carpenter, and the son of a carpenter, he wrought also at his trade blamelessly enough until he was about thirty years of age. After that he took to himself certain men of the baser sort, gathered from among ignorant fisher folk, and even publicans; these men he called his disciples. Then went he forth and began to teach strange and ungodly doctrines to the people. He taught them that the Sabbath was not to be observed after the law, that the priests and rabbis were hypocrites; yea, he even said that we were as whited sepulchres, fair to look upon, but within full of dead men's bones and all uncleanness. Extortioners also he called us and unjust." And the speaker's voice shook with passion. "He pretended to do wondrous miracles, and all manner of wild tales began to fill the mouths of the common people. Even of our own number were led after him certain ones—Joseph of Arimathea—may God smite him, and Nicodemus also, so thou canst perceive the cunning of the Evil One. He came boldly up to Jerusalem at the time of feasts, he even made pretense of keeping the feasts also with his disciples, yet was he always undermining the law and teaching others so. Repeatedly did he heal on the Sabbath day."

"What meanest thou?" said the young man, knitting his dark brows. "Did he heal then, of a truth?"

Annas hesitated a moment, he shifted uneasily about in his place. "Thou wilt hear wondrous tales of his doings," he said at length, dropping his eyes to the floor. "But—" and his voice gathered in firmness, "it is all lies—all lies. The man paid money to vile beggars to pretend that they were blind and halt, then, forsooth, he loosed them from their infirmities."

"It was reported in Tarsus that he had raised a man from the dead," said Saul, fixing his candid dark eyes on the downcast face of his companion.

"Reported?"—yes! I also heard of the marvel. The High Priest sent his servant, Malchus, to inquire into the matter."

"Why did he not go himself?"

"What need? the man was faithful."

"Where is this Malchus? I should like to speak with him."

Annas looked alarmed. "The man hath died since," he said frowning.

"What said he of the matter?"

"What could an honest man say?" replied Annas with a crafty smile. "Can a carpenter build anew the life which God hath taken out of a man? But I have not told thee all. This carpenter also declared that he was the Messiah."

There was silence in the room for a moment, broken only by the quickened breathing of the young man.

"He said further in the presence of the holy Council of Sanhedrim that he was the Son of God, the King of Israel, and that hereafter he would come in the clouds of heaven to judge the earth."

Saul of Tarsus sprang to his feet, lightnings played within his eyes. "Blasphemer!" he cried in a choked voice. "Why did not Jehovah smite him to the earth?"

"Jehovah did smite him by the hand of his servants; not many hours after he had uttered those sayings he died the accursed death—But hark! I hear a sound of turmoil; what hath befallen? Alas for Jerusalem! she is sorely vexed by the heathen within her gates. Ever and anon the Roman soldiers smite the inhabitants and there is the clash of weapons and the shedding of blood even at the very gates of the temple."

His companion glanced out the window. "The people are running from every direction," he said eagerly. "Let us see what hath happened."

THE PHARISEE FROM TARSUS. 51

"Go thou, my son. I must needs sanctify myself for the temple service."

Descending into the street and following the steps of the hurrying stragglers, the young man soon found himself in the meaner and more crowded portions of the city. Here the narrow streets were choked with people, all running, pushing, struggling towards a common centre.

The Pharisee of Tarsus shrank back with disgust into the doorway of a synagogue near at hand, and from this coign of vantage looked forth on the crowd. The white turbans of Jewish rabbis, the red-bronze faces of Egyptian camel drivers, and the gay robes of Asiatic merchants all mingled in the shifting mazes of the multitude. A jargon of tongues also, like the buzzing of a gigantic swarm of bees, filled the air. From somewhere not far away, he could hear the loud tones of a man's voice, rising and falling as if in passionate exhortation.

"What hath befallen?" he asked at length of a man dressed in the garb of a Greek sailor, who, like himself, had sought refuge in the doorway of the synagogue.

"Fire from heaven hath fallen on the followers of the Nazarene," replied the man, without looking around.

"Dost thou mean the followers of the man called Jesus, who hath lately perished on the cross?" said Saul, regardless for once of the defilement which he brought upon himself by speaking with this Gentile.

"The same," replied the Greek, glancing carelessly at his questioner. "The man Jesus was a worker of miracles. He revived after being buried three days, and went up bodily to dwell with the God of the Jews."

"Dog of a Gentile," cried Saul angrily, "thou art accursed because thou art a Gentile, but doubly accursed because thou hast also blasphemed."

The Greek shrugged his shoulders. "Do I care for thee, Jew?" he said, showing his white teeth in a wicked laugh. "Thou also art accursed, and thy temple shall be torn down, so that not one stone shall stand upon another. I heard the Nazarene say it, and, by Bacchus, I believe it."

"Thou shalt be scourged, fellow, and thy scurrilous tongue cut from thy head," hissed Saul between his shut teeth. "I am a Roman, and I will see to it."

At this the man turned pale, for all his swarthy skin. With a sudden, quick movement, he snatched his garments from the grasp of the Pharisee and fled away into the crowd, doubling and twisting under the arms and betwixt the legs of half-naked barbarians till he was lost to view.

Saul looked after him for a moment in speechless rage.

"Thou art a stranger, then, in Jerusalem," said a voice at his side, "and knowest not what wonders have come upon the Holy City—wonders and terrors also."

The young Pharisee turned and looked at the speaker. He was a Jew, and wore a broad phylactery upon his arm. "I have heard all," he said shortly. "But what hath befallen the followers of the man? The knave yonder said that fire from heaven had fallen upon them; I hope that they be burned to ashes, as were the dwellers in Sodom."

"They are unharmed," said the newcomer gravely. "If, indeed, fire hath fallen upon them, it was a fire that enlightened their understanding, for even now they are preaching to the people of the risen Galilean, so that of all these foreigners every man hears in his own tongue."

"Nay, son of Abraham," cried another voice, "the men are drunken with new wine, and babble as is the custom of wine-bibbers and gluttons."

Saul recognized in the speaker one of the members of the Sanhedrim. "Why then do ye, who are in authority, suffer such unseemly conduct in these men? Why not deal with them also as thou has dealt with their Master?"

"Thou art zealous," said the other in a low voice, and with a gesture of caution. "Yet would such measures be untimely. This," indicating the mixed multitude with a contemptuous wave of his hand, "is a beast, which hath not been tamed either by the church nor yet by the Romans. When it hath tired of these babblers it will rend them, even as it rent the Nazarene, for it was this very multitude that shrieked, 'Crucify him! crucify him!' for the space of three hours. Come, let us be going. We defile ourselves by remaining in this place."

CHAPTER VIII.

A BELIEVER IN THE NAZARENE.

F only I had been there, perchance upon even me might a little of the blessing have fallen. And yet, was it not by the mercy of the all-seeing One that I was chained to the side of him who slew Jesus? We are one flesh, as it is written in the law; if he is accursed, I also am accursed."

"Knowest thou our Lord so little that thou dost believe what thou hast said?" said Stephen, a smile dawning in his dark eyes.

The wife of Caiaphas wiped away one or two slow tears. "How can I know him?" she asked bitterly.

"Once when Jesus was upon earth," said Stephen, looking away towards Calvary, which they could see plainly from their breezy nook on the terrace, "he said this—I did not hear it—but John, whom Jesus called the beloved, one of the disciples, had asked the Master how they should pray, and he told them the very words they might use acceptably; but he also said, If thou hast desires bring them to the Father. He will give to thee even as an earthly father, and much more; if a child should come to his father and ask for bread, will that father offer him a stone? or if he crave fish, will he thrust a deadly scorpion into his hand? How much more then will your heavenly Father give his spirit to them that ask him. It was because we asked that it was given. Thou also shalt ask and shalt receive."

"Wilt thou tell me about it?" said Anna, in a low voice, fixing her eyes wistfully upon the speaker.

He was no longer a lad, she could see it; the awful experiences through which his soul had passed had swept him suddenly and forever away from childhood. His child nature had been crucified with those whom he loved, and upon his face there had come a look such as the strong young angels wear who wait in the presence of the Almighty to do his pleasure.

"We were together in the upper room," said Stephen, after a little silence, "the disciples, the mother of Jesus, and all the others. After we had eaten of the bread and drunken of the wine—as also he commanded to do in remembrance of his death—we continued in prayer, sometimes spoken, sometimes in silence—for there is no need to speak aloud to reach him who is 'with us always even unto the end of the world.' He was there, though we could not see him. All of us knew it; and we asked him for the fulfillment of his last promise—the Spirit, that we being weak, might receive power to be his witnesses before men. John the beloved spoke to him, after that there was silence for a brief space, then on a sudden there came a sound, faint at first, but growing louder by degrees till it filled all the place. It was like nothing I have heard upon earth, and yet was it most like the sound of the viewless wind when it rushes through the thick forest. But it was not wind. I knelt at the side of the Lord's mother, my eyes were upon her at the moment, and the light tresses that fell about her forehead did not so much as stir."

"Was that all?" whispered Anna, leaning forward and clasping her hands.

"As I kept my eyes fixed upon Mary," continued Stephen—"for it seemed to me that she was looking at him—I saw from in the air above her head a tremulous light, it wavered and brightened till it had the look of a cloven tongue of flame. As I feared and trembled greatly at the sight, on a sudden a voice cried out, 'The promise hath been fulfilled unto us!' Then did I see that upon every head hovered the heavenly fire."

"And then?"

"And then," cried the young man, a great joy in the solemn tones of his voice, "all things were made clear to us. We knew what the Lord meant when he said 'Ye shall be witnesses unto me both in Jerusalem, and in all Judea, and in Samaria, and unto the uttermost parts of the earth.' We were no longer filled with fear, thinking only of how to escape the hands of them that had murdered our Lord—nay, rather, that in the infinite and unsearchable knowledge and wisdom the Father had lifted him up upon the cross to be a light unto the world. We rushed out into the street, and the Spirit also drew together out of all the city devout men from every nation under heaven. They gathered in a great multitude that they might hear of the Saviour, not of the Jews only, but of the world."

"How, then, could they understand?" asked Anna, her worn face reflecting the glow upon the face of the young man, as the mountain top clad in its pallor of eternal snow reflects the radiance of the dawn.

"What is the weakness of mortal understanding when the eternal God sheds upon it his spirit of might? Did he not make the tongue of the Asiatic as well as the tongue of the Greek; the tongues of the Parthians, Medes, and Elamites also, as well as the tongue of the Hebrews? Are not all languages understood by him? He spake through us, and behold, every man heard the message in his own language. After that did Peter speak unto the people, and he mightily convinced them, so that many cried out, 'What shall we do?' 'Repent and be baptized,' he answered them, 'every one of you, in the name of Jesus, the Christ, for the remission of sins, and ye shall receive the gift of the Holy Ghost. For the promise is unto you, and to your children, and to all that are afar off.' "

"Said he this to the Gentiles?" asked Anna, in amazement.

Stephen looked troubled. "Nay," he said, "I know not if they were Gentiles, they had by inheritance a part in the blessing, even as I had through my mother; but of a surety God created all men. It will be made plain to us," he added, after a pause, a smile of heavenly sweetness touching his lips.

"And who is it that the wife of the High Priest honors thus with her hospitality?" broke in a sneering voice.

Anna started up with a faint cry, her eyes fixed with manifest terror on the gaunt figure that stood before them.

"Ah! thou dost not answer. Didst thou think, then, that I should remain chained to my couch forever? I am minded to see what is passing in my house. It is time."

"Do not stand," gasped Anna. "Thou art not strong. I thought that thou were asleep."

"Time hasteneth with rapid foot when a lady entertains so comely a young man," said the High Priest with a terrible gentleness. "Once more I ask of thee, who is thy guest?"

Stephen had risen to his feet and was looking with troubled eyes into the face of her whom he had learned to love almost as a mother. He waited for her to speak, Her lips moved, but no sound came from them. He turned and fixed his eyes upon the man. "I know not who thou art,' he said in a clear voice, "nor why thou dost question this beloved lady so harshly, but I can answer for myself. My name is Stephen."

The High Priest took a step forward; he did not speak, but death looked out from his eyes.

"Go! Go!" whispered Anna, turning her white face upon the young man. "Thou dost not understand, but go!—I beseech thee."

"Nay, I will not go till I am assured of thy safety. Who, and what manner of man is this?"

The smouldering fire in the eyes of Caiaphas leapt up into a lurid blaze. "Dost thou, the murderer of my son, defy me in mine own house?" he cried in a choked voice. "Because thou art in mine house, I will not kill thee, but—" and his voice died away into a silence more terrible than speech.

"Go!" repeated Anna imploringly.

But Stephen did not appear to have heard. "What dost thou mean?" he said, his voice full of horror. "Thou hast called me a murderer!"

The High Priest looked at him contemptuously. "Son of a malefactor, dost thou not know that upon thy head rests the blood-guilt of thy father?"

"No!" thundered Stephen, his eyes blazing. "The fire of God could not rest upon a head whereon is also blood-guilt. I am innocent; God hath witnessed it."

"Accursed murderer and blasphemer!" hissed Caiaphas. "Get thee hence, or not even the sacred law of hospitality shall refrain my hand from thy throat." Then he sank trembling onto a bench.

True to her wifely instincts, Anna sprang to help him, but he put her away roughly. "Stand before me, woman," he said, fixing his savage eyes upon her. "Thou shalt answer me somewhat that I shall ask of thee. Now that the murderer of thy son hath rid us of his presence thou canst perhaps attend to what I shall say." Anna stood before him, motionless and rigid, her eyes wide with an unnatural calm fixed upon his face. "Hast thou known who and what this young man is before to-day?"

"Yes."

"Hast thou before received him into my house?"

"Yes."

"Is he a follower of the accursed Nazarene?"

"Yes."

"Art—thou—also one of his believers?"

A change swept over the marble features of the woman, she lifted her face, a mysterious light from above seemed to shine upon it.

"I am," she said simply, but in those two words there sounded a very pean of triumph.

"Flesh of my flesh and bone of my bone," said Caiaphas in a low measured voice, "thou art anathema. As I would cut off my right hand should it become polluted beyond cleansing, so also will I sever thee from my life. Get thee hence unto thine own; thou hast no longer part nor lot with me from henceforth and even forever. And so let it be."

The woman looked dumbly into the pitiless face of the man before her; her slight figure swayed a little, then noiselessly as a snow wreath she fell forward and lay prone upon the marble pavement at his feet.

The man stared at the silent figure; he did not touch it. After a time he arose and walked heavily away without once looking behind him.

CHAPTER IX.

IN THE DESERT ENCAMPMENT.

"THOU mayest fetch the lad and the maiden and set them in my presence. I would question them of this thing."

The woman bowed herself humbly before her lord and retired; presently she returned, leading by the hand a slight figure clad in the shapeless blue gown of an Egyptian peasant girl. Behind lagged with unwilling feet a half-grown lad.

Abu Ben Hesed fixed his piercing eyes upon the twain. "Thou mayest go till I shall call thee," he said to the woman. She lingered yet a moment to whisper, "The maid is blind, my lord!"

"Come hither, my son," said Ben Hesed after a short survey of his two guests, "and tell me how it befell that thou wast in the desert alone? Didst thou know," he added somewhat severely, "that thou wast brought to the borders of the encampment only that thou mightest be buried safe from the vultures? Had not one of the women discerned signs of life, when no other eye could see it, thou wouldst even now be sleeping beneath the sand."

The boy shuddered slightly; he opened his lips as though to speak, but the girl broke out impetuously: "I

IN THE DESERT ENCAMPMENT. 61

alone am in fault," she cried. "It was I who would not listen to my brother when he said, 'we shall perish by the way if we go forth into the wilderness.' It is true," she continued, turning to the lad, "folly dwelleth in the heart of a woman; I am minded to let thee beat me. I have deserved it."

Abu Ben Hesed smiled in the midst of his great beard, but the smile looked also out of his eyes, so that the lad was emboldened to speak.

"We fled before the face of an enemy," he said, looking squarely into the bright eyes of the man before him. "He would have made slaves of us in the city; death in the wilderness is better."

"Thou has spoken a word of wisdom when thou hast so said, my son," cried Ben Hesed, his eyes flashing. "And who is it that would have caged the wild eaglets of the desert?"

"I know not," replied the lad. "I saw not the man, I only heard him speak. We were hidden in the abiding place of the dead; he would have shut us up there to perish, but Sechet smote him in the act and we left him on his face in the sand."

"Thou art Egyptian," said Ben Hesed after a pause. "How comes it that thou canst speak the tongue of the desert?"

"It was my mother's language; my father was a Greek."

"Where then are thy parents?"

"Dead, many years dead," said the boy looking down, and digging his bare toes into the hot sand. A single tear rolled swiftly down his brown cheek.

Ben Hesed saw it, his keen eyes softened. "No longer shalt thou look for a place to bide in safety from thine enemy," he said gently. "Where else should the young eaglets fly but to the nest of their kind? Thou art safe here, my children."

"Thou art good," replied the lad simply; 'but—my sister is blind."

"I am not ignorant of that, my son," said Ben Hesed with a stately inclination of his head. "There is no need that she labor with her hands. Plenty dwells within the borders of my land, though it be not the plenty of Egypt; there is no lack of either flesh nor bread, nor yet of the milk of many herds. Thou art strong, son, and thou shalt labor as becomes a man; the maid shall dwell with the women. Go now in peace, and think of thy past distresses no more," and he waved his hand in token of dismissal.

"Come, Anat," said the lad, drawing her gently away. "It is impossible for us to repay thee thy goodness," he added, lingering wistfully. Yet—"

"There is no need," said Ben Hesed, a slight shade of impatience in his tone. "Go now, my son will tell thee of thy duties."

"Nay, brother, do not hold me, I must tell him," cried Anat. "We cannot remain here."

"How now, damsel, art thou not satisfied with what thou hast received at my hands?" and Ben Hesed drew his bushy brows together with the look before which his wives, his children and his tribe were wont to tremble.

Seth also trembled. "I pray thee, my lord," he said, instinctively bowing himself almost to the ground, "that thou wilt not deal harshly with the maid, my sister. She is blind, and we were seeking a great magician who can heal blindness by a word. Thou knowest that it is an evil thing not to look upon the sun, and upon the stars, and upon the faces of one's kind."

Ben Hesed was silent for a moment. He looked keenly into the lad's flushed face. "It is in Egypt that the magicians dwell," he said at length. "Hast thou not heard how Moses, the mighty man of God, fetched out the Israelites with a strong hand from among the Egyptians; how he worked marvels also and great plagues with the rod of God, and the magicians of Egypt did so with their enchantments, save certain things which they could not do?"

"I know not Moses," said the boy, shaking his head. "Though I have heard many marvels of the great gods of the Greeks and Romans also. Yet is there no magician in Egypt who can cure blindness, for the land is full of it."

"And wherefore didst thou look for this magician in the wilderness?"

"The man said that he dwelt beyond the wilderness and that his name was Jesus," said Anat in her low, sweet voice. "I have not forgotten the name, Jesus. He healed the man, he will also heal me if only I can find him."

Ben Hesed fingered his beard for a time in silence. "What manner of man was he that told thee of this thing?" he said at length.

"He came out of the desert on a swift dromedary," replied Seth. "He was of great stature and his beard descended upon his breast. I gave him to drink of my goat-skin. He said, moreover, that the magician dwelt at Jerusalem."

"A year ago I went up to the Holy City," said Ben Hesed, "that I might offer sacrifices in the temple. I care not to go again. God is a God of the wilderness; he answers also in the wilderness. Of the rocks of the desert have I builded me an altar, even as did Abraham in the days of old. Jerusalem is desolate and her holy places are waste. Why should I go any more into a temple which is daily defiled by the feet of wicked men?" The voice of the speaker shook with passion as he said the last words. Then his head dropped upon his breast and his lips moved, though no sound came from them. The children waited before him in silence, not daring to move.

After what seemed to her a long time, Anat allowed a long-drawn sigh to escape her, by way of a delicate reminder of their presence. "Thou wast in Jerusalem?" she ventured timidly.

Ben Hesed looked up; something in the flowerlike beauty and innocence of the child-face, guarded by its pathetic, unseeing eyes, moved him strangely. The gloom lifted from his brow.

"I was in Jerusalem," he said gravely, "and I saw this man Jesus with mine own eyes."

Anat clasped her hands joyfully. "Ah! then thou canst tell us of him. Dost thou think that he would heal me? I have no money nor treasure to give him, except this," and she laid her fingers on the necklace of coins.

"He would not ask thee for treasure, my child," said Ben Hesed, "for I saw him heal a beggar, who lay upon his bed unable to move, and the man gave him no reward. I came away from Jerusalem in the same hour and saw him no more. I have thought since that sometime I will again seek for him, though I need not to be healed."

"It is a good word that thou hast given to us," said Anat in a tone of joyful conviction; "and now wilt thou further give a handful of parched corn that we may eat by the way? My brother will fill the goat-skin with water, and we will depart."

"Art thou not afraid of the vultures, little one?" asked Ben Hesed with a grave smile. "And how will the flint of the desert bruise those tender feet of thine now that thy beast is dead."

Seth looked depressed. "We cannot go," he said at length, "my goat-skin is not sufficient, and we do not know the way."

"Nay, but we must go!" cried Anat impetuously. "I care not for the vultures, and we have already come a great distance. Did I whine or complain when we thirsted?"

"Thou didst not; but could I bear again to see thee sink to the earth, thy tongue like a parched leaf within thy mouth? And the vultures—thou couldst not see them, but it was horrible—horrible! They stared at us with their red eyes, they waited for us to die. I kept up as long as I was able and drove them away, then did I call aloud upon the god of the land to save us; after that I hid our faces and waited for Anubis to take us."

"The God of the land heard thee, boy," said Ben Hesed solemnly, "for he is not a god like to the gods of the Egyptians. He saved thee, even as he saved the child Ishmael, whom Abraham cast forth into the desert to die. In the desert also did the child Ishmael remain; and God made out of him a great nation which hath ruled over the wilderness until this day. Ay! and shall rule as long as the desert itself remains, for his word is from everlasting to everlasting. Listen now to what I shall say unto thee: thou shalt go in search of this man Jesus, for I believe that he is able to do this thing whereof thou hast spoken. I will send thee to the borders of Judaea with food and water and beasts of burden also, that ye perish not by the way; after that shall ye with ease find Jerusalem, for the way is not long and the land is fertile. Enter freely into the villages and ask for bread, the inhabitants will not say thee nay. And when the maid shall be healed of her blindness, perchance thou wilt again remember the wilderness; return if thou wilt. To-morrow shalt thou set forth."

"I will return, my lord," said the lad, "and by all the gods of the sacred Nile, I swear unto thee that hereafter I will serve thee as a bondman during the years of my life—if it be thy will; because thou hast saved us from death, and because of all thy goodness unto us."

"Nay, rather, thou shalt be to me in the place of my son Eri, whom God hath taken from me," said Ben Hesed. "Go now in peace, and rest until the morning."

So the two were feasted that night, because that they had found favor in the eyes of Ben Hesed. And afterward they slept soundly in the tent of goat's hair, beneath the striped blanket with which they had hidden themselves from the fierce eyes of vultures. And Seth dreamed that he had grown to be a man, and that he was riding upon a swift horse, the wild desert winds blowing in his face, and he laughed aloud in his dream for joy. But to the blind girl came a gentler vision of one who laid a healing hand upon her sightless eyes, and behold! she saw the face of him that had healed her, but it was not the face of mortal, for upon it shone a light beyond the light of the sun.

CHAPTER X.

THE WHITE DROMEDARY.

ONG before the first streaks of light in the east proclaimed the dawn, Seth was awake. Outside he could hear the grunting of the sleepy camels, as their drivers aroused them to fasten the heavy loads on their patient backs. He raised the flap of the tent and looked out. A keen sparkle of stars overhead and a whiff of cold air greeted him. Yet he knew that it must be near the time to start, and he felt a thrill of boyish excitement at the prospect. Among the dark figures which were moving about near the dying fire he thought he could distinguish that of Ben Hesed himself. Presently he slipped out, leaving Anat peacefully asleep. Shivering a little in the cool breeze, he made his way towards the place where the most active preparations were in full tide of progress.

"Make haste!" he heard in the authoritative tones of Ben Hesed's voice. "Thou shouldst have prepared the waterskins last night. Feasting is good, but fasting is better, since it giveth diligence rather than sloth. I would not that ye press on through the fiercest of the midday heat," he added; "the maid hath imperfectly recovered as yet."

"They will walk with the drivers, my lord?"

"Nay, not so. Thou shalt put the saddle upon Mirah, it will suffice for both."

Marvelling greatly at this mark of favor, the men brought the great white dromedary, the favorite of her master, and threw upon her the broad saddle, gay with scarlet leather and tinkling bells.

Seth stared with amazement and delight at the docile beast that stood with outstretched neck snuffing at the fresh wind.

"What dost thou make of such favor to these beggar brats?" said one of the men in low tones to his companion, as he bent to fasten the saddle girth.

"Nay, I know not; 'tis a marvel," answered the other, looking cautiously about him. "Adah told me last night that he had promised to take the lad after his return in the place of his son Eri."

"Ah, sayest thou so? Let me tell thee then that the lad will not return. Why should such a thing be, when the son of his sister is among his tried followers?"

"What wilt thou do to prevent it, son of my lord's sister," said the other, with a low chuckle—"and a kid slain also, in the very midst of the mourning, that the heathen beggars might be feasted!" he added with malicious enjoyment.

Seth prudently drew back in the darkness quite unnoticed, but not before a fragment of the reply reached him; it was this, and it filled him with vague alarms. "What befell the lad Joseph in the days when he dreamed dreams, may also again happen."

Who was the lad Joseph, he wondered, and what befell him? But he presently forgot this in the bustle and excitement of starting forth upon their journey. Anat had been aroused, and the two, perched securely on the back of the gentle Mirah, were the centre of a group of women, some of whom held up their little ones to see, while others pushed parcels of fruit into the hand of the blind girl, wishing them prosperity in their journeyings.

At length all was ready, the last strap adjusted, the last farewell spoken, and the little cavalcade, consisting of some three or four camels and as many men, moved slowly away, followed by the stately Mirah, the two children, unaccustomed to the peculiar swinging motion of her gait, clinging fast to the saddle and scarcely remembering to look back into the kind faces of their rescuers.

All that day they traveled, stopping only for a brief space at the noontide hour. Seth, remembering the command of Ben Hesed, wondered a little at this, but he said nothing. In the man who seemed to be in command of the expedition, the lad had recognized with a feeling of uneasiness the one who had spoken the mysterious words, "What befell the lad Joseph may also again happen."

"Hast thou ever heard of the lad Joseph?" he said to Anat, when they were once more under way. They had grown somewhat accustomed to the long, swinging strides of the dromedary now, and were consequently more at their ease.

"The lad Joseph?" repeated Anat, in her clear, penetrating voice.

"Hist! do not let them hear thee. Yes, the lad Joseph, something strange befell him; it is a legend perhaps. I heard it spoken of in yonder encampment; thou knowest many such tales, for myself I have no mind to remember them."

"There is the great canal of Joseph in the land of Egypt, as thou knowest," said Anat, after a few moments of thought; "there is a tale concerning him who caused it to be made, I know not how long ago. I have heard it many times from our mother. He was a great prince—"

"Nay, then he was not the one; it is of the lad Joseph, and what befell him, that I wish to know," broke in Seth impatiently.

"If thou wilt hold thy peace, water-carrier," replied Anat with dignity, "I will tell thee the tale as it was told me."

"Thou mayest say on; it will help pass away the time."

"He was a great prince," resumed Anat, still with dignity, "but he was also a lad first. I had the tale from our mother. As I have said, it was told to her when she was a maid and dwelt in the borders of the wilderness; it is a true tale. As a lad this Joseph dwelt in the wilderness, the youngest of twelve brethren, the others were grown men; they hated Joseph and were envious of him because their father, who was very rich, gave him many things which they received not, an embroidered tunic, a chain of silver, and such like. The lad also dreamed dreams—"

"Ah!" exclaimed Seth eagerly, "He dreamed, sayest thou?"

"Of a surety," replied the blind girl; "he dreamed that when he bound his sheaf at harvest time, the sheaves of his father and mother and of his brethren came and bowed themselves before it, and other dreams of the like which signified that he would become a great prince, and that all they of his household should do reverence before him. He should not have told such dreams," she added sagely, "for of course his brothers only hated him the more. One day he was sent into the wilderness to fetch dates and honey to the eleven men, his brothers, who were herding the flocks; they saw him coming, wearing his fine, many-colored tunic, and they made up their minds to put him out of the way."

"What did they do?" said Seth breathlessly.

"I was just coming to that, impatient one. Canst thou not hold thy peace? Thou art as greedy over this tale as a flock of sparrows over a measure of corn that hath been spilled on the ground."

"I will hold my peace, queen of my soul," said Seth meekly; "only, I pray thee, tell me what befell the lad."

Somewhat appeased by his humble demeanor, the imperious little maid proceeded with her story. "First," she continued impressively, "they thought that they would kill him, and take his fine tunic home and tell their father that a beast had slain him, but just as they were turning the matter over in their minds they spied a caravan coming towards them, so they changed their wicked purpose to a wickeder yet, and sold him for a slave. Yes, their own brother for a slave," she repeated, much gratified by the involuntary cry which her listener gave at this. "They took him to Egypt—" she went on.

But Seth did not hear the remainder of the story; he was clenching his brown hands in silent anguish of soul. It was all clear to him now. They were to be sold as slaves after all of their sufferings and dangers; they would never see the Holy City, nor the man Jesus who could heal blindness. He groaned aloud.

Anat, in the full tide of her narrative, mistook this for a note of admiration or wonder. She had just arrived at the point in her story where the unfortunate hero is cast into prison. "What wouldst thou have done then?" she asked abruptly.

"I—I—am sure I cannot tell thee, little one," answered Seth, rousing himself with difficulty.

"Thou wouldst have remained there till the day of thy death, no doubt," with superb scorn, "but not so Joseph; he—"

"I am drowsy, little one; Sechet rages fiercely in the heavens; let us leave the tale till to-morrow," said Seth in a smothered voice.

Anat touched his cheek with a cautious forefinger. "It is true, thy flesh hath over-much heat. See! I have here a pomegranate; thou shalt eat of it and be refreshed."

After this the travelers spoke but little. Tirelessly the white dromedary strode onward under the blinding glare of the sun, her broad feet making no sound on the yielding sand; the landscape quivered in the intense heat, melting into golden, pink, and violet fires in the far distances, while near at hand the scarlet blooms of the cactus glowed like live coals. Once they came upon a flock of vultures gorging themselves upon the carcass of a camel; they rose with hoarse croakings and withdrew themselves to a little distance, till the living should pass by. "As yet, we have no concern with thee," they seemed to say to the white dromedary, "but so shall it be with thee also, for man is ungrateful." Then they again descended, a dismal crew, upon the stranded wreck of the desert ship. And the stately Mirah strode onward tirelessly.

That night they pitched a tent and built a fire of the dried shrubs. The man Pagiel spoke roughly to the children; he bade the lad gather the fuel; as for the maid, he pushed her aside with his foot, as though she were a dog. Seth's eyes burned when he saw the thing, but he said nothing; he thought instead. The white dromedary crouched upon the sand, chewing her cud, her large eyes fixed thoughtfully upon the distance. The boy approached her cautiously and caressed her snowy neck; the beast permitted it with a low sound in her throat.

"That wouldst thou not venture with every beast in the flock," said one of the men good-naturedly. "They be ugly save with those who know them. Yonder camel can be touched by no other save Jered, his driver; but Mirah there is of another sort; I have seen my lord's little ones climb upon her back when they were babes. For speed she is a marvel; thou hast not seen it, for the camels travel but slowly."

"She can outrun them then?" said Seth, his heart beating violently.

"Assuredly, boy, there is nothing swifter save the wind."

"Fetch fuel, beggar!" cried Pagiel, accompanying his words with a fierce look, "and do thou afterward get into the tent and sleep, thou and the girl."

"Why dost thou speak thus harshly to the lad?" questioned the other after Seth had withdrawn in obedience to the command.

"He is a heathen beggar; why should he receive kindness at my hand? Listen! tomorrow we come to the fountain of Hodesh, 'tis but a day's march from the river; we will tarry there till a caravan shall pass by, then will we sell the lad and the maiden for gold. The gold shalt thou divide between the three of you, and thou shalt say naught to Ben Hesed concerning the matter; it will pass from his mind, even as the mist dissolves before the rising sun. But thou shalt have that wherewith to comfort thyself."

The man listened with bent brows. "What is comfort to me," he said sullenly, "if I have not thy daughter to wife; she is comely, and I love her better than gold."

Pagiel stared at the speaker with amazement. "Thou hast forgotten thyself," he said haughtily.

"Nay, I have not forgotten; thou art the son of my lord's sister, I am the son of Kish the herdsman. Yet in the desert what matters it, am I not a man like unto thee?"

Pagiel was silent a moment. "It shall be so," he said at length. "It is true thou art a man, and my daughter is, after all, only a woman; I have sons also, thanks be to Jehovah!"

"And the gold?"

"Shall be for the maid's dowry, in addition to what she hath already."

"Thou hast dealt graciously with me, my lord, I am henceforth as thy son, and as thy son will I obey thee."

On the morrow they came to the fountain of Hodesh, and they encamped there, waiting for a caravan. On the third day during the heat of the noontide the men slept within the tent, but Seth rose up softly, and went out. He filled his goat-skin at the fountain and bound it upon his back; he took also of the parched corn a small measure, and of the dates a double handful; "for," he said to himself, "it was for us that these things were given by the lord of the desert."

"Why dost thou fill thy goat-skin, brother?" said Anat, hearing the familiar tinkle of the brasses.

"Wake not the men yonder," answered Seth in a cautious whisper. "They would deal with us after the manner of the brethren of Joseph. We will get us away upon the white dromedary, nor shall they be able to overtake us."

So the two went softly to where Mirah crouched beneath the shadow of the palms, and they climbed upon her back.

"It is a good thing for us that Pagiel commanded her to be saddled," quoth Seth. "He had the intent to ride after his sleep."

Then he spoke softly in the ear of the beast after the fashion of her driver; and she rose up with them, and went silently away into the desert towards the range of hills, beyond which lay the land of Judaea.

But Pagiel awakened out of his sleep and stood in the door of his tent. And when he saw the dromedary fleeing away, he made a great outcry and awakened the others also; and they pursued after them for many hours, but they were not able to overtake them because the gentle Mirah was very swift. Anon she disappeared from before their eyes like a white sail on the distant verge of the sea.

When Pagiel saw that she was gone, bearing the two whom he would have sold into slavery, he tore his beard and wept with rage because he had promised his daughter to the son of Kish, the herdsman. For he feared his women, notwithstanding he was a man, and of great stature.

CHAPTER XI.

AT THE GATE BEAUTIFUL.

HE long hours of the morning had worn themselves away, the sunshine had ceased to glitter on the wonderful carved brass of the great gate Shushan some three hours since. One without, standing on the marble pavement, might admire the marvels of Corinthian workmanship without an undue dazzling of the vision; so also might the lame man, who lay on his mat a little to one side of the entrance. Yet was he paying scant heed to the grandeur of his surroundings. He lay at the gate of the temple, which was called "Beautiful," not because it was beautiful, but because through it passed a stream of worshippers to and from the well-nigh ceaseless services of prayer and praise within. These all carried their money within their hand, since it was not lawful to enter the sacred enclosure having one's gold or silver within a purse nor indeed anywhere about the person save in the hand only. So the lame man profited by the law, inasmuch as many cast a coin into his bosom who might otherwise have been in too much haste for prayer to have fetched out their purses for a beggar.

On this day, however, the hands of the many had remained tightly closed upon their treasure, not only when they went in to bow themselves before the All-Giver, but also when they came out.

The lame man looked at them as they passed by him with unseeing eyes. He wondered what blessing these men with their hard, worldly-wise faces and closed fists had asked of the Almighty; he also wondered if they had received. He himself went but seldom within the gates. He could not approach too near the Holy Place because of his infirmity. God had declared that such as the lame, the halt and the blind were unholy and displeasing in his sight, so the priests taught. But he had been lame from his birth and was sadly accustomed to this and other miseries of his lot. For forty years his soul had looked from the windows of his prison-house upon the world. In these forty years he had ceased to look for happiness, but he had learned to be silent and to endure, which is perhaps better.

He had heard tales of the man Jesus, who had healed many; once he had begged his bearers to carry him to the healer that he also might be restored, but they had refused.

"Thou art able to earn the bread which thou eatest, and also to recompense us, who fetch thee back and forth from the temple gate; if thou art healed, what canst thou do more? thou art already old. There is no profit in having thee healed, therefore remain as thou art."

So he had remained as he was, and now the man Jesus was dead, crucified, and there was no further chance that he might be healed. He regretted it patiently; one learns to be patient even in one's regrets during forty years. But he often thought of the man who had been crucified. The priests had done it, he had been told; in secret he hated the priests, and for this thing he hated them the more. Why should they kill the man because he had healed upon the Sabbath day? he thought bitterly; but he said nothing, for there was no one who cared for his thoughts.

Presently he bethought himself to take account of his gains for the day, since the hour of sunset was drawing on apace. "'Tis not enough," he muttered, as he counted the copper coins from his greasy pouch. "I must pay Nicolas and Obed, else they will not fetch me home; I like not to stay here by night, the wind from the valley is chilly." Then he lifted his head and saw two men ascending the marble steps. They were not rich, his experienced eye told him that, but it was not from the rich that he expected alms. They were too busy thinking of the ritual which they were going to repeat, or which perchance they had just repeated without a flaw; and the pieces of money within their hand were sure to be gold, or at least silver, neither meet for a beggar. No, it was from women going humbly in to their outer court of worship, or from children, that he received, or from such men as these in the plain garb of Galilean peasants. Therefore the beggar lifted up his voice with some confidence and cried aloud in the words which his mother—when she found that he was a hopeless cripple—had taught him, and which he had repeated many times each day since.

"Sons of Abraham! Chosen of Jehovah! have mercy, I beseech thee, on one lame from his birth! Give unto me from thy heaven-bestowed bounty; so will God recompense thee fourfold."

The two men stopped and looked at him intently, and the beggar repeated his cry, stretching forth his lean hand imploringly and lifting his ragged robe to show the helpless and shrunken limbs beneath. "They will give," he thought within himself. "It will not be much, but it

AT THE GATE BEAUTIFUL.

has been a bad day with me so far, and every little bit helps."

"Look on us," said the older of the two men imperatively.

The beggar obeyed, marvelling within himself at the singular brightness of the man's eyes. He began to think that perhaps for once he had been mistaken, and that these men, despite their humble apparel, were after all rich and important.

"Silver and gold have I none," said the man, still holding the beggar's expectant gaze with his powerful eye, "but such as I have, give I thee. In the name of Jesus Christ of Nazareth, rise up and walk."

A thrill of hope passed into the beggar's starved soul; his heart beat violently, his eyes grew dim, he again stretched forth his hand, scarcely knowing what he did; it was seized in a strong grasp, and he felt himself raised to his feet—the feet upon which he had never stood in all the forty years of his life. His heart leaped within his bosom with a strange and wonderful joy. Involuntarily his feet leaped also, he could not help it. He clung to his deliverers, weeping out incoherent blessings and prayers. Then, walking and leaping, he entered into the temple with them, and remembering that he was no longer a cripple, and that now he might approach God freely, he cried aloud in his joy, not standing according to the law, with feet close together, hands upon his breast and head bowed, but walking and leaping and praising jubilantly with a loud voice. He knew that he had received, therefore his full soul overflowed its bounds.

As for the rest of the worshippers, who had prayed according to the law, and in whose souls there surged no tumultuous happiness—and why indeed should there?— they were greatly disturbed at this unseemly exhibition. They looked askance at the strange ragged figure singing aloud of his wonderful deliverance, and they shook their heads and frowned. "Go forth into the porch," commanded certain who were in authority, "until we shall look into this matter."

And the beggar, nothing loth, obeyed, still clinging to his deliverers and praising more loudly than ever.

"Who art thou?" he cried. "Tell me, for I would know; mayhap ye be of angels in the garb of men."

"Nay, we are but disciples of the crucified one, Jesus of Nazareth. 'Tis by faith in his name that we have been able to heal thee, and not by our own power."

And when the beggar heard the name, Jesus, he praised God yet more loudly.

Now all the people hearing the voice of the beggar ran together in the porch, which is called Solomon's, to see what had happened; and when they saw him that had been lame, walking and leaping as he praised God, they were filled with wonder. Some ran to the gate Beautiful to make sure that it was he and no other, but they found there only the empty mat on which the beggar had lain, and they returned marvelling more than ever.

"Behold!" they whispered, pointing out Peter one to another, "It was the man yonder who performed the miracle. It must needs be that he is most holy, that he hath kept the law without failure of jot or tittle, that he can do such marvels."

But when Peter perceived this he said unto the people: "Ye men of Israel, why wonder ye at this, or why look ye so earnestly upon us, as though by our own power or holiness we had made this man to walk? The God of Abraham, and of Israel, and of Jacob, the God of our fathers hath glorified his son Jesus, whom ye delivered up and denied in the presence of Pilate when he had determined to release him. Ye rejected the holy and righteous one and asked that a murderer should be

AT THE GATE BEAUTIFUL. 81

granted you; but the giver of life ye killed. Yet hath God raised him again from the dead, whereof we are witnesses. By faith in his name hath this man been made whole, whom also ye see and have known. Yea, the faith which is by him hath given him this perfect soundness in the presence of you all. And now, brethren, I know that in ignorance ye did these things, as also your rulers; what God before announced by the mouth of all his prophets that the Christ should suffer, he thus fulfilled. Repent, therefore, and turn ye, that your sins may be blotted out, so may the times of refreshing come from the presence of the Lord. And he shall send the Christ who hath been before proclaimed unto you, even Jesus; yet he must needs remain in the heavens till the time cometh when all things shall be restored, which time hath God spoken of by the mouth of his holy prophets since the world began. For Moses said unto the fathers, 'A prophet shall the Lord your God raise up unto you of your brethren, like unto me. To him shall ye harken in all things whatsoever he shall say unto you. And it shall come to pass that every soul which will not hear him shall be utterly destroyed from among the people.' Yea, and all the prophets from Samuel and them that follow after, as many as have spoken, have likewise foretold of these days. Ye are the sons of the prophets, and of the Covenant which God made with our fathers, saying unto Abraham, 'and in thy seed shall all the kindreds of the earth be blessed.' Unto you first, God, having raised up his son Jesus, sent him, that he might bless you in turning away every one of you from his sins."

And all the people paid heed unto him; and many wept aloud for joy when they heard that they might be forgiven for their part in the crucifixion of Jesus. They had not forgotten that day, nor how they had cried "Away with him—away with him! Crucify him—crucify him!"

Nor had they forgotten the terror of darkness at midday and the earthquake, nor the terrible sentence which they had pronounced upon themselves: "His blood be upon us and upon our children." Many times had they cried in secret what also they had said on that day, "We are undone—we are undone!" Therefore believed they with gladness the word which Peter had spoken unto them, and they prayed aloud that God would forgive them their blood-guiltiness. But as Peter and John would have spoken further unto them, the Priests and officers of the temple and the Sadducees came suddenly upon them.

"What mean ye, blasphemers?" they said, "that within the sacred precincts of the temple ye do preach in the name of an accursed malefactor the resurrection from the dead. These things shall not be." And they locked them up until the next day, for it was now eventide. As for the beggar that had been healed, they put him in hold also, that they might examine him at their leisure.

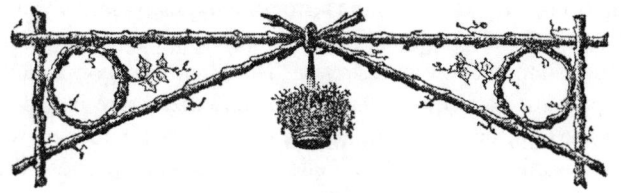

CHAPTER XII.

IN THE COUNCIL CHAMBER.

NNAS sat quite alone in the council chamber of the Sanhedrim. He had come early in order that he might set in order certain papers, and also that he might with due deliberation determine the course of procedure for the morning's session. But this was not easy; things looked dubious for the success of his enterprise; he was forced to acknowledge as much to himself.

"This miracle now," he thought, stroking his hoary beard reflectively, "was a most unfortunate thing—most untimely. The multitude seems quite carried away by it. Should we adopt violent measures with these pernicious persons it would, I fear, fail to commend itself to the populace."

At this point in his cogitations he was disturbed by the sound of a slow heavy step ascending the stair; the door opened and Caiaphas entered. Annas looked at him in surprise, noting with cold disapproval his haggard face, his disordered apparel, his shaking hands.

"I am astonished," he said, bringing his critical gaze to a standstill upon the uneasy eyes of his son-in-law, "astonished, indeed I may say that I am not well pleased to see thee here this morning, my son. Thou hast the look of a man who should be within the walls of his sick chamber. The ministrations of my daughter's skillful hand will surely prove more acceptable to thee in thy present state than the deliberations of statecraft. I pray thee let me command for thee a litter."

"Hold!" said Caiaphas, grasping the old man by the arm. "Hear what I have to say to thee first," and he lowered his voice to a husky whisper. "Thy daughter is no longer my wife."

"What dost thou mean, man? Thou art mad!"

"Nay, I am not mad; would that I were!" said the other faintly.

"I repeat that thou art mad," cried Annas, his eyes blazing with a scornful fire. "What! my daughter repudiated by *thee?*"

"She hath become a follower of the Nazarene," said Caiaphas dully. " Could she longer be wife of mine?"

"Where is she?"

"She hath gone to them."

Annas was silent for a time. "If what thou sayest be no figment of a disordered brain," he said deliberately, "then I say thou hast done well. No longer wife of thine, she shall be no longer daughter of mine. She is henceforth one of the followers of him whom we hanged upon the accursed tree. As for them, shall I tell thee what shall shortly come to pass?"

The younger man made no reply.

"When men would plant grain in a field which hath been a wilderness," continued Annas, still in the same icy, deliberate tones, "they root up the tares and utterly destroy them with fire. This shall we do with these mischievous and deadly weeds that be winding their poisonous roots about the only props that remain to our suffering nation, the temple and the home. But let not this thing be spoken of—the matter of the woman, I

IN THE COUNCIL CHAMBER.

mean. There is no need to make our name a byword and hissing; she hath for the present gone to pay a visit; later we shall, perhaps, devise a way to secretly rid ourselves—"

"What!" cried Caiaphas, starting up. "Wouldst thou—"

"Hist, man, the others are coming!—wilt thou remain? We shall this morning concern ourselves with this very matter."

"I will remain."

And when presently the council was convened, he took his old place upon the right hand of Annas. In his sick heart he wished for death, yet there burned within him the miserable desire to avenge himself upon them at whose door he laid the loss of both his wife and his son.

"Thou mayest fetch hither the two men whom ye put in hold," commanded Annas, "likewise the beggar."

"Ye behold in these," he continued, fixing his piercing gaze upon Peter and John, as they stood before the semicircle of their august judges, "two men who were prominent followers of the Nazarene, who was recently put to death because of his crimes against church and state. Wise men would have taken a wholesome warning from the fate of their false teacher, but these follow in the footsteps of him who was crucified, not remembering apparently that those footsteps led to the cross. Yesterday there was a tumult raised in the holy temple, a beggar whom God had justly afflicted because of the sins of his fathers was, forsooth, healed; healed by these men. It is not meet that such things be permitted. I therefore command that ye tell us straightway by what means and by what name ye have done this thing?"

"Ye rulers of the people, and elders of Israel," said Peter, and at the sound of his voice the beggar who had involuntarily shrunken back abashed stood boldly forth. "If we this day be examined of the good deed done to the impotent man, and if ye will inquire by what means he is made whole, be it known unto you all and to all the people of Israel, that by the name of Jesus the Nazarene, the Messiah, whom ye crucified but whom God raised from the dead, even by him doth this man stand here before you whole. This is the stone which was set at naught of you builders, which is become the head of the corner. Neither is there salvation in any other, for there is none other name under heaven given among men whereby we must be saved."

Something of the same feeling which had overwhelmed Annas on the night when he had essayed to question the man of Nazareth came upon him. He tried to speak, and his voice failed him. Meantime a murmur of surprise ran about the circle.

"How is it," whispered one to his neighbor, "that these ignorant men can speak in such a manner?"

"They have learned it in the company of the Galilean," replied the other. "Dost thou not remember his sayings?"

"What shall we say?" queried a third. "The man there will spread the thing far and wide."

"Remove the prisoners," commanded Annas, somewhat recovering himself. "We must confer in private concerning this thing. This is a most untoward happening," he added, when they were alone, looking about him at the circle of attentive faces. "What now shall we do with these men?"

"Let them be stoned for blasphemy," said Alexander, drawing his heavy brows together. "Did they not call the crucified Galilean the Messiah, and declare that God had raised him from the dead? This also they preach openly to the people. For myself I am of the opinion that our case is worse than before; the Galilean himself was but one man, and could be in but one place, now, forsooth, we have a thousand men in his stead, all haranguing,

IN THE COUNCIL CHAMBER.

healing and creating a very fire of heresy amongst the populace. The thing must be stopped, else will our power be short-lived. These men be worse than the Romans, for they at least suffer us to be in peace."

"Suppose that we stone them," remarked one of the sons of Annas with a sneer. "How then are we bettered? The whole city would take up the cry against us, more especially the lower classes who envy us our wealth. 'These holy men have wrought a notable miracle,' they would howl, 'and the Sanhedrists have stoned them for it.' Could we crush the whole mob of the so-called disciples with a single stone, and perform the deed quietly, then should I cry with a good will, 'Let them be stoned.' As it is, such a course would only add fuel to the flame."

"Thou hast spoken wisely, my son," said Annas, "The miracle is a notable one; all Jerusalem knows it, and we cannot deny it. But that it spread no further among the people, let us straitly threaten them, that they speak henceforth to no man in this name. Fetch now the men," he added, turning to the temple police who waited their pleasure.

"We have considered the matter of your doings with care," he continued with portentous solemnity, when the prisoners had again been set in his presence. "The matter of the healing we are disposed to overlook, though it is not seemly for children of dust to assume the prerogatives of the Almighty; by his hand hath this man been laid low, he should have remained as he was. It is not our custom to heal beggars, nor should it be yours; it savoreth of a compact with the evil one. The matter of your speaking to the people is far more serious. Dost thou know that thou hast laid thyself open to a death by stoning? For verily thou hast blasphemed foully; our ears and the ears of them that have heard thee are polluted by the unholy words which thou hast spoken. Yet are we merciful and inclined to pardon even this iniquity, on the one condition that from henceforth ye speak to no man in this name of Jesus—a name I like not to utter. If now ye are ready to comply with this our reasonable request, ye shall at once be released."

Then did John, the beloved disciple, fix his calm eyes on the man who had spoken; with something of the divine prescience of the Master did he read the false soul behind the lying lips. "Whether it be right in the sight of God," he said solemnly, "to obey you rather than God, judge ye. For we cannot but speak the things which we have seen and heard."

"Continue to speak them," cried Caiaphas in a fury, as he thought of his lost wife, "and a fate more terrible than stoning shall befall thee. Shall we endure to see—"

But Annas laid a warning hand upon his arm. "Remove these men," he said hastily to the temple guard. "Let them go."

"And the beggar, my lord?"

"Release him also, but bid him hold his peace concerning his healing, both in the temple and elsewhere, lest a worse thing than lameness come upon him."

But the beggar followed after the disciples as they went away, and when they saw him they said, "Dost thou join thyself to us because thou believest on the name of Jesus?"

And he answered them humbly, "By the name of Jesus was I healed of mine infirmity, how then can I help but believe?"

And they suffered him gladly because of that word. And when they were come to the place wherein were gathered many others that believed, they told all that the chief priests and elders had said to them, and they lifted up their voice to God in one accord and said:

IN THE COUNCIL CHAMBER.

"O Lord, thou that didst make the heaven, and the earth, and the sea, and all that in them is, by the mouth of David thy servant thou didst say:

> " 'Why did the nations rage,
> And the people meditate vain things?
> The kings of the earth set themselves in array,
> And the rulers were gathered together
> Against the Lord, and against his Anointed.'

"For of a truth, in this city were gathered together against thy holy servant Jesus, whom thou didst anoint, both Herod and Pontius Pilate, with the nations and the peoples of Israel. And they did what thy hand and thy counsel had determined should come to pass. And now, Lord, look upon their threatenings, and grant unto thy servants to speak thy word with all boldness, and stretch forth thy hand to heal, that signs and wonders may be done by the name of thy holy servant Jesus."

And when they had thus prayed, behold the place where they were assembled was shaken and they were all filled with the Spirit, so that they had no fear in their hearts of what might befall them at the hands of their enemies. And on that day and every day they continued to speak the words which God gave them with great joy and confidence.

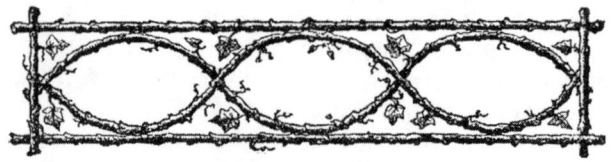

CHAPTER XIII.

AT THE FEET OF THE APOSTLES.

 O Anna, in the house of Mary, there had come peace. When she had awakened from the death-like swoon in which she had sunken at the feet of Caiaphas, to find herself alone, she scarce knew at first what had befallen her. But memory, too faithful, repeated to her shrinking soul the words which had struck at the very fountain of life; she turned them over dully in her mind, "As I would cut off my right hand, should it become polluted beyond cleansing, so also will I sever thee from my life."

"How can that be," she thought, staring at the light branches of a rose tree that swayed from the trellis above her head; the sun struck vivid sparks of emerald fire from its translucent leaves, the breeze shook a full-blown blossom, and a handful of the odorous petals fell upon her face. She inhaled their fragrance as in a dream of pain.

"So I will sever thee from my life," she repeated, looking at the shattered rose. "Ah, it can never bloom again!"

And with the thought came a sudden frightful realization of what had happened. She sprang up and looked wildly about her. "I must find him! It cannot be!" Then she sank feebly upon her knees beside the bench, and buried her face in her hands.

Is it for naught that misery instinctively assumes this attitude? Nay, rather, it is a divine impulse of the suffering soul, a blind and voiceless feeling after a hand in the darkness. And the hand is always there.

To Anna thus bowed there came at length the thought of God, of Jesus, the all-Comforter; of Stephen, his dark eyes full of loving light; of Mary, the mother of Jesus, like herself, desolate. And presently, though, she scarce knew why, she grew quite calm and strong. She arose. "I will go," she said aloud, "to them; they will tell me what I must do."

And so it was that she came to the house of John, the beloved disciple, where abode Mary, whom the dying Lord had given into his keeping, and with them Peter, and Andrew his brother, also Stephen.

"I am desolate," she said humbly, "for my husband hath cast me off, because I believe that the crucified Jesus is the Messiah of Israel."

"Then art thou welcome here," said the master of the house, gravely. But Mary fell on her neck and kissed her, and she wept with her, because she knew that tears are healing, if only they be wiped away by the hand of God.

And so, after many days, there came to her peace; nay, more, there came joy. Involuntarily songs broke from her lips, lips for many years silent; she smiled often even when alone, for a strange delight filled her soul, her deep eyes shone like stars.

Stephen saw the change in her and he rejoiced.

"The Lord is with thee, mother of my Titus," he said, tenderly.

"I scarce know why I am so happy," she replied. "Is it meet that I should rejoice when my son is dead, and when I am more desolate than a widow?"

"It is the gift of him who sitteth at the right hand of the Father," said Stephen. "Did he not say, 'Peace I leave with you, my peace I give unto you. Not as the world giveth, give I unto you. Let not your heart be troubled, neither let it be afraid.' And this good word of peace he left with his chosen ones on the very night before his death. The world cannot give peace in the midst of sorrow, but he can, and he hath given it unto thee, beloved. And thou dost rejoice, and thy joy shall no one take from thee."

"But my husband?" said Anna eagerly.

"Ask the Lord that it may be granted unto him to see the truth. I will also ask, then shall it be done for us according to his promise which cannot fail."

"And he will again love me?"

"Love is the fulfilling of the law," said Stephen, smiling. "He will again love thee, and the love that he hath had is as nothing to that God will give him, for God is love, and he is also the all-giver. All love is from God, and without it would the world fall from its place in the heavens into the darkness which is outside of love—if indeed there be any place where the light of God doth not penetrate." He paused, and looked thoughtfully away into the sunset, as if he would pierce with his longing gaze beyond the gold and the crimson to that place where dwelt the risen Lord.

The days went swiftly in this new life, for none were idle. Indeed, there was never a company of folk since the world began into whose lives crowded more of service, of love, of joy. The sick, the unhappy, the poor from all the city and the country round about came for healing, cheering, help; nor was any turned away. The disciples

AT THE FEET OF THE APOSTLES. 93

were ever mindful of the word of their Lord, "Freely ye have received, freely give." They remembered also with awe how he had washed their feet on that last night before he was betrayed. So there was no service too lowly, no labor too arduous for them to undertake in the strength of their new joy.

"Did he not say unto us," said Peter, his face glowing with divine enthusiasm, " 'As the Father hath sent me into the world, so send I you?' "

To be a Christian in these days meant simply to live as Christ had lived. And so the women were busy from dawn until evening in fashioning garments for them that had none; in preparing the simple food, which they ate from house to house with gladness and singleness of heart, every meal a memorial feast of him who had gone to prepare a place for them in the heavens. And the men, in proclaiming the amazing tidings of salvation from sin in a world given over to sin, of joy in a world wherein was weeping and pain and woe, of peace in the midst of strife, of a great light that had shined in the darkness. It was so real, so wonderful, so new. They had not read of these things in an ancient book. They had not heard them with cold dead ears 'as a tale that is told,' but they had seen the Lord living and walking among them; they had seen him upon the cross; they had seen him in the tomb dead—his hands and feet torn with the cruel nails. And they had also seen him alive again and received into the glories of a visible heaven. Upon their heads had the pentecostal flames rested, and they beheld their mortal bodies endowed with divine powers. Little wonder then that they rejoiced, little wonder that a holy fear came upon every soul and that they had favor with all the people. Yet for our comfort is it written that the Lord once said unto Thomas, "Because thou hast seen me thou hast believed; blessed are they that have not seen and yet have believed."

Now because very many that were poor came to the disciples to be fed, and because the apostles had now no time for fishing, being made fishers of men as the Lord had promised, and for the reason that then as now no one can live in the world without money, they asked of the Lord concerning this thing, indeed they still asked about all things just as when he was on the earth. And it became very clear to them what they must do. And they did it in all simplicity and singleness of heart. They that had lands or houses sold them, and brought the prices of the things that were sold and laid them down at the apostles' feet, and distribution was made unto every man according as he had need, so that there should no longer be among them any that was rich, for had not the Lord said to the young ruler, "Go sell what thou hast and give to the poor, and thou shalt have treasure in heaven," and also, "How hardly shall they that have riches enter into the kingdom of God." And because they thought much about heaven in those days and because they longed to enter into the kingdom, it was not hard for some of the rich to do this. Their possessions were as nothing to them compared with the riches which God was giving so freely.

"He is the same yesterday, to-day and forever." And alas! humanity is the same yesterday and to-day, but to-morrow, which shall also be forever, when we shall be like him!

There was in Jerusalem a certain man named Ananias, and he was married to a woman called Sapphira. They had heard the preaching of Peter and they believed, and came and joined themselves to the church. They were rich people and owned land outside the city. Now when others who had possessions sold them and brought the money to lay at the apostles' feet, they were ill pleased.

"Why should this be?" said Ananias to his wife. "If we give a tithe of what is ours is not that all that the law demands?"

"It is unjust," declared Sapphira, "we also shall be beggars if we do this thing, besides it hath been told me that the scribes and elders have the intent to crush these apostles as well as all that believe; for myself I have no mind to be stoned."

"Let us withdraw then."

"Nay, not so, for God is with these men as also thou hast seen," said Sapphira. "And if the Master presently come back from heaven—as indeed they all expect—he will establish a kingdom here in Jerusalem, and it must not chance that we be found on the wrong side when that shall come to pass."

"They do not demand that we sell our lands," said Ananias, knitting his brows thoughtfully. "Let us be prudent and reserve our possessions till we shall see what is going to befall."

"Only this morning Joses brought money and laid it down at the apostles' feet, said Sapphira. "He hath sold every cubit of his farm in the hill country. They know that we also have lands," she added fretfully, "and they expect that we will do the same. There are already five thousand persons in the church, and very few among them own earth enough to be buried in."

"It is a hard case," whined Ananias, "if honest, industrious folk must give up all that they have to beggars. They will devour it up like grasshoppers; as for us who have given it, what shall we have for a time of adversity, or for our old age?"

"What indeed?" echoed his wife. "But we must do something or we shall be talked about. What if—" and she lowered her voice to a whisper—"we sell the land, and also freely tell of the matter, but of the price that is received we will give a part only, the remainder we will bestow in safety till we shall ourselves have need of it."

"Thou art a prudent woman!" cried her husband. "I know a man who will give me a good price for the land."

"Go then and sell, but let no one know of the amount which thou receivest. That shall be secret betwixt the two of us. The man Peter shall suppose that we have given all, even as did Joses."

So Ananias went and sold the land and he received for it a goodly sum, which the two took secretly and buried in the earth, keeping out a part only; this the woman laid in her lap.

"It is a great sum," she said, looking regretfully at the pieces of silver. "With it we might buy fine raiment for ourselves; or I might put them upon a string for my neck. I have no necklace."

"Spoken like a woman, and therefore foolishly," said Ananias, lifting a handful of the coins and letting them slip through his fingers one by one. "For my part I should buy a vineyard. One could then have an abundance of wine."

"Neither of these things can be," said Sapphira with a sigh. "We must give it, else when the Messiah shall come, the man Peter will say, 'These people having land sold it, but gave no part to us;' then the Messiah will give us neither place nor power."

"Suppose he comes not?" said the man doggedly.

"We shall at least stand well with the apostles and the rest. They be all prating of the generosity of Joses to-day. 'Such a man! So holy!' they cry. To-morrow they shall speak of us also; what we shall give will be much more than his paltry bit of silver." And the woman tossed her head.

AT THE FEET OF THE APOSTLES.

"Well, I will give it."

"But do not let them know about the other," whispered Sapphira.

"Thou mayest trust me for that!" said the man with a harsh laugh.

On the morrow, when all were gathered together according to their custom, came Ananias bringing the money—Sapphira remaining at home to guard the buried treasure; and he laid down the silver at the feet of Peter saying, "I have sold my lands for the service of the Lord, and here is all the price of them."

And the people looked at the money which he had laid down, and they marvelled at his generosity, saying one to another, "Joses truly was righteous, but this man hath brought a greater sum than he."

But Peter fixed his inspired eyes upon the giver. He read his soul. And he said to him: "Ananias, why hath Satan filled thine heart to lie to the Holy Spirit, and keep back part of the price of the land? Whilst it remained was it not thine own? And after it was sold, was it not in thine own power? Why hast thou conceived this thing in thine heart? Thou hast not lied unto men, but unto God."

And when Ananias heard these words, it was as though the light of God had been flashed into his soul. A fierce agony fell upon him. He saw clearly what he was, and what God was; and because this may not be endured by a mortal, he fell down at the feet of the apostle dead. He had passed into the presence of the Love which is also a consuming fire.

And the young men arose, wound up his body in grave clothes, and carried it away. And it was about the space of three hours after when his wife, not knowing what was done, came in. And Peter said to her, "Tell me whether ye sold the land for fifty shekels?"

And she said, "Yes, for fifty shekels."

Then Peter said unto her, "How is it that ye have agreed together to tempt the Spirit of the Lord? Behold! the feet of them which buried thy husband are at the door, and shall carry thee out."

Then fell she down straightway at his feet and expired, and the young men came in and found her dead, and carrying her forth, buried her by her husband. And great fear came upon all the church, and upon as many as heard these things.

CHAPTER XIV.

A CUP OF COLD WATER.

"THEN the beast is not thine own?"

"I have said that it belongs to Abu Ben Hesed, who dwells in the wilderness of Shur. For this journey alone was it ours. I must return it to its owner after that I have accomplished mine errand in yonder city."

The man looked at the boy steadily for a full minute; a slight smile curled the corners of his lips, but he turned his head so that the lad should not see it. "And thy business in Jerusalem, what might it be? Thou art perhaps a merchant seeking goodly pearls, or a purchaser of slaves, or—perhaps a pilgrim?"

"My business is naught to thee; I have asked of thee a question, wilt thou care for the beast till I shall return? I will pay thee for it."

The man ran his eyes once more over the white dromedary, she shook herself and all the silver bells of the bridle rang merrily. "I will take care of her," he said, nodding his head once or twice and smiling again broadly; "and when wilt thou be pleased to return?"

"This very day at evening, if I shall find the man I would see. His name is Jesus. Canst thou tell me where to find him?"

"There be half a score of that name in the city. Dost thou mean Jesus Barabbas?" and the man laughed aloud, as if his thoughts afforded him secret pleasure.

"Is he a magician?" asked the lad eagerly.

"A magician? Dost thou mean a man whom the gods granted to be born under a lucky star?"

"Assuredly!"

"Then he is the man."

"What is thy name?" broke in a clear sweet voice.

"My name?" said the man looking startled, "Oh, 'tis thou, maiden. My name is Gestas, my pretty one. Why dost thou ask?"

"That we may find thee when we shall return from the city. Can this Jesus Barabbas of whom thou hast spoken heal blindness?"

"Art thou blind?"

"Yes I am blind; I would be healed, and I have heard that a man named Jesus can heal blindness."

The man looked soberly for a moment at her blank eyes, he opened his lips as if to speak, then scratching his shaggy head reflectively, he again glanced at the white dromedary. "Go into the city," he said at length, "and ask for the man, some one will tell thee; I will care for the beast whilst thou art gone."

"Come, Anat, let us make haste," cried the lad joyfully. "We must find him at once."

So the two went away towards Jerusalem, which lay not far distant, its walls and towers gleaming as whitely as though no lurid shadow of destruction hung from the avenging heavens above it.

As for the man whose name was Gestas, he laughed aloud as he seized the stately Mirah by the bridle. "Truly the gods love me," he said. "This beast will bring a goodly sum," and he struck the white dromedary across the face with his staff in order to let her know that she had a new master.

"Yonder is a venerable man," said Seth to the blind girl, when the two had entered within the gate, and he ran forward and plucked the man by the sleeve.

"Canst thou tell me where to find the man Jesus, who can heal blindness?"

The old man turned upon the lad with blazing eyes. "Beggar!" he cried, "Get thee gone! How dost thou dare pollute mine ears with that name?"

Seth stared at him in amazement as he strode onward, muttering angrily to himself, his snowy beard blowing over his shoulder in the light breeze.

"By the sacred Nile!" he exclaimed, "in what have I offended? Praise be to the gods, they have no such customs in Memphis. Well, I must even ask another."

Taking the blind girl once more by the hand, they walked a little further on. It was as yet early in the day, but the streets were alive with people hurrying to and fro. Merchants sitting comfortably at their stalls cried lustily to the passers-by to come buy of their goods; beggars whined out their piteous tales of woe, and displayed their gruesome deformities to the averted eyes of the hurrying crowd; water-carriers clinked their brazen cups and bawled loudly of the cooling draughts which they carried in the goat-skins upon their backs. Once the two adventurers had to squeeze themselves back into an angle of the wall, while a platoon of Roman soldiers marched by, the sun glittering in dazzling splendor on their burnished shields.

Seth's heart had suddenly grown heavy within him, though he could scarce have told the reason. He almost feared to ask the question which hovered upon his lips of any of these busy, indifferent-looking people. Presently his eyes fell upon a blind man, feeling his way slowly along with a staff and whining out a dolorous cry for alms as he went. His heart sank lower still. "If there is a great magician who can heal blindness in this place," he thought, "why is not this man seeking him?"

Darting forward, he touched him upon the sleeve. "Canst thou tell me," he said timidly, "if there is a man called Jesus anywhere about—a man who can heal blindness?"

The beggar stopped short and turned his head. "There was such a man," he said, "but he is dead—crucified, three months since. I never found him," he added bitterly; "I came too late." Then he went on his way, and the boy heard his shrill voice rising and falling dismally down the street. He stood still in the place where he was, staring stupidly after the man, the words "too late" still echoing in his ears.

"Curses upon thy stupid head! Why dost thou block the roadway?" And a smart blow across his cheek from the whip of a muleteer served to bring him to his senses. At the same moment he heard a cry from Anat; looking quickly around he saw her fall to the ground beneath the hoofs of the laden ass which the man was driving.

With a shrill cry of fear the lad sprang forward, and dragged the girl out from among the confused tangle of men and animals, the muleteer shrieking curses upon him, the other passers-by merely pausing an instant to stare curiously at the scene. No one offered to help him, and cold with fear he lifted the slender form in his arms.

There was a projecting arch near by, with a great doorway sunken deep into the wall of masonry, in the shelter of this he laid his burden down, and looked into the beloved face in a very agony of terror.

"Anat! Anat!" he cried, bending over her. But there was no answer; the peach-like bloom of the brown cheeks had changed to a curious dusky pallor, the fringed lids had fallen over the sightless eyes, the slender hands were cold.

"Anat! Anat!" he repeated in a frenzy. "Awake!" and he shook her by the arm, scarce knowing what he did. "My God! if she is dead!"

Just then with a harsh sound of rusty hinges the great door behind them swung open, and a turbaned head peered cautiously out. The lad started to his feet with sudden hope. "Kind sir!" he said beseechingly. "My sister hath been grievously hurt; nay, I know not if she be alive. Wilt thou give me a cup of water that I may try and bring back her soul?"

The man looked at him coldly. "This is the house of God," he said. "'Tis not meet that its threshold be defiled with that which is dead, 'tis an abomination in the sight of Jehovah. Get thee hence, the hour for prayer draweth nigh."

"Nay, but I beseech thee, by the love of Isis! Give me but a cup—a small cup of water!"

"Get thee hence!" said the man with a gesture of abhorrence. "There is naught here for such as thou," and he made as though he would have pushed the senseless form of the blind girl into the street with his foot.

Seth's eyes blazed. "The curses of Sechet light upon thee!" he cried fiercely; "thou hast the withered heart of a mummy a thousand years dead!" Then he caught up his burden once more and fled away, the furious imprecations of the Jew sounding in his ears.

Hurrying blindly forward, he neither knew nor cared whither he was going, but he became conscious after a few moments that he had come into a quieter place. With a dim sense of relief he once more laid the limp figure down upon the pavement; this time, to his great joy, he heard a faint sound. She was trying to speak. He kneeled at her side and lifted her head to his knees. "Water! Water!" she moaned feebly.

He looked distractedly about him. The long narrow street was suffocatingly hot, on either side of it stretched blank walls of rough-hewn masonry, pierced occasionally with a deep-set door; two or three dogs skulked in the black shadow of an archway near by, and a flock of swallows swooped back and forth in the dazzling sunshine, crying out to each other with wild sweetness, but there was no human being in sight. He could hear the distant cries of the venders, and the shouts of the muleteers from the busy street which he had just left. It seemed to him presently, as he listened, that somewhere near by he could hear the cool tinkle of a fountain; he looked up, from the top of the wall above his head there fluttered a glimmer of green leaves. There must be— there was a garden there, and water, he was sure of it. He sprang up, and laying Anat's head carefully down, pulled impatiently at the bell which hung at the side of one of the sunken doorways. After a long delay, every minute of which seemed a separate eternity to the boy, a panel in the door swung open, and the head of a man was thrust out.

"What wilt thou?" he said in a surly tone, as his eye fell upon the boy.

"Water! for the love of all the gods, water! my—"

"What dost thou mean, fellow," interrupted the man, scowling, "by coming to the palace of the High Priest for water? The public fountains are for such as thou." And without further ado he shut the door with a decisive clap.

Seth stood for a moment as if stunned, then he threw himself down upon the hot stones with a smothered cry of despair, and bowed his head upon his knees. After what seemed a long time a touch upon his shoulder aroused him, he looked up dully, his eyes red with weeping.

"What aileth thee, lad?"

He stared at the face of his questioner without answering. It was like no other face he had ever seen, and yet, strangely enough, something in the dark eyes brought back to him the dim memory of his mother. The young man—for it was a young man who had spoken—repeated his question, and this time the lad answered.

"My sister hath been trampled upon by a beast of burden. She is dying for water, no one will help me, my bottle is empty, and I know not where to find a fountain."

But the stranger did not wait to hear all, he was already sprinkling the face of the girl, who had again lapsed into unconsciousness.

"She is not much hurt, he said at length. "See, she is reviving already." And indeed under his skillful ministrations the color had begun to return to the cheeks and lips of the injured girl.

"But she is blind," said Seth, looking up wistfully into the face of the young man, "and we have come from Egypt, seeking for the man Jesus who can heal such. A beggar told me that he was dead, but it is not true?"

The face of the stranger glowed with a smile so angelic that the lad involuntarily cried out with wonder.

"Nay," he cried, "He is not dead, he liveth forever more at the right hand of God."

Then he fixed his eyes upon the lad. "Tell me," he said gravely, "All that hath befallen thee, and how it is that ye seek Jesus in this far country."

So the lad told him all. How that their parents had passed into the regions of the dead, leaving them alone; and how for many years he had cared for his blind sister; of the man who would have sold them into bondage, and how fleeing from before his face they had first heard of the man who could heal blindness; of their awful journey in the wilderness; of their deliverance from the vultures, and their escape from the hand of Pagiel. When he ceased from speaking, the young man was silent for a space.

"Of a surety," he said at length, "the Lord hath led thee." Then raising his head he looked up into the dazzling blue of the sky.

"Thou who hast said, 'Lo, I am with thee alway even unto the end of the world,' look now upon this child who hath sought thee for healing, through weariness, and thirst, and pain, lo, these many days; and heal her, I beseech thee, by the hand of thy servant, according to her great faith."

Then stooping, while the lad held his breath with awe, he laid his hand lightly, tenderly, upon the sightless eyes of Anat. "In the name of Jesus Christ of Nazareth," he murmured, "receive thy sight."

And into the dark eyes of the maiden, erstwhile as irresponsive as soulless jewels, there flashed a look of intelligence. She gazed steadfastly into the eyes of the stranger.

"Art thou the man Jesus?" she whispered softly.

"Nay, my child," he answered, "I am but his servant Stephen."

CHAPTER XV.

IN PURSUIT OF THE FUGITIVES.

O Abu Ben Hesed, sitting, as was his wont at the sunset hour, in the door of his tent, came Pagiel. It was the evening of the fourth day after he had seen the two children disappear from out his sight on the back of the white dromedary. He had not made haste to return; he needed time to think, for he was slow-witted, and the matter in hand was weighty.

"There is no place like the solitude of the wilderness for meditation," quoth Pagiel. So he abode quietly in the place where he was for one full day. Not so the son of Kish the herdsman; he was impatient.

"Let me return, I beseech thee," he said to Pagiel, "I would fain look upon the face of my bride."

"What art thou saying, man?" cried Pagiel hotly. "Dost thou think that now I shall give to thee my daughter?" Our matter is ended."

But Ben Kish loved the daughter of Pagiel; he was therefore bold and determined. Moreover, he saw that the man was afraid to return. "My father is wroth," he said, "because the two Egyptians have fled away with the beast. I will return to my lord and I will tell him what they have done. Surely it was meet that such should be sold into slavery and that their value be given the daughter of Pagiel for her dowry."

"Nay, thou shalt not return!" cried Pagiel. "If the thing be told Ben Hesed then should I be cut off from among my kinsfolk and brethren."

Ben Kish smiled. "Is it better for thee to be thus cut off," he said, "or to have for thy son the son of Kish? For of these two things, one shall assuredly come to pass."

"Swear to me that thou wilt keep the thing secret," said Pagiel, "and I will give thee my daughter, even as I have said."

"Swear to me that thou wilt give me thy daughter," replied Ben Kish, "and I will keep the thing secret."

So they both sware a great oath; and they builded that day of the stones of the place a memorial, in token that as the stones which endure without change, even so must their compact remain. Then they gat them up and made haste to return, and the son of Kish laughed within himself because he had prevailed; but Pagiel was so busy inventing a tale which should explain the loss of the white dromedary, that he thought no more of the matter.

"Ben Hesed is a hard man," he thought. "If I say thieves came and stole the beast while we were returning, he will say, 'Why then didst thou not pursue and slay them? Thou hast no wounds.' If I say the beast fled away from us into the desert, he will laugh me to scorn. Nay, I will tell him the truth; it is after all best; moreover, God loveth a truthful man. I will say this; the Egyptian brats rose up whilst we were asleep in the midst of the day, and they took the beast and fled. We pursued them also till the going down of the sun, but could not overtake them."

So he told Ben Hesed this, and when he had done speaking he waited to hear what his lord should say. For

IN PURSUIT OF THE FUGITIVES. 109

a long time he said nothing, because he was very angry, and it was his wont to refrain from speaking when he was thus disquieted.

"Shall a man rage like a wild beast?" he would say. "Nay, for in so doing he is no longer a man; let him rather remain silent, remembering that God made him in his own image. The heavens are voiceless even when the earth beneath runs red with blood. Men blaspheme the name of Jehovah, yet there is no answering bolt of wrath to slay them. Let us then be patient as befits them that are but a little lower than the angels, created in the likeness of the Eternal One."

On this occasion Ben Hesed was silent so long that Pagiel was frightened; he had bowed himself to the earth, and he still remained in this humble posture that he might escape the lightnings which leapt up in his lord's eyes as he heard the tale.

After a time he became very uncomfortable, the sand on which his forehead rested was hot, his knees shook beneath him. "Why do I abase myself before this man," he said within himself. At the thought he too grew angry, and because anger is stronger than fear, he leapt up and stood before Ben Hesed.

Ben Hesed also arose. "I will myself pursue these Egyptians," he said, "and I will bring them again into the wilderness; the wilderness shall avenge me."

Then he made haste and gat him gone within the hour, but Pagiel remained behind; he had now the matter of the marriage in hand. Remembering this as he went to his own tent, he again tore his beard and cried aloud to God to help him in his extremity. But for the life of him he could think of no other word save that which the psalmist David wrote,

>   "The wicked plotteth against the just

> And gnasheth upon him with his teeth,
> But the Lord shall laugh at him,
> For he seeth that his day is coming."

And in this there was so little comfort that he prayed no more.

Ben Hesed arrived at the borders of Judaea after a journey which consumed but half the usual time, for he tarried not to rest at noontide nor at night. Once beyond the river he began to make inquiry among the people concerning the white dromedary, and because beasts of that sort and color not often passed that way he soon found them that had seen her. In this place had the runaways stayed for a night; in another had they bartered a coin from the girl's necklace for provender for the beast.

"At least they have not abused the animal," said Ben Hesed to himself, and insensibly his anger cooled day by day.

"I shall hear what the lad hath to say before I pass judgment upon him," he said to his son who accompanied him. "It is best to look at both sides of a matter—yea, and within it also. When a man hath done this to the best of his ability how far short doth he fall of the complete knowledge of God, who made the soul and to whom it lieth open like a parchment that is unrolled; therefore should man leave punishments to God. I will not lift my hand against the two as I at first purposed in my heart; and lo, this thou seest, my son, how wise it is to make haste slowly in matters that pertain to revenge. The hours that pass cool the angry heart even as drops of rain quench the glowing coals. This is good; a year from now I shall think little of the loss of the beast, and if I shew mercy it will endure in my heart for many years as a sweet savor. Look always at a present calamity as if it had happened many moons since, then shalt thou be able

IN PURSUIT OF THE FUGITIVES.

to judge whether it be worth thy while to be angry and to avenge thyself."

Beguiling the way with good words of the like, and at the same time keeping a wary eye out for the white dromedary, the worthy man journeyed on towards Jerusalem, for it was there that he confidently expected to find the fugitives.

When at length they came within sight of the holy city, lying fair and white amid the green and gentle mountain slopes, the travelers were amazed to see the numbers of folk who were going into it by every road.

"What may this mean?" said Ben Hesed. "It is not feast time." Presently they passed one of these companies, and they saw that in the midst was a sick man on his litter; he was groaning dismally as his bed shook beneath him with the unevenness of the way.

"Why dost thou fetch this man into Jerusalem?" asked Ben Hesed of the bearers.

"To be healed," they answered him. "Happy shall we be if we get him there alive; already this is the third day since we started with him, and death pursueth after us faster than we can journey."

Ben Hesed marvelled at their answer, but he forbore to question them further, for he saw that they had no mind to talk. Presently he came upon a woman sitting by the wayside and weeping bitterly.

"Why dost thou weep, woman?" he asked of her, for he was not of those who reckoned it a defilement to speak to a woman.

"I weep," she answered him, "because, although I am in sight of the Holy City, I can go no further and my child must, after all, perish."

She thrust out her feet from beneath her robe, and Ben Hesed saw that they were horribly bruised, cut, and blistered, as if she had walked a long way. As for the child, it lay waxen-faced and silent in her arms, the purple eyelids half dropped over the dull eyes. Ben Hesed shook his head gravely as he looked at it; it seemed to him that it was beyond help.

"Thou shalt ride upon my beast," he said, "and thus reach the city speedily. I will walk beside thee."

The woman smiled through her tears. "Now may the God of Abraham, Isaac, and Jacob bless thee!" she cried; then she looked down at her babe, and her face whitened. "It may be too late," she murmured.

"From whence hast thou come?" asked Ben Hesed gently.

"From beyond Jordan, in the hill country. I heard of what was being done in Jerusalem, and so when my babe sickened I rose up with him and hastened to come hither, but the sickness hath increased by the way. I fear—"

"The man Jesus is of great power," interrupted Ben Hesed hastily. "It hath been said of him that he hath even raised the dead."

The woman looked startled. "Thou art, then, a stranger in these parts," she said, "and hast not heard what hath come to pass of late in Jerusalem?"

"I am from the wilderness; what is it that hath come to pass?"

"The man Jesus hath been slain—crucified!" said the woman, her heavy eyes blazing with indignation.

Ben Hesed was silent for a moment. "Why did they slay him?" he asked at length.

"Nay, I know not," said the woman wearily, holding the child close to her bosom. "I saw him once in my own village. He did there many mighty works of healing, and of the things which he said, I remember much even to this day. He was a great prophet, and now is his power fallen on his disciples, even as the mantle of Elijah fell upon Elisha when he ascended in the chariot of fire and had, therefore, no further need of a mantle."

Ben Hesed looked once more at the city to which they were now drawing very near. "Thus saith the Lord God," he murmured, "This is Jerusalem; I have set it in the midst of the nations and countries that are round about her. The end is at hand, behold it watcheth for thee, O thou that dwellest in the land! The time is come, the day of trouble is near. Now will I shortly pour out my fury upon thee and accomplish my anger upon thee. And I will judge thee according to thy ways, and will recompense thee for all thine abominations, for the land is full of bloody crimes, and the city is full of violence."

And when they were now come to the gates, they had much ado to enter in, because of the great multitude of the sick, lame, and blind which were coming from every quarter. The streets were filled with them, and with the noise of their groaning and wailing. Ben Hesed, his son, and his two servants, together with the woman, who still held the quiet child close to her bosom, followed on with the others.

After a time it became impossible to proceed further, so they waited where they were. Near them two men were holding a demoniac, who bellowed loudly from time to time, and tore at his clothes, which were already in ribbons, and at the hair and faces of his guardians. A little further on, the keen eye of Ben Hesed descried a palsied man lying on his bed, his emaciated face the color of death. Beyond him were a group of blind men, waiting with the hopeless apathy of accustomed misery for something, they scarce knew what. Save for the moans and cries of the sick ones there was scarcely a sound; the sun beat fiercely down from above, the yellow dust rose in stifling clouds from beneath, and still they waited.

At length from somewhere afar off there rose a cry—a wild, jubilant, inarticulate sound; a deep answering murmur rose from the ghastly throng of sufferers about them. This strange pean of joy rose and fell, now swelling loudly, now dying away, but always drawing nearer. Ben Hesed looked at the woman; she was fumbling wildly at the wrappings which swathed her babe; she bent her head as if to listen to his tiny chest.

"My God!" she cried, "it is too late; he is dead." Then she dropped back breathless and waxen as the little form which she still held close in her arms.

Ben Hesed caught her as she fell; he looked about him for help.

"Here is water," said a voice at his side, and looking up he saw, to his intense astonishment, Seth, the Egyptian lad. At the same moment the boy recognized him, and started back with a little cry.

"This is no time to speak of what concerneth thee and me," said Ben Hesed sternly. "Give me the water!" And he fell to sprinkling the face of the woman with no sparing hand.

"They are coming!" shouted the lad. "Stay! I will bring him hither," and he darted away into the throng.

Ben Hesed looked after him quietly. "The wicked flee when no man pursueth," he said under his breath, "yet shall sure wrath overtake him, neither shall a swift foot deliver him. Come!" he added, turning to his son, "let us bear this woman hence; there is now no further need to wait for them that heal."

CHAPTER XVI.

A ROLL OF PARCHMENT.

HOU canst hear for thyself how Jerusalem is in an uproar; the credulous and ignorant from all the country round about are crowding into the city bringing their sick with them."

"'Tis worse even than when the man himself was alive; but what can we do?"

"Shorn of our powers as we be, what indeed? But shall we then sit quietly down and allow these men to snatch from us the little that remains?" Annas arose from his place as he spoke and opening a small receptacle of carved ivory, removed from it a roll of parchment. "Let us now consider this matter between ourselves; later it must be presented before the council, but I tell you plainly that in the council itself there be them that are of two minds. I have written here," he continued, "the names of them that are principally concerned in the present disturbances; let these be either slain or forced into banishment, and the thousands who now claim to believe will quickly lose their fervor—which is after all simply a frenzy of excitement, skillfully produced by these apt pupils of the man from Galilee."

He was deliberately unrolling the parchment as he spoke. "I have prepared this list after most careful inquiry and investigation," he went on, looking keenly from one to the other of the two attentive faces before him. "To thee, Saul of Tarsus, this information should prove most useful. Other names may be added from time to time as shall appear necessary, but at present I have set down only some seventeen names, including the twelve who companied with the Nazarene. These are now I am told known as apostles; and it is they who are the principal inciters of the unseemly gatherings which daily take place within the confines of our Holy Temple, and which as yet we have not been able to put a stop to. To our shame be it said!"

"The names! the names!" cried Caiaphas impatiently; "read them, I pray thee, without further delay."

Annas frowned. "Thou art zealous in the cause, my son," he said with a warning gesture. "I commend thy diligence; would that all the Sanhedrim were of like mind with thyself. The names of the twelve who must be crushed at any cost are as follows:

"The first is Simon, also called Peter—without question the most dangerous of them all, in that he is absolutely unbridled of tongue and apparently without fear of God or man. He is an ignorant fellow, having been taken from his fishing boat on Gennesaret by the Nazarene, as one well fitted to become his disciple."

"Was he not the one who declared with curses that he never knew the Nazarene, on the night when the man was so cleverly given over to us by that other follower of his, Judas?" said Caiaphas.

"Thou art in the right, my son," replied Annas, stroking his beard thoughtfully, "though I had entirely forgotten the circumstance; indeed all of his followers forsook the man and fled at the time of his arrest."

"Didst thou say that this Peter denied his Master?" asked Saul.

"He not only denied knowing him, but cursed and blasphemed foully in the faces of them that inquired of him concerning the matter, and that without provocation, since there was no effort made to molest the followers of the Nazarene, it being deemed sufficient by us at the time to put an end to the man himself—a mistake in judgment which we are like to repent bitterly."

"Then the man is a coward!" exclaimed Saul contemptuously, "a loud-mouthed braggart; doubtless a Roman scourging will suffice to close his mouth for the future."

"The suggestion is a good one," said Annas approvingly, "it can be brought about with ease; though for myself I am in favor of measures which shall entirely rid our city of the whole blasphemous brood. The second name I have set down is that of John, he is always to be found with the man Peter, of whom we have just been speaking. He is, in his way, quite as dangerous, since in common with the other he possesses some means of deluding the multitudes into supposing that he hath healing power."

"There is a way provided by the law for dealing with such as have familiar spirits and by means of them work deeds of darkness," growled Caiaphas.

"Quite right," assented Annas, "we shall come to that presently; of the others I need say nothing except that they follow the same practices as the first two named, and are occupied night and day in spreading the pernicious teachings of what they are pleased to call the good tidings. I will name them in order, commencing at the beginning once more. Simon, who is called Peter, and Andrew, brother of the same; John and James, sons of Zebedee; Philip, Bartholomew, Thomas, Matthew, a tax gatherer; James Ben Alphaeus, and Lebbaeus, surnamed Thaddeus; another Simon, who is a Canaanite, and Matthias, whom I find they have chosen to take the place of the man Judas, who served us well and cheaply you will remember in the capture of the Nazarene, but committed the incredible folly of hanging himself immediately afterward; a pity, since we might have found him useful now. To these twelve names I have also added Mary, the mother of the Nazarene, she had best be made an example of, together with some of the other women, who consort with the men and brew mischief among them as only women are able."

Caiaphas started up. "Thou hast rightly said," he cried in a hoarse shaking voice, "the devil led captive the first woman, and they all do follow him to this day if he but put on the guise of a fair youth. I pray thee to add yet another name, the name of Stephen. Murderer and thief! I will kill him with my hands—I hate him—I—"

"Assuredly; all whose names are written here are under sentence of death," said Annas, laying a warning hand on the speaker's arm; "but I pray thee, attend me while I finish the reading of the parchment, after that must we take immediate action. I have here further set down for your consideration the apostates, Nicodemus and Joseph of Arimathaea, formerly members of the Sanhedrim, but now delivered over unto ungodly lusts and blasphemies in the company of the Galileans. Of Joseph it is further known that he openly begged the body of the Nazarene from Pilate and made a great ado over its sepulture, buying spices and fine linen as if for a rich man, and laying the fruit of the accursed tree in his own new tomb, from whence it also disappeared on the third day through the further machinations of these same apostles."

"I once knew Joseph of Arimathaea," remarked Saul thoughtfully; "he was a fair-minded man, I will speak with him concerning the matter—"

"Not so, my son!" cried Annas hastily. "I forbid it in the name of the holy council; it is not meet for one that is sanctified to the service of Jehovah to consort with them over whom Satan hath gotten the victory. But hold! I hear some one at the door; it may be news of some fresh disturbance, I ordered the captain of the temple police to bring me word should such occur. Enter, I pray thee, Caleb. What is it that hath befallen?"

"A great tumult, my good lords," said the man, bowing himself reverently before them. "The men have wrought many wonderful cures upon the halt, the maimed, and the blind; the whole city is at the doors to see them. They are bringing out their sick and laying them on the stones of the street, crying out that if only the shadow of Peter fall on them they shall be healed."

"This is monstrous!" cried Annas, starting up. "Do thou, Saul of Tarsus, go with this man and see to it that these fellows are put in hold; their shadows will go with them. Thrust them into the common prison, and let the jailer look to it that they escape not. Take with thee a sufficient number for thy security, and accomplish the matter quietly but with all speed. To-morrow we will consider their case."

Saul of Tarsus was already girding himself. "Thy commands, my lord, shall be obeyed," he said bending his haughty head, "and I rejoice that I am counted worthy to be of service in bringing to naught these workers of iniquity. If it meets with thy approval I shall also put in hold any others whom I shall find engaged in this blasphemous wickedness."

"Go forth, my son," quoth Annas, rolling up his eyes, and spreading abroad his jewelled fingers, "and take with thee a High-Priestly blessing, may it enable thee to prevail gloriously. Deal with the men as thou wilt; only remember that we must be prudent, and that too great zeal in the beginning oftentimes cripples an enterprise which would otherwise have grown mighty and irresistible, therefore temper thy burning zeal with all caution and diligence as befits a truly wise man." He rubbed his hands together with an air of satisfaction as the door closed after the young Pharisee. "A most admirable man for the occasion!" he exclaimed, turning to Caiaphas. "Most admirable! Full of courage, full of determination, withal easy to be controlled; but I would not that he talk much of the matter with any other save ourselves. If he should hear the talk of Nicodemus, Joseph, or Barsabas, I fear me that he might receive an impetus in the wrong direction; and once started, there would be no halfway measures with him. He would speedily develop into another Peter on our hands."

"Dost thou in truth believe that these men are of the devil?"

Annas started, the self-satisfied smile faded; he looked sharply into the worn face before him, at the eyes with their feverish glitter, at the thin, nerveless hands, at the bowed shoulders; then he frowned.

"Thou had best go to thy chamber—" he began irritably, but Caiaphas checked him with an impatient gesture.

"Prate not to me of my chamber! I am sick, yes, but it is a sickness of the soul. Thou dost not know all, I have not told thee; but hear now that my son, my son David, was crucified as a thief at the right hand of the Nazarene." His voice rose almost to a shriek at the last word and he tore at his hair as one in uncontrollable agony.

Annas started to his feet. "Thou art mad!" he cried. "For God's sake, do not shriek forth such foul ravings, lest it come to the ears of them without."

"Nay, I am not mad," said Caiaphas. "If I were mad, I might sometimes forget. Thou knowest how we lost him," he continued, sinking his voice to a husky whisper. "He was stolen by a thief who bred him to his own damnable trade, and who also was crucified. This Stephen, who preaches to the people of the Nazarene, is his son. It was Stephen who taught the woman who was my wife to believe that the Nazarene was the Messiah of Israel. What if it were true! My God, if it were true!"

"Fool!" cried Annas, clenching his hands. "Breathe to another human soul what thou hast told me and I will thrust thee into a dungeon where thou shalt cool thy hot brain to eternity. Wilt thou drag our ancient name in the foul mud of the streets and make it a by-word and a hissing? This fellow Stephen shall die, and that speedily; now look to it that thy tongue is forevermore silent in the matter! Dost thou hear me?"

Caiaphas cowered beneath the murderous eyes of the old man. "It shall be as thou hast said," he faltered weakly. Then he burst into a passion of sobbing like a sick child.

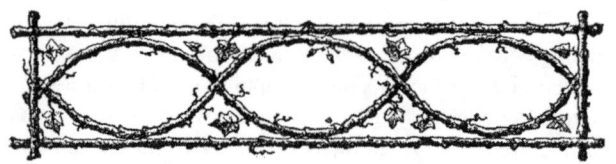

CHAPTER XVII.

IN THE PRISON HOUSE.

T was very dark in the prison, and the straw which littered the earthen floor of the place was damp and filthy. Abu Ben Hesed found a difficulty in breathing the stagnant air, he groaned aloud and beat upon his breast. "Alas!" he sighed, "how have the wicked prevailed against the innocent. We are as birds in the snare of the fowler." The babe in the arms of the woman beside him stirred, then wailed loudly.

"I have no food for him," said the woman plaintively. "Nevertheless he hath the strength to wail for it, thanks be to the Almighty. But how doth the bitter and the sweet always commingle. No sooner is my child restored than I am thrusted into this noisome place; for what reason I know not, I but praised him by whose name was the healing wrought."

"Thinkest thou not that he who hath restored thy babe is able likewise to deliver thee from prison?" said a deep voice from out of the gloom.

The woman drew a little nearer to Abu Ben Hesed. "Who is it that speaks?" she whispered timidly, while the child again wailed loudly.

Ben Hesed turned his piercing gaze toward the place from whence the voice had come. He thought he could distinguish a number of dark figures huddled together in one corner. "Who are our companions in this misery?" he asked.

"We are the apostles of the Lord Jesus, in whose name we are able to heal them that are sick. By the command of the chief priests we are thrust into this place; the officers who seized us are well known unto us. But praises be to the Eternal One that we are accounted worthy to do the works which the Lord did, and to be partakers of his sufferings. For unto us shall be also a share in his glory which he hath with the Father. But how is it that ye are come with us into this place?"

"I am from the desert," answered Ben Hesed. "As I journeyed I found by the wayside this woman, who had essayed to bring her baby to Jerusalem for healing. When I perceived that she could go no further by reason of her weariness, I set her upon my own beast and fetched her into the city. As we waited, hemmed in on every side by the multitude, it seemed to us that the child was dead, therefore I bore her away a little from out the throng, because the spirit was well nigh gone out of her by reason of her grief. Then it was that a little lad called Seth, brought unto us a young man, who laid his hands on the twain and healed them. I saw it with mine own eyes as did they that were with me, and we all cried aloud and praised God for his mercy, the woman also with a voice of thanksgiving. But as we rejoiced, there came a certain man who commanded us to be silent. 'Shall I be silent,' I answered him, 'when mine eyes have seen wondrous things?' Then I bade him begone, for it is not my custom to hear or to heed commands from any, since I am lord in mine own land. But even as I spoke I was seized on a sudden from behind by them that bound me and haled me away hither, together with the woman. For this also shall vengeance overtake the man, for I will neither eat bread nor drink wine till I have accomplished my wrath upon mine enemy. I, Ben Hesed, have spoken it."

"Nay, my brother," said another voice, "I will show thee a more excellent way. The Lord Jesus, when he was betrayed into the hands of cruel men—who also accomplished their desires upon him, reviling him, beating him, and at last crucifying him—though he was endued with all power from on high, offered no resistance; even as it is written by the prophet Isaiah, 'He was despised and rejected of men, a man of sorrows and acquainted with grief; he was wounded for our transgressions, he was bruised for our iniquities; the chastisement of our peace was upon him and with his stripes we are healed. He was brought as a lamb to the slaughter, and as a sheep before her shearers is dumb, so he opened not his mouth.' If the Holy Jesus, Lord of all the heavens, could endure such suffering with patience, is it meet for sinful man to seek for vengeance?"

Ben Hesed listened attentively. "I would hear more of this man Jesus," he said. "I once saw him in Jerusalem. He seemed to me a man, even as others, though it was told me that he had the power to heal them that were afflicted with diseases."

Then they told him all the story of Jesus of Nazareth; and when they spoke of his awful death on the cross, the old man wept aloud.

"Would to God that I had known it!" he cried; "I would have come with my tribe like a swift whirlwind from out the desert, and would have snatched him from the hand of the oppressor. In the desert God reigns."

"Doth not God reign over all the earth, for he made it?" cried Peter. "Yet he suffered these things so to be; it

IN THE PRISON HOUSE. 125

was his will concerning him, as also our Lord told us many times before his death, yet because of our blindness we heeded him not. Yea, I even denied that I knew him, in his extremity; yet he forgave me, as also he will forgive and save all that come unto him."

"How can he forgive when he is dead?" said the woman sadly. "Behold there is no hope in the grave; they that go down unto death return not for either loving or forgiving, though we weep tears of blood in our anguish."

"Hast thou not heard," cried Peter in amaze, "how that the grave could not hold him? On the third day he became alive again, and we all saw him and knew by many infallible proofs that it was he and no other. And as he arose from among the dead, even so shall every one that believeth on him also become alive again. Death is swallowed up in victory. After many days, with our own eyes did we behold the heavens receive him. Yet is he even now with us to help and to comfort, and shall be always even unto the end."

While he yet spake, lo! all the place became light about them, and they saw that the doors of the prison stood wide open; and while they marvelled at the sight, a man in bright raiment stood before them and said:

"Go, stand and speak in the temple all the words of this life!"

And they went forth, all of them, into the night; but the keepers of the prison continued to stand before the doors, neither seeing nor hearing what had happened, for their eyes were holden by the angel.

Ben Hesed was baptized in that same hour, and so likewise was the woman, because they believed what the men had told them concerning Jesus of Nazareth; and they tarried for the night at the house of John. But in the morning very early the Apostles went into the temple that they might speak to the people, even as the angel had bidden them.

About the third hour of the day at the bidding of Annas came the members of the Sanhedrim, with the chief doctors of the law, and all the great rabbis that were at Jerusalem, that they might take council together concerning them which Saul had made fast in the prison. And when Annas had spoken before them at length concerning the matter, and with great power and subtilty had convinced the greater part of them that these men were of the devil, and that upon the Senate thus convened rested the honor and safety of Israel, he commanded that the prisoners should be brought. And the officers went as they were bidden, and when they were come to the prison they asked of them that stood on guard before the door, whether the prisoners had been troublesome during the night.

"We heard them speaking one to another about the third watch," the officer of the guard made answer. "But there has been neither sound nor motion from within for many hours; they sleep heavily and late."

"They must even awake now, that they may appear before the council. Fetch them out at once, for I must make haste."

Then the officer of the guard, whose name was Chilion, opened the door of the prison and went in. "Awake, sluggards!" he cried loudly, "and come forth."

But when there was yet neither voice nor motion, he drew his sword and thrust it in among the heaps of mouldy straw. "If ye will not come forth peaceably," he said, "then shall I fetch thee forth at the point of the sword." But no shriek of pain answered the weapon. So he strode forth into the light. "Fetch hither a torch," he roared, "there is the darkness of the pit within, and the rascals make me no answer."

IN THE PRISON HOUSE.

So they made haste and fetched lights, and they searched the prison with all diligence. The prisoners were gone.

"Thou hast been drunken in the night and so have the fellows eluded thee," said Caleb, the chief of the temple police, when he had satisfied himself that the men had indeed made good their escape. "For this shalt thou answer with a scourging."

"Thou liest, man; I have neither eaten bread nor tasted wine during the night," cried Chilion, choking with rage, "and these shall bear me witness. We have stood continually before the doors, even as thou didst find us; it is from within that they have gotten away."

Then they again examined the floor and the walls of the prison; but there was no place where so much as a mouse could have crept through.

"I am undone!" cried Chilion, rending his clothes, "if they be not found. 'Twas by their magic powers that they have done this thing. Thinkest thou that men who can open the eyes of the blind, cannot also open the doors of a prison house?"

So Caleb returned unto the council; and when he had made obeisance before them, he said, "I am most unhappy, my lords, in that I am the bearer of evil tidings; the prisoners whom I was sent to fetch have somehow made good their escape during the night."

"How is this?" cried Annas angrily. "Who guarded the prison?"

"The detachment of Chilion, with Chilion himself in command, my lord. The prison was shut with all safety, and the keepers found we standing without before the doors; but when we had opened, there was no man within."

"A most singular story this, my lord," remarked Alexander sarcastically. "It will doubtless transpire that the fellows reasoned with the keepers during the night watches, and so converted them from their duty to their own interest; this do they with all men."

"The guard, Chilion, hath been bribed," suggested another. "Fetch him hither, and try the effect of a scourging. A bleeding back createth an honest tongue oftentimes when nothing else will suffice."

But as they thus talked together, Chilion himself knocked at the door; and when he was admitted, he cried out before them all that he was innocent of any failure in his duty; he was, moreover, ready to swear to the truth of this upon the high altar of the temple, than which there was no oath more sacred. "As for the men whom ye put in prison," he added, "they are at this moment standing in the temple teaching the people!"

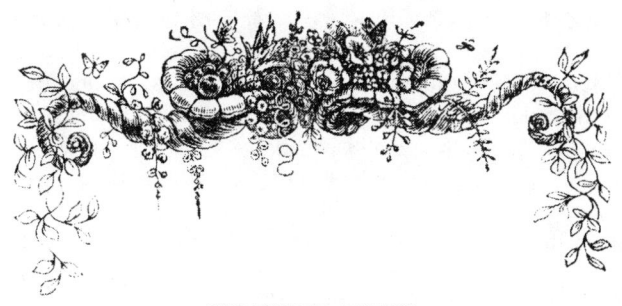

CHAPTER XVIII.

"WHOSE WE ARE AND WHOM WE SERVE."

AY I advise, my lord, that these men be at once apprehended and brought hither?" The voice was that of Saul of Tarsus; he had arisen in his place, and the eyes of all were fixed upon him. "We shall then be able to examine them of the truth of this man's statements. It would seem most necessary that our prisons be made secure, since I opine that we shall have need of them before we have seen an end to this matter."

"It is well said," murmured several who were high in authority, "let them be fetched with all speed; we will not go hence until we have seen them."

So Annas commanded the officers, "Fetch hither the men, but without show of violence, for they have a great following among the people. A popular enthusiasm," he added, "when bred at the wrong moment and on the wrong subject, is most disastrous; though what it may accomplish when properly directed, those of you who were in the city at the time of the execution of the man from Galilee will remember. The populace must be with us now as they were then."

Caleb therefore with a chosen few of his men sought the temple; and there they found a great multitude assembled in Solomon's porch, listening to the apostles who spoke to them of Jesus, the crucified carpenter of Galilee. Him they declared boldly to be the Prince of Israel; assuring the people that though he had been rejected by them and cruelly slain, yet was he able to save them from out the sin and misery of their present lives, and furthermore give them everlasting life in place of death. So that for them that believed there was now no further terror in the grave, since he had promised and was able to raise their corrupt bodies into the likeness of his own glorious body. And all the people heard their words with joy; and they cried aloud to the Crucified One to forgive them their sins and to remember his promises to them also.

When the chief captain of the temple police was seen to approach stealthily, a man whose long, silvery beard descended upon his breast, and in whose eyes burned the fire of desert suns cried out: "Seest thou these men? They are even as the leopard of the mountain which steals upon his prey unaware. Look to it now that they do the men of God no violence!"

And the people answered with a great shout, "Let us stone them forthwith; if they be dead they will trouble us no more!" And Caleb feared exceedingly lest they should lay hands upon him; but being a discreet man and in pursuit of his duty furthermore, he made a bold stand before them.

"Ye men of Israel," he cried, "there is no violence intended these men, if they will but come with me peaceably. The council and senate of the people of Israel would hear them of these matters whereof they are now preaching, and for this purpose have they even now assembled themselves together. Let the apostles go, I pray ye, that those in high places may also receive the Gospel." This he said, not because he himself believed, but because he was a man of wisdom, and knew that unless he could placate the multitude, great harm might come not only to himself but to the senate also.

"Should these men once accuse the chief priests of the murder of the Nazarene," he said within himself, "the mob would immediately hale them forth from the council chamber and tear them limb from limb." And for a moment he was half minded to send word to the citadel asking for a detachment of Roman soldiers, but he bethought himself that this would only betray his fear. So he again spoke, and this time in the ear of Peter.

"I beseech thee, good Rabbi," he said, with apparent humility, "that thou wilt appease the people, since thou art obeyed of them; and I, despite mine office, have no authority at all over them."

"Call not thou me good, who denied the Lord of Glory," answered Peter. "I will go with thee." Then he beckoned with his hand unto the multitude that they should pay him heed, and when they were silent, expecting that he would command them concerning the officers, he said: "Ye men of Israel, this Jesus, whom we preach unto you, while he was yet alive, commanded that they which would follow him should do no evil to any man. Yea, he declared that if a man should smite his neighbor on the cheek, that the smitten one should also suffer his enemy to smite again without resistance or anger; and when, on the night before his death, the chief priests sent a company of men armed with swords and staves for to seize him, I was filled with indignation and smote the high priest's servant with the sword, so that his ear was severed from his head; but the Lord rebuked me, and bade me put up my sword into its place, then he reached forth his hand and touched the wounded man and healed him. Furthermore, ye remember how that afterward, when he was mocked and scourged and spit upon by his enemies, he opened not his mouth with revilings, but bore all with patience, though there remained within his call more than twelve legions of angels, armed with the fiery swords of heaven. If then ye would follow him on whom ye have believed, give place to wrath and conduct yourselves peaceably. For ye may have confidence that the Lord Christ, whose we are and whom we serve, will not suffer us to be tried above that we can bear, but will with the necessity provide a way of escape."

And when the people heard these words, they suffered the apostles to go away with the officers. But Ben Hesed, and with him others of them that were strong-hearted, followed hard after, and waited near the door of the council chamber.

"For," said Ben Hesed grimly, "it is also written concerning the Lord, 'With the merciful thou wilt show thyself merciful, and with the froward thou wilt show thyself froward. The Lord will save the afflicted people, but he will bring down high looks,' and further, 'He teacheth my hands to war, so that a bow of steel is broken by my arms; I have pursued mine enemies, and overtaken them, neither did I turn again till they were consumed.' "

And when Caleb perceived that the men were even at the doors, he wrote upon a table, saying: "Be discreet, I pray thee, in thy dealings with these apostles, for there be them without which are able to make of thee and of all that are within, even as the small dust of the balance." And this he caused to be given to Annas privily.

When Annas had read these words, his heart burned like a live coal within him. Yet was his brow calm and unruffled as he fixed his keen eyes on the men who stood humbly enough in the presence of that imposing assembly. "Again hath it become necessary to rebuke you openly because of your blasphemous conduct. Stiff-necked and ignorant fishermen, how is it that ye do thus persist in doing the things which work only for unrighteousness? Did not we straightly command you that ye should not teach in this name? And, behold, ye have filled Jerusalem with your doctrine, and intend to bring the blood of the slain Nazarene upon us."

"We ought to obey God rather than man," affirmed Peter simply.

Annas trembled with his pent up anger, but he still spoke with calmness. "This have ye before declared as the reason and excuse of your disobedience to this most holy council of the People of Israel. Dost thou think then that the God of our fathers speaks no longer save to fisher folk, publicans and malefactors? Nay, for upon us doth rest the power of God and the wisdom of God; in that we would defend from scurrilous and wicked hands the faith which we have kept unsullied from the days of our father Abraham even until now."

"We have but one answer to make to this," said John, looking squarely into the furious eyes of the man who had spoken, "and it is this. The God of our fathers raised up Jesus, whom ye slew and hanged on a tree. Him hath God exalted with his right hand to be a Prince and a Saviour, that he might give repentance to Israel and forgiveness of sins. And we are his witnesses of these things; and so is also the Holy Spirit, whom God hath given to them that obey him."

"Hearest thou these sayings?" cried Annas, starting to his feet. "What is this else but foul blasphemy? It is poison of this kind that these fellows spread industriously amongst the people day by day. The Nazarene, a prince and saviour forsooth, and we are his murderers! If the people once come to believe this, what shall come to pass? We shall be overthrown and the whole nation given over to blasphemy and idolatry."

"We shall be doing God service if we immediately put these to death," said Jochanan. "It must needs be done, the public weal demands it."

"I am of the same mind," exclaimed Alexander.

"And I—and I!" shouted half a score of voices.

"Let them be stoned!"

"Give them over to the Romans!"

"I beseech your indulgence, my good lords!" interrupted a grave deep voice from the inner circle of the assembly, "that ye may grant a brief hearing to one, who, because he is still somewhat unfamiliar with these new doctrines, perchance looks upon them from a slightly different standpoint from those of you who have patiently borne the heat and burden of the day."

"Gamaliel! Gamaliel!" cried several voices. "Let us hear what he hath to say."

The speaker was a man of powerful physique, and of calm and dignified bearing. As he looked keenly about over the excited assemblage with an air of conscious authority, every eye was fixed upon him with grave attention. "May I request," he continued when the tumult of excited voices had died away into silence, "that the persons under discussion be put forth for a little space."

This command being obeyed with alacrity by the underlings of Caleb, the speaker resumed in a deep measured voice. "As I have listened to the sayings of these men," he said, "my mind hath sought the past, for it is in the experiences of years gone by that man hath ever found the best council for the exigencies of the present. To adopt excessive measures for the disruption of this new sect would, in my opinion, be not only unwise in the present disturbed state of the populace, but actually dangerous. I have mingled with the multitude and I know that whereof I speak; therefore take heed to yourselves what ye intend to do as touching these men. Turning, as I have suggested, to the annals of the past, we find that before these days there rose up a certain Theudas, boasting himself to be somebody, to whom a number of men, about four hundred, joined themselves. After a time he was slain in a brawl, and all who believed on him were speedily scattered and brought to naught. Again, somewhat later appeared Judas, a Galilean, in the days of the taxing, and drew away much people after him; he also perished, and those who had obeyed him were dispersed. So now I say unto you, refrain from these men and let them alone, for if this preaching and healing which they do be of men it will speedily come to naught. But if, on the other hand, it be of God, ye cannot overthrow it, lest haply ye be found to fight against God."

A deep murmur of approval followed these words, after which a number of the more influential ones expressed themselves as in favor of adopting the safe and conservative course recommended by the wise doctor of the laws who had spoken.

Presently, when all had been said, Annas arose and looked about him. In the hush that followed, the tumult of the surging multitudes without could be distinctly heard.

"Though I believe that these men and their works are neither of man nor of God, but of the devil," he began, his voice shaking with suppressed excitement, "yet is the devil ever watchful of his own, and the populace are not to be trifled with at the present moment; therefore do I agree with the worshipful Gamaliel in thinking that the safe course for ourselves and for the cause which we serve will be, as he hath suggested, to let the men be for the present. I am not without hope of interesting Herod in the matter. Let it come to his ears once that these fellows are preaching to the people that their Master is shortly coming back to establish his throne in Jerusalem—as I can bring witnesses to testify—and he will speedily take care of them that say such things. I will therefore command that the men be scourged in our presence, which may prove a wholesome corrective to their mistaken zeal; after that they shall be released." This accordingly was done, the dignitaries looking on calmly whilst the scourging was administered by the underlings of the temple police.

When the sickening sound of the blows had at length ceased, Annas again spoke. "There is somewhat that ye have still to answer for," he said. "How is it that ye made good your escape from the prison? These your guards declare that they stood continually before the doors from the evening when ye were incarcerated even until the morning."

The face of John glowed with a celestial light. "The angel of the Lord, whose we are and whom we serve, came and fetched us out, and the eyes of the keepers were holden that they wist not when we went by them."

Annas eyed the speaker with a mocking smile. "How is it," he said slowly, his eyes lingering with manifest satisfaction upon the crimson marks of the scourging, "that he who delivered thee from the prison house, was not able also to deliver thee from the hands of them that beat thee?"

"We were delivered from the prison that we might speak to the people of him who is able to save them from their sins," answered John. Then he also smiled, but it was as an angel might have smiled, on whom the King immortal, invisible, had conferred some high and heavenly boon. The servant is not above his Lord," he said, "and if we suffer with him, we shall also reign with him; he hath gone to prepare a place for us, that where he is, there we may be also."

Then Annas rose in his wrath. "Let what ye have received at our hands serve to remind you that ye are forbidden to speak the name of the crucified Galilean in Jerusalem. Further disobedience shall meet with a punishment to which this shall be as nothing." Then were the apostles thrust out from the council chamber; and they departed, rejoicing greatly that they were counted worthy to suffer shame for his name. And daily in the temple and in every house where dwelt them that believed, they ceased not to teach and preach Jesus Christ.

CHAPTER XIX.

IN THE SHADOW OF THE WALL.

"HEN thou wilt not go with me this morning?" "Nay, I must not; this morning I am to learn how to spin. The mother of Jesus will teach me; afterward I shall make for thee a tunic. Now thou seest what a thing it is to have eyes." Anat looked down at the small hands which lay folded in her lap. "These," she continued, spreading out the slender brown fingers, "have hitherto been as idle as the hands of a princess, but the lady Mary says that they must learn many things, if with them I would serve him that healed me."

Seth looked half regretfully into the eager face. "Then we shall no more dwell by ourselves as heretofore? Hast thou forgotten the desert?"

"I have not forgotten, but I would like to stay here."

"And the dromedary?"

"Thou must find it. It was not I who would leave it without in the hands of a stranger. The lord of the desert is just in requiring it at thy hands."

The lad turned away. "Be it so," he cried angrily. "Till I have found it, thou wilt see my face no more; if that be never, why then—"

"Seth, Seth! Stay a moment, my brother! do not leave me so!" But he was gone, and without turning his head.

"How can I find the beast?" he muttered to himself crossly, as he plunged into the labyrinth of narrow streets. I have asked everywhere for the man Gestas, no one knows him; as for the white dromedary, men look at me as if I were a witless fool when I speak of it. If now I were in Egypt, I should offer a libation to Ptah Hotep, or fetch a garland to the temple of the sacred bull, then might I receive wisdom; if I pray to the gods of this land, how will they heed me who am an alien?" At this point in his meditation the lad flung himself down in the shadow of an archway, his eyes following idly the darting flight of the sparrows overhead; something in their noisy crying brought back the memory of the day when he bent half distracted over the unconscious form of Anat. "There is a God who can hear somewhere," he said half aloud. "For he both heard and answered the man who healed Anat; yet is it a great thing to heal blindness, I dare not ask him to help me find a beast of burden. Is there not some smaller god who cares for common things? 'Not a sparrow falleth to the ground without your Father.' " Where had he heard those words? It was John who had spoken them after the scourging before the council. "That means his father, not mine;" he went on meditatively, "I am not a Jew. Yet are there sparrows in Egypt also; if I pray to this God, he will not, I suppose, strike me dead; I will try and see what comes of it. God of this land—Jesus—if that be thy name! I am as thou seest an Egyptian, and I know not what offering is pleasing unto thee; and if I knew I could not provide it, for I am poorer than yonder sparrow. Yet if it be true that thou dost care for such, help me also, I pray thee, to find the white dromedary, which is justly required at my hands by the lord of the desert."

When he had prayed thus, a vague comfort stole into his heart; he opened his eyes and looking down the street, saw coming toward him two men. One of them he instantly recognized as the man in whose keeping he had left the dromedary; with a little cry of joy he started to his feet, but shrank back again into the archway, and seeing a broken place in the wall, he squeezed himself into it and stood motionless. "I will follow after them when they have passed by," he thought within himself. "It may be that so I shall come upon the beast unawares; if he sees me, it will not come to pass."

But the two paused beneath the archway, and finally sat down on the stones, neither of them noticing the motionless figure in the black shadow of the broken wall.

"Give me thy flask if thou hast in it a swallow of wine; I am parched with the heat," said the one who was called Gestas.

"I have no wine," replied the other; "water is better."

"Pah!" grunted Gestas testily, motioning away the proffered flask. "I do not drink water; 'tis fit only for the beasts."

"Thou art assuredly right, good friend; the best of the wine is not too good for thee. Do but a trifling service for me, and thou shalt not lack for the necessary gold."

"What wouldst thou?"

The Jew hesitated for a moment as if he scarcely knew how to proceed. Seth cautiously peered out from his hidden nook; he saw that the man was well dressed and had, moreover, an air of importance. He listened eagerly for his next words.

"Thou art the man who witnessed before Pilate against the malefactors, Dumachus and Titus, who afterward suffered with the Nazarene."

Gestas started visibly, he drew away a little and fixed his small twinkling eyes on his companion with a mixture of bravado and apprehension.

"What if I be?" he said at length. "I was discharged by the governor with but twenty stripes."

"Ay, but since then thou hast also—" here the speaker lowered his voice so that Seth lost what followed.

Gestas sprang to his feet with a great oath, and half drew his knife. "Thou knowest too much by half," he cried; "I am minded to send thee where thou mayest prate of this to the shades."

"Peace, braggart!" said his companion, a shade of contempt in his voice. "I am not unarmed. But thou canst see that had I spoken the word thou wouldst even now be rotting without the walls. I did not choose, because—thou canst serve me. Sit down and listen."

Gestas obeyed. "It is murder, I suppose," he said sullenly. "I know you all, you rich men! You force us poor devils to accomplish your black deeds, and dole out to us a scanty pittance from your hoarded gold; but if there be other recompense, such as the scourge or the cross, it is ours without grudging. Thirty pieces of silver they paid for the Nazarene; I know, for I saw it."

"What if it be thirty pieces of gold this time?" said the Jew softly. "The Iscariot was an ignorant Galilean; he was satisfied with the silver. It was enough," he added with a shrug, "for he hanged himself immediately thereafter because of his remorse. Now thou wouldst not do that, I dare venture?"

"I? Never! Else I had been dead a score of times already. But the matter in hand, what is it? I make no bargain, understand, till I know."

"'Tis simple enough—and—safe. Only the disposal of a man without family, and—yes—without friends. He is moreover blood-guilty; his removal is therefore lawful."

"Why then dost thou—"

"Why do I not perform the deed myself? A proper question; thou hast understanding. It is—most sapient Gestas—not my affair. I represent another; that other is not in a position to avenge himself personally, nevertheless he will be avenged. Wilt thou undertake this—for thirty pieces of gold?"

"Ten pieces now—thirty afterward, and I will do it."

"Say five now!"

"Nay, ten; I have no mind to risk my life for a pittance."

The other produced his wallet, albeit with some reluctance, and passed it into the hand of Gestas. "There are just ten pieces within," he remarked. "Thou mayest count them."

Gestas fumbled over the coins deliberately, counting them in a sibilant whisper. "One—two—three—four—five—six—seven—eight—nine—ten. Yes, ten—and a bit of silver." Then he lifted the pouch to the light and looked at it critically; "I will keep this also—and the silver," he added with a knowing leer.

"Of course, keep that also," said his companion, eyeing him with an inscrutable smile. "But I have not told thee the man's name. His head must thou deliver to me this very night at midnight, if thou wouldst receive the thirty pieces. It is known to me where thou art encamped with thy followers."

"I make no secret of that," said Gestas with a boastful laugh. "There is good water for our beasts in the valley of Hinnom, and it is not too far from the highway. If therefore thou wilt be in waiting just without the Jaffa gate, the head shall be delivered into thy hand at the hour named; if not to-night, why then to-morrow night; one must have time to snare the bird. But thou hast not yet told me the name."

"True; well then listen!" leaning forward, the Jew whispered for a little space into the ear of Gestas, who nodded twice or thrice as if he understood.

"I know the man," he said. "No one better; he should by right be about another business," then he laughed aloud as if something afforded him much secret amusement. "I have done for the father, I am once avenged; now I will be twice avenged, which is better. I know also how to lure him into a safe place. Thou wilt not fail with the thirty pieces?"

"I swear by the Temple that I will not fail."

"Good! Now there is another matter; I have in my camp a dromedary of great swiftness which I wish to dispose of at a fair price; the animal is young, docile, well trained; it is moreover of a white color; I have never seen the like. I bought the beast of a caravan and paid for it a great sum."

"No doubt," replied his companion suavely; "but let us first finish the matter in hand. One thing at a time, and diligently done, maketh a well ordered life," he continued piously. "So then I leave the affair in thy hands."

"Thou mayest trust me!" cried Gestas with a great laugh; he rose as he spoke and brought down his broad palm on the other man's shoulder with a sounding thwack. "Thou hast made no mistake in putting the matter into my hands, it will—" here he stopped short and stared fixedly into the shadow of the arch. "Body of Jove!" he exclaimed. "It seems that we are not alone!" And reaching forward, he grasped Seth by the shoulder and dragged him forth into the sunlight.

"What wast thou doing there, thou devil's imp? Nay, but thou shalt answer dearly for this."

But Seth had not shifted for himself all his thirteen years of life for naught. He instantly perceived that the man did not recognize him; rubbing his eyes stupidly, he stammered out something about sleeping soundly. Then he stretched out his hand toward the Jew who was regarding him suspiciously from under his bent brows, and whined out a petition for alms.

"Wilt thou that I give thee a gold piece?" said Gestas in the Greek tongue.

Seth regarded him blankly. "I do not understand, honored sir," he said humbly.

The companion of Gestas looked relieved. "It is safe enough if the beggar understood us not," he said. "Best take him along with you and make him secure till afterward; then release him."

"It may be that he doth not understand," rejoined Gestas, staring fixedly at the lad with his fierce red eyes; "yet there is but one kind of a man who can be trusted to tell no tales, and that is a dead man. All languages are alike to the tongue that hath ceased to move; any other tongue is to be feared."

The other shrugged his shoulders indifferently. "Ah well, do with him as thou wilt; life can be nothing to such as he. Only take him away. Till the hour and place of our agreement, farewell!" and turning he walked rapidly away, without once looking behind him.

For an instant Seth meditated flight; but the burly figure of Gestas was planted directly in front of him; to elude him would be impossible. Raising his eyes he saw the brown head and bright eyes of a sparrow, perched securely upon the ledge of the arch above him; the little creature was regarding the scene with apparent curiosity. Presently with a wild cry it darted away to join its fellows. The lad followed its flight with envious eyes, and for the second time he remembered the strange words of John, "Not a sparrow falleth to the ground without your Father." Again he prayed to the unknown

God who minded even the little wild things of the air, and as before he was comforted.

Gestas was evidently considering the situation with care, for he continued to stand silent before his prisoner, his arms akimbo, his small savage eyes riveted upon the figure before him. "Wouldst thou that I release thee?" he asked suddenly in the Greek tongue.

"If it please thee, good sir," responded Seth, quite off his guard.

Gestas smiled evilly. "It doth not please me, boy. Now march before me—so. Remember that I have in my hand a knife." And grasping the boy by the shoulders, he shoved him with a kind of terrible gentleness into the street.

Like one in a dream the lad walked before his captor. From time to time he looked wildly about in the vain hope of rescue, but the few passers-by went about their business with unseeing eyes, and an occasional prick of the knife from behind warned him that instant death awaited him should he venture to cry out. At length they had passed quite out of the city; here Gestas paused for a moment, and seeing that no one was by, he proceeded to bind the lad's hands securely behind his back.

"Thou art such a proper liar," he remarked with a grin, "that I am minded to leave thee alive for a while longer." Seth made no reply, nor did he cry out when Gestas playfully thrust the knife within a hair's breadth of his throat.

"If I must die," he thought, "I will at least die like a man." Then he remembered Anat sitting happily at her spinning at the feet of the gentle Mary; the tears rose to his eyes and brimming over rolled in great drops down his brown cheeks. He shook them off valiantly. "Tears do not become a man," he said to himself sternly.

"Come, come, my lad," cried Gestas, "my business requireth haste as well as diligence. We must be getting on." Then feeling very merry indeed, he put up his knife and fetched out his newly acquired pouch; shaking it so that all the gold pieces within clinked musically, he strode along, chanting a pagan rhyme of Bacchus and the pleasures of the vine.

After a time they reached one of the narrow defiles which wind between the hills on either side of the Valley of Hinnom, and here they presently came upon the encampment, cunningly placed within a copse of low-growing trees on the edge of a stream.

Half a score of men were scattered about upon the greensward, some of them eating and drinking, others playing at dice, and others still stretched out at full length in the shade asleep.

The arrival of Gestas and his prisoner was greeted with a shout of laughter. "Ha! our worthy chief hath made a notable capture," cried one, sauntering up to Seth and looking down at him. "A mighty man of valor is he truly to accomplish the overthrow of such as this. How many bags of gold didst thou take from him?"

Gestas winked significantly. "I shall take three, if the gods prosper me," he replied; then he bound the lad's ankles together, and bidding the man keep an eye upon the prisoner, he threw himself down upon the ground and demanded food and drink. Two or three others gathered about him, and to these he talked rapidly in low tones as he ate; but nothing of what was being said reached the ears of Seth, who was beginning to suffer intense agony from the tightness of the cords with which his wrists and ankles were bound.

He ventured at length to speak of this to the man who had been detailed to watch him; his guard good-naturedly

IN THE SHADOW OF THE WALL. 147

loosened the bonds, then relapsed into a doze, which presently deepened into a heavy sleep.

As the hours crept slowly by, Seth worked cautiously and unceasingly to loosen further the cords at his wrists. Towards evening he found to his intense joy that his hands were free. No one noticed him; the man at his feet still slept heavily; and after awhile he ventured stealthily to undo the thongs which bound his feet together; then he sat motionless, not daring to stir till the shadows should deepen.

As evening drew on, Gestas accompanied by two of the other men left the camp; he cast a glance in the direction of the lad as he passed by him, and hesitated for a moment as if he were minded to examine his bonds, but finally went his way. No sooner had he disappeared, than the lad crept away among the trees and bushes; before many minutes he had reached the edge of the thicket, here he paused breathlessly to listen, then rising to his feet, ran like the wind in the direction of the city.

"I must find Ben Hesed," he said. "He will know what to do."

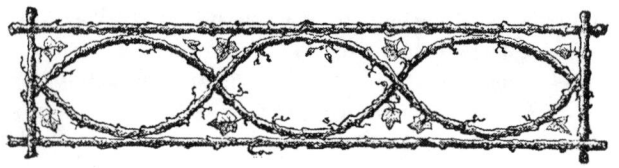

CHAPTER XX.

WITHOUT THE JAFFA GATE.

HE sunset hour was always a time of peace and peculiar joy in the house of John. The toils and dangers of the day being well over, the family were wont to gather upon the housetop, there to talk over what had happened during the hours that were passed. The golden glories of the dying day served to bring to their minds, each recurring evening, that place beyond the toils and sorrows of earth which their Lord had gone to prepare, and toward which each day's journey was swiftly hurrying them. Here the mother of Jesus sat enshrined in saintly peace; here also were John and Peter with the other apostles; Anna, the wife of Caiaphas, Stephen, and of late the black-eyed Egyptian maiden, together with many others who came to them for help, instruction, or healing. The number of such homes was daily increasing in Jerusalem; yet it was at this door, perhaps more often than at any other, that wretched humanity knocked for admittance, and admittance was always granted. For to these had been committed the ministry of the ascended Christ, with all that this signified of power and of blessing.

To-night into their midst came Ben Hesed, to talk once more with the apostles concerning the Crucified One. He brought with him the scrolls of the Prophecies, for he was troubled about certain points therein.

"How is it," he said, "that it is written, 'Accursed be every one that hangeth upon the tree. Surely God's Anointed could not be accursed."

"Dost thou doubt concerning him already?" asked Peter sternly.

"Nay, I doubt not, man; my spirit witnesseth within me that the thing is true. But I would fain be able to speak convincingly to them which believe not, when I shall have returned into the wilderness. It is not granted to every one to behold the angel of deliverance."

"Thou has spoken wisely, who art wise," said John gently. "The young man Stephen doth without ceasing make study of that which hath been written aforetime concerning the Christ. Yes, the spirit also hath revealed to him many things which have been hid from the eyes of the wise; and this to our profit who are sorely beset with the duties of our ministry. Read, I beseech thee, my brother, from the scroll which thou hast prepared."

"Concerning him which hath been hanged, it is written in the law thus," said Stephen, who a little apart from the others had been poring in silence over a number of parchments. " 'If a man have committed a sin worthy of death, and he be put to death, and thou hang him upon a tree. His body shall not remain all night upon the tree, but thou shalt surely bury him that day; for he that is hanged is accursed of God. That thy land be not defiled which the Lord thy God giveth thee for an inheritance.'

"But and if a sinless and holy man be put to death by false accusation, how is it that he is accursed? Herein is a great mystery, which as yet we see only in part, nor indeed can it be apprehended of mortals, that God gave his only begotten Son, not only that he should live amongst us a holy and sinless life, but that he should yield up that life in all meekness at the hands of his enemies. This also being the will of the Father concerning him; as he himself said, and as the voice of many prophets declare—who being dead yet speak to us in the words of the scripture. Are we not every one accursed, for we have sinned in the sight of God; and he, the sinless one, hath through the infinite compassion of the Father become accursed in our place. Even as it is written by the hand of the prophet Isaiah, 'He was wounded for our transgressions, he was bruised for our iniquities, the chastisement of our peace was upon him and with his stripes we are healed.'

"And behold these sayings—'I gave my back to the smiters, and my cheeks to them that plucked off the hair: I hid not my face from shame and from spitting'—'The assembly of the wicked have closed in upon me, they pierced my hands and my feet'—'They parted my garments among them, and cast lots upon my vesture'—'They gave me also gall for my meat, and in my thirst they gave me vinegar to drink'—'I became a reproach unto them, when they looked upon me they wagged their heads.' And this, 'his visage was so marred more than any man, and his form more than the sons of men'—'He was despised and rejected of men; a man of sorrows, and acquainted with grief; and we hid as it were our faces from him'—'He was taken from prison and from judgment and who shall declare his generation, for he was cut off out of the land of the living, for the transgression of my people was he stricken'—'And he made his grave with the wicked and with the rich in his death.'

"All these sayings I found concerning him," continued the young man gravely, "written many generations before his birth; they might have been writ yesterday by one who witnessed his death. Also by the hand of the prophet Daniel is this: 'And after three score and two weeks shall Messiah be cut off, but not for himself, and the people of the prince that shall come shall destroy the city and the sanctuary; and the end thereof shall be as a flood, and unto the end of the war desolations are determined.' "

"The end is yet to come," said Ben Hesed, involuntarily clenching his strong hands and looking toward the walls of the mighty temple, which shone white and mystical in the soft light of the rising moon.

"He himself foretold all that hath happened," said John sorrowfully, "and what is yet to come; how that he should be delivered up to the Romans, and should be mocked and spitefully entreated, spitted upon, scourged and crucified. It lay heavily upon him so that even he, who walked over in the light of God, was exceedingly sorrowful; and when he looked to us for sympathy that last awful night, we—slept. God forgive us!"

"He hath forgiven us all things," said Peter. "He bore our sins in his own body on the tree. For the love of him, shall we not gladly suffer what shall yet befall us? for he told us plainly that the world would hate us, even as it hated him; that we also should be persecuted, scourged, and put to death. Yet how soon will all be past, and then we shall go to him."

In the silence which followed these words a loud knocking was heard at the outer gate of the courtyard. Stephen arose quietly from his place and descended the stair. When he had opened the door, he saw standing in the street a man. He was meanly clad, as Stephen could see by the dim light; therefore his voice was more gentle than usual as he said:—

"What wilt thou, friend?"

"Is there here a young man called Stephen?"

"I am he; wilt thou enter?"

The man shuffled uneasily on his feet, then looked furtively up and down the street. "There be a sick man who hath need of thee for healing and strong words of thy faith," he said at length, fixing his eyes upon Stephen.

"Wouldst thou not rather inquire for one of the twelve?"

"Nay, it was for one Stephen, a Greek, I was bidden to ask. The man I have spoken of is also a Greek, and would not ask for healing at the hands of a Jew."

"The healing cometh from God," said Stephen gravely. "I will come though. Where is the sick man?"

"I will show thee where he lieth," said the man eagerly; "and I pray thee to make haste, for his case is desperate."

"Let me first speak to them that are within, I will join thee immediately," said Stephen, stepping back into the courtyard and leaving the door partly open.

The man listened to the sound of his retreating steps as he ascended the stair. "They be all above," he uttered, stepping softly within. "Now if by any chance—Ha! what is this? A capital warm cloak, 'twill serve to shelter me these chill nights. Body of Jove! but I am always in luck of late!"

When Stephen returned, the man was waiting humbly without as he had left him. The two immediately set forth, the man going before; they walked swiftly through the dark narrow streets, the stranger glancing frequently over his shoulder to make sure that Stephen was following. After a time he paused, "'Tis without the walls," he muttered hoarsely. "We must pass through the Jaffa Gate."

"There is moonlight," said Stephen rather absently, raising his eyes to the heavens, where in truth his thoughts had been as he followed his strange guide.

"There is moonlight," repeated the man with a hoarse chuckle. "So much the better."

Stephen looked at the speaker more attentively than he had done at first; the white light which poured down from above revealing clearly every feature of the brutal face before him. He started visibly. "I have somewhere seen thee before!" he exclaimed. " Nay I now know, thou art of them who formerly—"

The man laughed aloud. "I am Gestas; second in authority to Dumachus, who was chief of our band—and your father. Since the Romans put an end to him, along with Titus and Nazarene, I have been chief."

"And is it one of your followers who is in need of healing?" asked Stephen, shrinking back a little with something of his old-time dread.

"It is. Art thou afraid?"

"No," returned Stephen quietly, "I am not afraid; surely of all men ye are most in need of the mighty help of the risen Lord; 'twere most fitting if so be that I may bring it into your midst."

Gestas looked at him with an indescribable mixture of contempt and pity. "Thou art a pretty enough fellow," he said, running his eyes over the slender but well-knit figure. "A thought too pretty indeed. Why art thou contented to pass thy days in the company of a band of crazy fools, who will end as their Master did—though he merited it not—on the cross? Why take the devil's wages without the devil's pleasures first? If now, I die on the cross, it will be for the reasons better than preaching, praying, and the healing of dirty beggar folk."

"Afterward is the judgment," said Stephen.

"A fig for the afterwards!" cried Gestas. "Who knows anything about that? But, come," he added with a sudden change in his tones, "it lacks but an hour of midnight; thou must be gone before that time."

"I am not in haste to be gone," said Stephen gently. "I will remain until morning, if I can do anything to help."

"There is naught that thou canst do—after midnight," said Gestas gruffly. "If there is an afterwards," he muttered, "it will make no difference to him."

The two walked silently for a time, pausing at length at the edge of a low-growing coppice, through the interlacing branches of which could be seen the fitful flash of a dying fire. Making their way through the thicket by a winding path evidently well known to Gestas, the twain presently found themselves in the centre of the encampment.

"Where is the dying man?" said Stephen, eager to begin his ministry of love.

For answer, Gestas seized him by the arm and hurried him forward into the midst of a dark group of figures which seemed to be awaiting their approach. "Thou art the dying man!" he whispered hoarsely. "Prepare for thy afterwards swiftly."

Half involuntarily, Stephen made a mighty unavailing effort to free himself from the grasp of the ruffian who held him; life on a sudden looked very sweet to him. It could not be that God had appointed such an end as this for one who would serve him long and faithfully. Surely he was too young to die. Yet not younger than Titus, who had gone by the horrible way of the cross to be with him in Paradise. At the thought, a great peace possessed his soul. "Not my will but thine be done," he murmured aloud, raising his eyes to the stars which glittered keenly through the interlacing branches overhead.

"So this is the man!" cried a rough voice, as a dozen hands bound him to the trunk of a tree. "It may be that if he hath the power to heal, as they say, he will be the master also of other magic arts, which he will use to our undoing. Best make way with him quickly."

WITHOUT THE JAFFA GATE.

Stephen looked about on the crowd of evil faces which surrounded him, and a great wave of pity for his tormentors swept over him. So far were they from God, so deep in unfathomable depths of misery. For himself he felt no fear; from earth to heaven was but a single step.

"Men and brethren," he cried, and his voice rang out clear and sweet upon the startled air. "Let me live for yet a little space, till I shall declare unto you the words of life. For such as you, Jesus died upon the cross; he will save you from out the misery of this present life, and afterward give you the life that endeth not. Only believe on him and forsake your evil ways."

"Prate not to us of thy Jewish Messiah," cried one. "He is not for us, even if what thou sayest be true. We must die as we have lived. We be uncircumcised Greeks that care not for an everlasting abode with them that spit upon us in this life."

"Nay, but he died for the sins of the world, and he is risen from death to abide forever with the Father which made the Greek as well as the Jew, and loveth both alike."

"Give to us a sign!" cried another. "If what thou hast said be true, let the man Jesus come down out of the heavens and deliver thee, then will we believe on him; nay, more, thou shalt be our leader in place of Gestas here—who is too stupid to be chief."

At this Gestas swore a great oath of rage. "Stand back, all of you," he cried. "I will smite him; and there is none that shall deliver him out of my hand, either on earth or in heaven."

Then he raised his arm; Stephen caught the keen glitter of the steel. He closed his eyes. His lips moved in prayer. Something smote him on the breast, but it was not the soul-delivering blade, as he dimly realized ere his senses left him. Gestas, stricken full in the heart by an arrow sped from the bow of an unseen archer, had leapt straight into the air without a cry, then falling limply, his head striking against the prisoner, he lay, a grim unsightly heap, at Stephen's feet.

The others stood for an instant aghast, then with wild cries of fear they fled away into the thicket.

"I fear the knaves have done for him, whoever he be," cried a voice, as the figure of a young man bounded out of the bushes.

"Nay, my son," said Ben Hesed, who had followed more deliberately, "the miscreant had but raised his blade when my arrow smote him; let us loose the man here and get away from this place with all speed, for they will return and fall upon us, if they find that we be few."

"I must fetch the white dromedary," said the voice of Seth, at his elbow. "It is in yonder glade."

"Be quick, then; there is no time to lose!"

The moon had looked down for a full hour longer upon the dark motionless something, which lay just where it had fallen on the soft grass, when the thicket again opened and a man peered out. He looked about him cautiously, then turned and spoke reassuringly to some one behind him.

"There is no one here, Joca; come on!"

"It was a bolt from heaven assuredly which smote him; for there is naught missing save the man," said the other, looking keenly about in his turn at the familiar scene; "Let us get away from this place; I am sick of it."

"Ay! we will return to Greece where the old gods yet rule; I like not the ways of the god of this land; but first—" And the speaker cautiously approached the body of Gestas. "He hath something about him, which we shall have more need of than he. Ah! here it is, ten good pieces—if he have not already spent some of them."

"But there were to have been thirty pieces more."

"Ay! and more's the pity that they be lost to us."

"Why need they be lost to us, man?"

"What meanest thou?"

Joca whispered something in his companion's ear, whereat the other chuckled hoarsely.

"Why not?" he cried, "thou art a son of Minerva to have thought it."

The servant of Annas had waited outside the Jaffa gate for nearly two hours; he was growing impatient at last.

"I will not stay longer," he muttered, "something hath miscarried in the matter; it will be to-morrow—if the knave hath not failed me altogether."

But even as he spoke he saw a man approaching him. He at once stood forth in the full moonlight, bidding his companions remain within the shadow of the wall.

The man came up to him swiftly. "Art thou he who hath thirty pieces of gold to give in exchange for a strange commodity?"

"I am he. Hast thou the commodity?"

"Ay! it is here; wilt thou see it?"

The Jew shuddered at sight of the bag which the other tendered him. "No!" he said shortly. "Take the money and be gone." Then he turned to one of the slaves who waited his orders. "Take this," he commanded, "and fetch it to the palace."

CHAPTER XXI.

NOT A SPARROW FALLETH.

OMETHING must be done. Our widows can no longer wait in their desolations. It has been almost the space of two years and our women continue to be neglected." They were conversing in low tones, but their excited gestures and gloomy faces betrayed the fact that the topic which they were discussing was not a pleasant one.

"There is unquestioned and open partiality on the part of the apostles toward them that be of Hebrew birth and descent," said one bitterly. "Though we be circumcised and walk after the law in all diligence, the fact that we are Greeks can be neither overlooked nor forgiven."

"I mind not what they think;" cried another sturdily, "a Greek is as good as a Jew any day, and we be all servants of one Master, even Christ; but it is not just that our widows and fatherless be spurned in the daily distributions, for we all have given freely of our substance into the common fund."

"I like not to boast, my Andronicus," said the third man almost in a whisper, "but I cannot forbear the thought that had I retained in mine own power what I aforetime laid down at the apostles' feet—freely and in all humility of mind, these tales of neglect would not now be coming to our ears."

None of the three had observed that a fourth man had joined himself to the group, till the newcomer spoke. "The neglect of which thou dost complain, my brothers," he said in a deep musical voice, "is not a neglect born of contempt for us because we are Greeks. I know these men through and through; they rest not day nor night, but labor incessantly, and in all unselfishness and love for the church, yet is the burden too heavy for them. Christ healed many that were sick and fed many that were hungry. Yet there remain multitudes of them that are blind, of them that are lepers, of them that hunger, who were also blind, leprous, and hungry, when our Master walked the earth. They came not unto him, and how could he succor them, being burdened with this humanity which doth irk us all?"

"What thou hast said, my Stephen, is true," admitted Andronicus. "But it is also true that among the Jewish widows there is no lack, while Priscilla and her little ones remained two days without food. Had she refrained from joining herself to us, she would have continued to receive aid from the Temple treasury; the woman herself declared it, and I could not gainsay her had I wished it. If there be not neglect born of contempt, there is assuredly a lack of wisdom."

"What hath been done for Priscilla?"

"My wife ministered to her necessities, as well as to those of Julia and Eunice."

"Hast thou spoken of this to Peter?" asked Stephen, looking troubled and turning to one of the others.

"Nay, I have not spoken of it; there should be no need to speak, say I."

"Forget not the word of the Master, 'Judge not that ye be not judged,'" said Stephen, gravely. We must look carefully within before we lightly censure any man—least of all the chosen and anointed ones of our Lord." Then after a thoughtful pause he added, "I will myself speak with John concerning these things."

The man who had first spoken, and who was called Apelles, looked after him as he walked away. "From him I can suffer reproof as from no other;" he said, "he hath within him the very spirit of the ascended One."

"Like the ascended One, he hath also enemies in high places;" said Andronicus, significantly, "the continued attempts made upon his life bear witness to the fact."

"What dost thou mean? He was threatened, it is true, by certain of the Sadducees because of his boldness in declaring the resurrection in their very midst, but no man laid hands on him."

"The Herodians, and especially the Pharisee from Tarsus, are bitter against him for some reason, which perhaps we understand not wholly. Hast thou forgotten his rescue by Ben Hesed more than two years hence; and also what happened thrice since—when by the barest chance he escaped with his life?"

"True, he has been mercifully preserved amidst great dangers; but each time there was a simple enough cause for the peril without attributing it to an enemy," said Apelles, thoughtfully. "Once it was from robbers, who would have slain him from the mere lust of murder, as is their wont. Again, a heavy stone fell from the wall above as he spake to the people, barely missing his head in its descent."

"Yes; I know all that thou wouldst say;" broke in the other, "but listen! Yesterday a basket of fruit was sent him, bearing a scroll inscribed thus: 'This fruit is for the saintly Stephen, from one who believes that the apples of Paradise are none too fair for such as he.' "

"A pretty conceit assuredly!"

"A most lovely conceit! Had he eaten, as the sender supposed that he would do, even now would the apples of Paradise be within his grasp."

"What meanest thou?"

" 'I will not eat of this fair fruit,' said Stephen, 'instead I will bear it to the aged Clement, who hath only of late joined himself to us,' but while he waited for a convenient season for taking the gift, the fruit stood without on the ledge of the window, and the birds came and pecked it. Before they could fly away after their stolen meal the little creatures dropped dead."

"Horror! the fruit was poisoned then?"

"Assuredly. Now thou seest that he hath an enemy."

"But who?"

"I have my suspicions, and have warned him. His answer was this, 'He is with me always even unto the end; until my appointed time there is nothing that shall be able to hurt me; neither shall I fear what man can do to me.' "

"Wonderful! I have confessed that Jesus is the Christ, but I fear my faith in him is but a poor thing compared with that of Stephen; had the like happened to me I should have fled the city."

"'Twas what I urged upon him. Go away from Jerusalem, I said. There be Jews in every city of Greece who would gladly hear thee of the Christ; in the land of thy fathers shalt thou dwell in safety. But he shook his head. 'The day is not far distant,' he made answer, 'when not alone to the Jews shall this salvation be preached, but unto every people and kindred and tongue beneath the heavens; for Christ came to save the world, and therefore shall the world be saved; but it is not I who am called to this work; my place is here.'"

While the two Greeks thus spoke one to another of Stephen, the young man himself was passing rapidly through the streets towards his home, his thoughts busied chiefly with what Andronicus had told him concerning the daily ministrations. "The matter must be looked to," he said to himself. "The twelve are not sufficient for the work, God be praised. So mightily hath the spirit worked with and for us, that the day is not far distant when the cross shall cease to be a symbol of shame and hissing among men and shall everywhere be hailed the sacred token of deliverance."

Communing thus within himself he lifted up his eyes and beheld the square which lay before the palace of Pilate. "It was here," he murmured, "that they brought him on the day of his death. It was here that the people cried out, 'Crucify him—Crucify him!' Ah, that awful day—nay rather that day of days, decreed from the foundations of the world!" Then he passed on into the square, being minded to look for a moment on the very place where he knew the Man of Sorrows had stood so patiently on that last day of his earthly life. As he approached the mosaic of many-colored marbles which marked the place of the judgment seat, a Roman chariot containing two men and drawn by a pair of powerful black horses dashed into the square.

"Dost see that fellow yonder, Herod?" exclaimed the man who stood behind the driver. "I mean the one with the white robe. 'Tis that beggarly Greek, Stephen, who hath been setting the city on an uproar of late with his driveling cant. I hate the whole blasphemous brood, but he is most contemptible of all."

"I will engage to run him down, if thou sayest it," said the man who held the reins, and across whose white tunic streamed a scarf of the imperial purple.

"Be it so!' answered his companion with a malignant scowl. "'Twill be a happy accident that rids the world of such a one."

"An accident of course," said the other with a brutal laugh. "Who would dare question it?" And he brought the long lash with a whistling curl about the glossy flanks of the horses; they leapt forward as one. Something else also leapt forward. There was a cry, and the sound of the iron hoofs was horribly dulled for an instant, then the chariot thundered on, and swept into the avenue beyond the palace.

"By the gods, Alexander!" cried Herod. "Didst thou see the man who leapt forward from behind? He dragged the beggar forth just in time; another instant and he would have been crushed beneath our wheels."

"I saw, yes," answered the other, grinding his teeth. "The wretch bears a charmed life."

"We will drive back to inquire of the accident," pursued Herod with a sneering laugh. "Pollux there struck something softer than the pavement. Hey! Pollux, my beauty? If it chanced to be the man's head he will prate no more of dead malefactors—nor yet of live ones. How now, fellow!" he shouted, reining in his struggling horses as they approached the borders of the crowds which had instantly gathered at the scene of the accident. "Was the man hurt seriously?"

"Not seriously, they say, your Highness," replied the man to whom he had spoken, bowing low at the sight of his royal questioner; "but the stranger who rescued him hath beyond doubt suffered a mortal wound."

"The more fool he!" cried Herod contemptuously. As the horses again sprang forward in obedience to the lash, he turned to his companion with a wicked laugh. "'Twere a pretty pastime for our leisure to root out these pestiferous fellows from the Holy City, and 'twould doubtless cover a multitude of sins."

"May we count on thine assistance, my prince?" said Alexander eagerly. "We who are against the Nazarenes grow fewer each day; already the greater number of Pharisees either believe or regard them with tolerance. These all declare openly that the dead carpenter of Galilee is alive and is like to return any day to rule over Israel."

Herod's face darkened. "Let him return and attempt it!" he cried angrily. "Behind me—is Rome."

CHAPTER XXII.

BY THE THORNY WAYS OF HIS SIN.

PON a couch in the house of John lay the stranger who had rescued Stephen from death. About him were gathered those of the household who chanced to be at home when the sad little procession had arrived.

"He gave his life for mine," said Stephen, solemnly, looking down at the quiet face across which the shadow of approaching death had already fallen. "And God hath accepted the sacrifice; it is not his will that he be restored. Would that I knew to whom I owe this debt of gratitude before he goes hence."

"He will recover consciousness, I think, shortly," said Mary, laying her cool white fingers on the brow of the sufferer. He is assuredly not a Jew," she added, gazing intently at the dark face upon the pillows. "Fetch me a basin and sponge, my daughter; it may be that the cool water will revive him."

The girl to whom she had spoken hastened to obey. As she stooped to pour water from a jar which stood without in the courtyard, a young man hurriedly entered the enclosure.

"Where is Stephen?" he cried, as his eye fell upon the maiden. "I heard but just now that Herod had crushed him beneath his chariot wheels. A brutal deed. He that told me was an eye-witness."

"By the mercy of God," answered the girl with a half sob, "he hath escaped with a bruise; another was smitten in his place, and he is dying. I must hasten with the water!" and she sprang up and hurried away.

The young man followed, and approaching the group that surrounded the couch, he looked over the shoulder of the young girl as she held the basin ready for the hand of Mary. He started as his eye fell upon the wounded man.

"He is an Egyptian!" he exclaimed.

Even as he spoke, the man opened his eyes. "Water!" he gasped faintly. Stephen raised the languid head while the skilful Mary held the cup.

"Lay him down again, gently—so," she said in a low voice.

Then Stephen bent over the pillow. 'Canst thou tell us who thou art, and why it was that thou didst choose the life of another rather than thine own?"

The dull eyes brightened a little, "Did I save him? Ay, yes—thanks be to the gods! thou art alive. Did any hurt befall thee?"

"Nay—but I lived, alas, because thou art to die."

"It is well, not only that thou wilt live, but that I shall die, if the God whom thou dost proclaim will but count my worthless life a sacrifice for my many sins."

"Nay, my brother," said Stephen, "if thou dost but believe on Jesus the Christ, there is no sacrifice needed for sin; he gave himself a sacrifice for our transgressions because of the love which he bare us."

"It cannot be that he loves me," said the dying man. "Listen till I shall tell thee all. I am an Egyptian, my name is Amu—"

The maiden who still stood at his bedside grew very white at the sound of that name, and the newcomer, who was watching from behind, reached quietly out and took the basin from her nerveless fingers. "Anat," he whispered, "'tis a common enough name."

"It is he," she returned, I know the voice—but listen!"

"Early in life," continued the Egyptian, his voice gathering strength, "I was even as others, neither better, nor worse—'tis not of those days I would speak, but of the days when I was a man grown—then it chanced that there came a certain stranger out of the wilderness with his wife and child, and sojourned in Egypt. He possessed gold and bought for himself a plot of land not far from the river. This he tilled with industry, so that after a time he gained more gold and bought still another bit of tillage. Not much, for land was costly in the neighborhood of the river. I was his neighbor and I was not unfriendly to him, for he was a stranger and knew not the ways of the people, nor at the first the proper grains to cast into the earth. And because I helped him in such small matters, he loved me and clave to me, as also his wife; and I was ever an honored guest in their house. After a time, there came a great sickness over all the region about the upper Nile, because the river failed to overflow its banks at the proper season. The people were wasted by it, and they died by hundreds and by thousands. My father and my brothers died; and the plot of land which had been theirs came to me.

"After a time the man who had come out of the wilderness was likewise stricken, and his wife; and when it presently appeared that they both must die, he sent for me and spake to me after this manner, 'My friend, who hath been to me even as a brother in this land of strangers wherein we have sojourned, I am sorely stricken, both I and the mother of the children, and it must presently come to pass that we be gathered to our fathers; but before my soul passes I would fain speak to thee of my little ones who will be left desolate, if so be that the plague spares them.' 'Speak,' I made answer, 'I will do with them as thou dost command.' Then he told me how that he was a Greek born in Antioch, and the son of a rich man. After his father died a fierce quarrel arose betwixt the two brothers over the division of the inheritance; and when after many days the bitterness still continued, it came to pass that he smote his brother and wounded him sore; then taking what he would he fled away into the wilderness. There he took to himself a wife from the tribes that wandered in the desert and afterward came to dwell in Egypt.

" 'Now I pray and beseech thee,' he said to me, 'by all that thou holdest sacred, that thou wilt take my two children and the price of the land—when thou shalt have sold it—and fetch them to my brother, for I have heard that he yet liveth, and say to him this: Thy brother is dead. He sendeth thee the money that he took away—and more; and here are also his two children. Let them find favor in thy sight, I pray thee, for they are desolate.'

"I promised my neighbor that I would do what he desired of me; and I sware it by the temple of Ptah Hotep, and by the sacred Nile, and by the soul of my father. And when he had told me his brother's name and how to find him, he turned himself about on his bed and spoke no more. In that same day both he and his wife perished. Of the two children one was likewise stricken, and I watched her many days till she recovered. Afterward I perceived that she had become blind by reason of the plague.

"That season I could not sell the land, for there were none to buy; so I planted the crops and reaped them, and the children ate and were satisfied; but the money I received for the grain I kept, for I said the laborer is worthy of his wages. The next season I also planted and reaped, and the next; and at the time of the third harvest a man came to me and said, 'Wilt thou sell this land for thy neighbor's children?' and I answered him 'Nay, I will not sell. My neighbor owed me money and he died without repaying me, therefore is the land mine!' And after a time I came almost to believe what I had said. But I waxed exceeding bitter against the two children, who were as yet only babes; so I sent them away to a woman who dwelt in the tombs above the river; and I paid her to keep them. Afterward she died, and the two continued to dwell alone in the tombs. They grew and waxed strong—though no one cared for them, for the boy was robust and brave; he had become a water-carrier. Still I kept a watch upon them, for I feared lest they should in some way find out what I had done; though I confessed it to no one, not even my wife. After a time the fear grew upon me so that I could neither eat nor sleep, and I resolved to rid myself of the two. I had not yet grown evil enough to wish to slay them, so I turned the thing over in my mind for many days; at the last I was resolved what to do. I would sell them for slaves, then would they be taken away and I should be free from my fears; not only so, but I should receive gold, with which to buy more land. But when I would have accomplished my desires upon them, they fled away into the desert, and assuredly perished; for though I searched for them long, I could never find what had become of them."

"Why didst thou search for them?" said Seth suddenly, as the man paused to drink from the cup which Mary again held to his parched lips.

"I searched for them," replied the man, his eyes resting upon his questioner's face with a startled expression, "because—Nay, I hardly know why. I had repented of my desire to make slaves of them, but I was not ready to give up the land."

"What became of Besa?"

"I found him dead in the tomb where he thought the twain were hidden," answered the Egyptian as if in a dream. "But who art thou that dost question me?" and he half raised himself in the bed, his livid face growing yet more ghastly with the painful effort.

"We are the children of the man thou didst wrong," said Seth fiercely. "Tell me, what was the name of our kinsman, that we may yet seek him as our father willed?

"His name was Erastus; but, alas, he is dead now these many years. I sought him that I might render an account of what I had done, for I feared death on account of my sin. Neither dared I pray any more to the avenging gods; for had I not foresworn myself in their names? So, because there was no longer any comfort for me in the lands which I possessed, nor in my children, nor in anything in the whole land of Egypt, I became a wanderer in far countries. Here in Jerusalem not many days since, I chanced to hear a wondrous thing, 'that they which had sinned might find peace and forgiveness in one Jesus of Nazareth, 'who had lived upon earth that he might save them which were lost.' That same day I beheld him that had spoken these words; and I drew near, desiring to ask him still further of the matter, when on a sudden I saw that he was in mortal peril. I scarce know what followed; but I longed to save him, if only that I might hear once more the strange story of the man Jesus. Tell me"—and the man's glazing eyes sought Stephen—"thou hast heard all—is there forgiveness for such as I?"

"There is forgiveness for every one that doth repent and believe in the Lord Jesus," said Stephen softly. "Surely thou mayest pass in peace, my brother; for God hath led thee even by the thorny ways of thy sin unto himself."

The dying man's eyes again brightened, his lips moved with the delicate expressions of repentance; then he stretched out his hand toward the youth and the maiden, who had sunken to their knees by his bedside. "Wilt thou also forgive?" he murmured.

"Yes—yes. We forgive thee fully, as also we hope to be forgiven," cried Seth, pressing his lips to the cold hand which had so cruelly wronged him.

"Thy mother—her name was Zarah," faltered the Egyptian—"she was the daughter—of—" his voice failed him; thrice he made an unavailing effort to speak, then the eternal silence fell softly upon him.

"He hath passed into the presence of the Love that hath led him through all the weary way of his life," said Mary solemnly. "There will he find peace."

CHAPTER XXIII.

IN THE SYNAGOGUE OF THE NAZARENES.

OR what have we been called together at this time, knowest thou?" asked a man of his neighbor in the crowd assembled before the synagogue of the Nazarenes. "Seeing that this is not the prescribed day for worship."

"'Tis that we may consider the matter of which the Grecians have been murmuring of late," replied the other. "Their widows, say they, are neglected in the daily ministrations."

"Not more than the widows of our own blood; the fault lieth with the young men to whom of late the apostles have been forced to give a part of the work. But see, the doors are opened."

The twain, together with the rest of the quiet and orderly multitude, passed into the porch, where each person paused for an instant to dip his hands into the brazen urn of water which stood without the door; this constituting the ceremonial washing of hands required before entering into the sacred enclosure.

The scene within did not differ materially from that which might have been seen in any other of the four hundred and eighty synagogues of Jerusalem. Against the wall opposite the entrance, beneath a canopy of purple cloth, stood the wooden chest or ark, containing the scrolls of the law. Above this ark burned the perpetual light, token of the visible glory of the Lord as it was revealed in that first temple which their forefathers had reared in the wilderness. This sacred light was a three-fold symbol, for it also served to remind the worshipper of the human soul, which is the breath of God; as it is written, "The spirit of man is the candle of the Lord." And of the divine law—"For thy commandment is a lamp; and thy law is light."

Here also facing the congregation was the desk from which the ruler of the synagogue was wont to preside over the worship; and at one side, elevated upon a raised platform, twelve wooden seats were provided for the twelve apostles—the visible heads of the Church; it being the custom in all synagogues to thus elevate above the common rank those who were considered the most enlightened. In these, as in all other respects, did the disciples walk orderly as after the law; being yet minded, despite the warning of the Master, to put the strong new wine of the kingdom into the ancient bottles of Judaism.

On this day, after that the congregation had seated themselves in due order—the men upon one side of the room, the women and children upon the other, separated by a low wooden partition—the service was begun by the chanting of the sacrificial psalms; after which the whole congregation arose and repeated as with one voice the benediction called "The Creator of Light."

"Blessed art thou, O Lord our God, King of the universe, who createst light and formest darkness; who makest peace and createst all things. He in mercy causes the light to shine upon the earth and the inhabitants thereof, and in goodness renews every day the work of creation. Blessed art thou, the Creator of Light."

And also this—"the Great Love."

"With great love hast thou loved us, O Lord our God; thou hast shown us great and abundant mercy, O our Father and King, for the sake of our forefathers who trusted in thee! Thou who didst teach them the love of life; have mercy upon us and teach us also to praise thee, O Lord, who in love hast chosen thy people!"

Then did Matthias—who on this day had been chosen to lead the worship, and who like the rest of the congregation wore the fringed garment prescribed by the law and the phylacteries upon his head and upon his left arm—arise, and cry aloud in the words of the ancient prayer which was called Kadish; all the people joining heartily in the Amens.

"Exalted and hallowed be his great name in the world which he created according to his will; let his kingdom come in your lifetime, and in the lifetime of the whole house of Israel very speedily!"

"Amen!"

"Blessed be his great name, world without end."

"Amen!"

"Blessed and praised, celebrated and exalted, extolled and adorned, magnified and worshipped, be thy holy name; blessed be he far above all benedictions, hymns, thanks, praises, and consolations which have been uttered in this world."

"Amen!"

"May the prayers and supplications of all Israel be graciously received before their Father in heaven."

"Amen."

"May perfect peace descend from heaven, and life, upon us and all Israel."

"Amen!"

"May he who makes peace in his heaven confer peace upon us and all Israel."

"Amen!"

Then followed the eighteen benedictions, of which the first sentence only was repeated in a loud voice by the leader, the rest being recited by the congregation in unison. Save this prayer, which all repeated aloud and with a joyous tone of full expectation; for they knew him to whom they prayed. "To Jerusalem thy city in mercy return, and dwell in it according to thy promise; make it speedily in our day an everlasting building, and soon establish therein the throne of David. Blessed art thou, O Lord, who buildest Jerusalem." And so to the end, closing with the words, "Our Father, bless us all unitedly with the light of thy countenance; for in the light of thy countenance didst thou give to us, O Lord our God, the law of life, loving kindness, justice, blessing, compassion, life, and peace. May it please thee to bless thy people Israel at all times, and in every moment with peace. Blessed art thou, O Lord, who blessest thy people Israel with peace!"

Then followed the reading from the scriptures. Afterward Peter arose in his place and spoke to the people; he brought again to their remembrance the words of their risen Lord, 'how that they should continue to dwell together in all peace and love, forbearing one another and loving one another in expectation of that great day, perhaps nigh at hand, when he should return bringing his reward with him for them that had been faithful in all things.' He spoke also of the matter which had been troubling the minds of many during the days that were past.

"God knoweth, brethren," he said, "that we would not willingly neglect any, who by the grace of our Lord have joined themselves with us; least of all them who by reason of their affliction are dependent upon our bounty. If any have been neglected it is because of the weakness of the flesh. The work hath waxed too great for us; for besides this duty of the daily distribution of bodily food to them that lack, there remaineth also the duty whereunto we were set apart by the Master himself—of preaching the good tidings of salvation from sin and from death unto all men. 'It is not reason that we should set aside the work of God to serve tables'—and it is manifest that we can no longer do both—'wherefore, brethren, look ye out among you seven men of honest report, full of the Holy Ghost and wisdom, whom we may appoint over this business. But we will give ourselves continually to prayer and to the ministry of the word.' "

And when he had finished speaking, Philip arose in his place.

"If I read aright your faces, my brothers," he said, looking around about upon the multitude, "this good saying hath pleased you all. Let us therefore choose, and that there may no longer be any thought of jealousy betwixt Jew and Greek—which thing also must be displeasing unto him, who according to his word, is at this time in our midst—let it come to pass that of the seven which we shall choose, three shall be Hebrews, three Greeks and one a proselyte. Then shall there be no longer need nor excuse that any should murmur concerning this matter of the dispensations."

And these sayings being approved of them which were assembled, one Aristarchus arose and presented the name of Stephen for the honorable office of deacon. "For he is," declared the speaker, "as is known unto you all, a man full of faith and of the Spirit."

And all the people cried with one voice: "Worthy! He is Worthy!"

Then did they in the same manner choose also Philip and Prochorus, Nicanor, Timon, and Parmenas; and also, according to the word of Philip, Nicolas of Antioch, who

IN THE SYNAGOGUE OF THE NAZARENES. 177

was a convert to the Jewish faith, but now to the risen Lord. And these seven stood up before the apostles and before all the congregation of the people; and when the apostles had prayed they laid their hands upon them, in token that thus were they set apart unto the sacred duties of their calling.

CHAPTER XXIV.

THE WARNING.

HE bell which hung beside the porter's lodge jangled sharply, and the porter, after first peering out to see who stood before the door, promptly opened. "My master is within," he said, making his obeisance. "I pray thee enter, reverend sir, thou wilt find my lord Annas upon the terrace. He is expecting thee."

Without a word the newcomer strode past and disappeared within. The porter stared after his retreating figure for a moment in silence, then he shook his head slowly. "His look is dark and threatening, he muttered, "it bodes no good for them that believe, when at night and at morning and also at midday those that hate us gather themselves in secret conclave. There be mischiefs brewing, I fear me; a dark cloud which will break ere long and bring swift destruction upon the church—unless the Lord send help, and that right speedily."

"And what hast thou found to grumble about now, Simon?" said a cheery voice at his elbow.

The old man looked up sharply. "Ah, Iddo, didst thou hear me? I am indeed falling into indiscreet habits in my solitude when I prate aloud of my fears. Had it been

THE WARNING.

Aaron now, in thy stead—but why do I say so? I am not ashamed to own that I believe on the Nazarene."

"Thou art in good company, assuredly," said the young man, "though an open avowal of thy faith would doubtless cost thee thy snug quarters. The lord of this house is not likely to be of them which are daily being added to the church. Hast thou heard that of the priests themselves we are continually gaining in great numbers? 'Tis wonderful; all Jerusalem will be with us in another year; as for these worldly old hypocrites, let them be; they will die in their sins and the world will be better without them. Even the Master had no good word for such. Whited sepulchres called he them, and pronounced against them the woes which they assuredly have merited. Nothing can stand against us now, for the Lord is with us!"

But Simon shook his head. "Thou art young, Iddo," he said querulously, "and hast much to learn. There is a storm at hand and it will blow no good to the church; I have said it, and thou wilt see. Do I not stand at this gate and see them that go in and out? I hear also many things—for the Lord hath persevered my ears, and they that enter mind me no more than yonder stone bench—listen!" and the old man held up a shaking hand. "Yesterday I admitted two—four—five of them that be rich and mighty—I will not name them. They remained within, three whole hours by the shadow on yonder dial, then they came out together."

" 'Tis a goodly thought of Annas to first put out of the way the pestilential Greek,' quoth one, 'the witnesses will not be hard to find.'

" 'I trow not,' said another with a laugh, 'words are cheap both for the buying and selling; as for the fellow Stephen, he doeth more mischief among the common people in a week than the slow-witted hinds whom they call apostles could accomplish in a month.'"

"Stephen," cried Iddo, aghast.

"Hist, boy! Now thou seest that though I am old—and as thou hast said, given to over-much foreboding—there is a deadly mischief on foot."

"The Lord will smite them if they lay but a finger on Stephen," exclaimed the young man indignantly. "'Tis such as he that the Lord's flock hath need of; daily doth he work great miracles of healing, and his voice is heard in every synagogue persuading men to believe on Jesus the Christ. Men listen gladly; and to listen is to be convinced of the truth."

"Ah, boy! 'tis because of these very things that they hate him; were he less than he is, they would not lay a finger on him."

"But surely God will protect him!"

"God spared not his own son," said the old man solemnly. "He suffered him to be tortured and to be slain at the hands of these very men; and the servant is not greater than his Lord."

The other was silent for a time; all the brightness had faded out from his face. "Who is within now?" he said, at length.

"Saul of Tarsus," replied Simon, briefly.

"I shall warn them of the household of John of this thou hast told me?"

"Assuredly, but let it not be bruited abroad; there is nothing to be gained by it, and perhaps much to be lost. If the young man Stephen—" but the clang of the bell interrupted him, and he hastened to open. "Enter, my lord, I pray thee. It is so, my lord Annas is within, and with him is the Rabbi Saul."

Iddo bowed with instinctive respect as the tall, gaunt figure swept by him and disappeared down the

THE WARNING.

passageway. "He is no longer High Priest," he said, in a half whisper, "and it perchance hath irked him to resign the office."

"There are other reasons for his haggard look," said the old man sagely; "but it is not for such as I to prate concerning the affairs of Caiaphas. The Lord hath dealt with him, as he doth also deal with all men; perchance that he may draw them to himself at the last."

"Nay; dost thou think then that it is possible for such as the murderers of our Lord to be forgiven?"

"'Tis assuredly not for us to set limits upon the compassion and love of the Father of our Lord Jesus—who also prayed for them in his agony. If he can save me, he is able to save any one; for I know my own heart how that it is deceitful above all things and desperately wicked."

"That is a true word, my Simon," said the young man, humbly. "No one knoweth it better than I, who was ever prone to do evil as the sparks fly upward—I must away; if Stephen could but be persuaded to leave Jerusalem—"

"'Twas what I would have said," broke in Simon, eagerly. "Let him go—and at once. There is no need that he remain to fall into the net which these are making ready for him. It may be that it was by the good providence of God that I chanced to hear what I did." Then as he opened the door that the young man might pass out, he whispered, "Let them all beware of the Pharisee from Tarsus."

"'Tis a word of wisdom," said Iddo to himself, as he strode rapidly away. "Yet would he dare molest us who walk orderly after the law? If now we kept not the fasts, nor observed the solemn feasts, nor prayed at the times of the morning and evening sacrifice,—but all of these things we observe and do. Yet have I heard Stephen proclaim in the synagogues that there was now no further need for the priestly slaughter of flocks and herds, because that Christ had given himself a sacrifice for the sins—not only of the Jews—but for the sins of the whole world. Even the apostles say not such things, it must be that he is over-bold—being a Greek. Some one should speak to him of the matter."

Revolving these thoughts in his mind, the young man came at length into the street where was the house of John the apostle. It was narrow, and still, and hot; the feet of the few passers-by—mostly women passing to and from the public fountains with their water-jars—making no noise in the yellow dust. Iddo paused a moment with bent head; he smiled, and his eyes sparkled with joy. "She is singing," he said aloud. And he hurried forward faster than before—almost stumbling indeed in his haste over some small brown object which squatted silently in the hot sunshine before the door which he sought.

"What is this?" he cried, looking down, and discovering that the obstacle was none other than a small brown child; that there were, in fact, three of them, a boy and a girl—and betwixt the two a baby, smaller and browner than either.

"We be listening," said the girl solemnly, shaking the dark curls out of her eyes and looking up at her questioner. "The baby hath gone to sleep because he likes it; we come every day. Wilt thou sit down here? the dust is soft, and the music is like angels singing."

Iddo smiled. "Thou art right, little one," he said; "'tis like the voice of an angel."

> "I lift mine eyes to the hills.
> Whence cometh my help?
> My help is from Jehovah,
> Maker of heaven and earth,"

THE WARNING.

chanted the melodious voice within, then it dropped to a pleading cadence,

> "May He not suffer thy foot to be moved!
> May He not slumber that keepeth thee!
> Behold, the Keeper of Israel
> Shall neither slumber nor sleep.
> Jehovah keep thee from all evil!
> He will keep thy life.
> Jehovah keep thy coming and going
> Henceforth and for ever!"

The listener sighed involuntarily; then he stretched forth his hand and laid it upon the bell—paying no heed to the solemn little voice at his feet, "If thou dost pull the rope the singing will stop."

Almost immediately the door opened, and a sweet voice cried, "Ah, 'tis thou, Iddo Ben Obed! Enter, I pray thee," then observing the young man's serious face, she added, "What hath befallen thee, friend? thou art as solemn as that great image in the desert which men call the sphinx."

"I have reason," answered Ben Obed, "as thou must hear presently."

"I must first speak to the little ones.—Enter, friend, thou wilt find my brother within. Why didst thou not knock, little one?" she continued, stooping to raise the sleeping child, "the sun is too hot for the babe; it breedeth mischief at this season. Stay—I will give thee some pomegranates, then must thou go home where it is cool. Tonight if thou wilt come and knock on the door thou shalt enter, then I will sing to thee, and also tell thee a story of how the babe Jesus came through the wilderness to the land of Egypt." And having kissed the smooth brown cheeks in token of dismissal, she watched the two as they trudged away down the street, the sleepy baby toddling between.

Ben Obed was already seated upon the stone bench in the cool shadow of the house, talking in low tones to a young man of about his own age, who with bent brows and serious air was paying him diligent heed.

"I can scarce believe that such talk is more than idle threatening," he was saying. "Since the day that Gamaliel gave counsel in the Sanhedrim that we be left in peace, there hath been no active persecution. They must see by this time that the Lord is with us, therefore is the good counsel of Gamaliel proven; surely there can be none amongst them bold enough to fight against God. And this said I to Simon—or words of like import. I reminded him also that we are well looked upon by all the people, and how—being in all points disposed to keep the law—even the priests are daily joining themselves to our numbers. But he hath a different opinion; moreover, he bade me tell all of this household to beware Saul of Tarsus."

"What danger is threatened?" asked Anat, anxiously.

Iddo Ben Obed raised his eyes to her face, and there was that in their fiery gaze that brought the warm color to the maiden's cheek.

"Danger is threatened to Stephen," he said slowly, "though how great is that danger we cannot tell."

The face of Anat grew deathly pale. "Tell me—" she said, breathlessly, "all that thou hast heard."

Iddo dropped his eyes to the ground. "They will imprison him if he continues to preach that the Christ is mightier than the law," he said coldly. "What more I know not. 'Twill be best for him to leave Jerusalem."

Anat turned swiftly and went away into the house.

That evening she told the three children the story which she had promised them; and sang to them wild songs of the desert—vaguely remembered from the days when she dwelt in Egypt; and afterward the Psalm of the watchful Love, which she had sung in the morning. Then she gave the little ones into the hand of their mother, and went softly up to the housetop. A lonely figure stood by the parapet, looking away toward the afterglow which burned in solemn splendor behind the mountains. She hesitated for a moment, then went lightly forward.

"Hast thou heard," she said softly, "the evil tidings which the son of Obed brought to this house to-day?"

"I have talked with John concerning it."

"And what said he? Surely he urged thee to flee the peril?" And the girl's voice thrilled with passionate entreaty.

The young man turned. "Anat—beloved," he said softly, "I know all that thou wouldst say; and there is much in my heart that I would fain say to thee—only that the time is short. Already for me the daylight fades and the night cometh when I can no more work for the Master, while for thee there yet remaineth many years wherein to glorify his name; and this shalt thou do, and in the doing find peace—the peace that passeth understanding."

The girl had sunken to her knees beside him, her slender frame shaken with a tempest of weeping; but a great calm fell upon her soul as Stephen rested his hands upon her bowed head—his voice tremulous in that sweetest of all benedictions: "The Lord bless thee, and keep thee: the Lord make his face shine upon thee, and be gracious unto thee: the Lord lift up his countenance upon thee, and give thee peace."

CHAPTER XXV.

THE WRATH OF MAN.

"HOU hast the witnesses?"

"I have the witnesses, my lord; but there was no small difficulty in persuading any man to serve. A score refused outright, reviling me moreover and threatening me with death should I dare to molest the fellow. I placated them as best I was able, saying that I but desired to assure myself that the reports which I had heard against so excellent a man were false. Yet do I fear that these may fetch him word so that he will escape out of our hands."

"He shall not escape. What witnesses hast thou?"

"One Esek—a money lender—who for the sum of ten shekels of silver hath consented to witness; and with him two of mine own underlings, who will speak that which is put into their mouths with all diligence, both on account of the reward which I have promised if they shall acquit themselves well, and because of the scourging which awaits them should they fail. One of them is Iddo Ben Obed—a young man of some promise, who hath by my orders frequented their synagogue much of late, and can therefore speak understandingly of the thing. To him have I promised sure advancement if he shall please the Council this day."

"Thou art a faithful servant, Caleb, and shall thyself not fail of thy reward," said Annas approvingly. "Now see to it that the Council Chamber be prepared with all speed; we must accomplish the thing quickly, lest this favorable opportunity pass by us. Hast thou the man under espionage, that thou mayest lay hands upon him without delay?"

"He is at this moment engaged in his duties of almoner, my lord, distributing amongst the rabble of Jerusalem that which is little better than stolen from the Temple treasury, in that it is withholden from us unlawfully. Afterward he hath the intent to harangue the people according to his custom."

"He will find a different audience to-day," interrupted Annas grimly, "and one that cannot be led away by specious words. In what synagogue wilt thou find him?"

"To-day they purpose to assemble in Solomon's Porch, that they may entrap the multitude. The fellow Stephen will interpret the prophets, wickedly alleging—as do they all—that holy men, such as Moses, Isaiah, and all the prophets, foretold as the Messiah the fruit of the accursed tree."

"Little need to suborn witnesses when they openly profane the holy places of the earth with such blasphemies. But go now; keep the fellow under thine own eye till I shall send thee word, then fetch him with all speed, together with the witnesses. Stay a moment— see that there is no tumult made when he is arrested."

Caleb smiled as he again bowed himself before his superior. "I have devised a cunning plan wherewith to entrap him without tumult," he replied.

"All is going well," said Annas to himself when he was left alone. "Our patient and apparently fruitless toil is at last about to be rewarded. Besides Caleb, who shall in no wise lose his reward, we must not forget that we owe much to the discretion and zeal of Malluch and Zared, who have diligently spoken against this man and his words to the people. The sum agreed upon was forty pieces of silver for each of them—a goodly sum for such as they, yet if to-day's descending sun finds the man dead I will command that it be made fifty. But here is our Pharisee from Tarsus; I must deal wisely with him. I would that he were a Sadducee, the doctrine of the resurrection is a mischievous one, and one moreover which these blasphemous Nazarenes preach without ceasing. Greetings to thee, my son. This will prove a glorious day with us, if it shall witness a signal victory over unrighteousness."

The newcomer received this friendly greeting with chilling hauteur. "God knoweth that I long to see the workers of iniquity put to confusion," he said, throwing himself into a chair and fixing his stern eyes upon his companion. "But lying and deceit are hateful to my soul. Neither shall anything prosper that is accomplished thereby."

The face of Annas hardened. "Thou speakest in riddles, friend," he said coldly. "Whom dost thou accuse of lying and deceit?"

"It hath come to my ears that certain ones have been hired to speak evil of the man Stephen; that these have stirred up the people against him so that they are ready to lay hands upon him. It is true that the man hath spoken freely and openly in every synagogue, alleging that the carpenter of Galilee was the Christ foretold by the Prophets, and that he hath risen from the dead and is become the first-fruits of them that sleep."

"And hath he convinced the learned Saul of the truth of these things?" said Annas with a sarcastic smile. "Nay, that were a victory indeed."

Saul laughed aloud, a harsh, unmirthful sound. "I am of all men least likely to become a victim of this monstrous delusion. The man should not be suffered to speak further, for he hath the cunning tongue of a great orator, and convinced the people mightily. Neither I, nor any who have disputed with him have been able to undo the mischief that he hath wrought. But I like not that we suborn liars to serve our cause."

"We forbade these men to speak the name of the Nazarene some three years ago, letting them go with but a scourging, according to the counsel of the most sapient Gamaliel, whose pupil thou art. But how did they obey the commands of the most holy Council, and how hath the advice of Gamaliel profited our cause? Since that day they have not ceased to bruit the hateful name of Jesus of Nazareth about Jerusalem, till the very beggars of our streets pray to him openly. If we have employed discreet men to assist us in rooting out this menacing evil, what is it but the part of wisdom? Do not the Nazarenes also feed and clothe the men who are daily spreading this poison to the confusion of Israel? This man Stephen, being a Greek, not only doth not himself observe the law, but he is forever bringing to the mind of the people the words and practices of the Nazarene, who would be well forgotten by this were it not for such pestilent fellows. He diligently reminds the multitude how that the man worked miracles on the Sabbath day, declaring that God would have mercy and not sacrifice, and how he openly prophesied the destruction of the Holy Temple. The carpenter from Galilee, he blasphemously alleges, was God made manifest in the flesh; therefore his acts and words are greater than the law of Moses, and rather to be observed than any priestly commands. For such as this fellow there is but one remedy, as it is written also, 'The mouth of them that speak lies shall be stopped.'"

Saul was silent for a moment. Before his mental vision there arose the face of Stephen, as he had seen him many times during the furious controversies which had of late taken place in the synagogues, glowing with high courage, hope and confidence, and illumined withal by a mysterious light at which he had more than once inwardly marveled. Then his face hardened. "It is just that this apostate be put to death," he said. "This is no time for half-way measures; but let it be done according to the law and without fear of the people."

"Thou hast said!" cried Annas. "This we will do, for the time is ripe. Listen, this very day he shall be brought before the Council; witnesses are at hand that every word may be established according to the law. As it is written, 'in the mouth of two or three witnesses every word shall be established.'"

"Who are the witnesses?"

"Reputable men—most respectable men. One Esek, a Jew, who dwells near to their synagogue, and—"

"Do these testify freely?—without money, I mean?" again interrupted Saul with an irritable gesture.

"It is the custom, my son, to compensate witnesses for the loss of time entailed upon them in the pursuance of their duty," began Annas smoothly.

But Saul broke in rudely. "I will have none of it," he cried, springing to his feet and striding stormily up and down the room. "Hired agitators amongst the people; hired witnesses against a man who, whatever his accursed beliefs, is at least incapable of such meanness."

Annas also arose, and with an air of awful dignity fixed his piercing eyes upon the flushed face of the young man. "Thou dost assuredly forget," he said slowly, "the respect due him in whose presence thou art standing. As the head of the high-priestly family, which for many generations has acceptably served Jehovah in that most holy office, I am not lightly to be accused to my face of that which my soul abhorreth, as also it is written: 'I hate and abhor lying, but thy law do I love.' Twice hast thou cast this thing in my teeth, and in so doing thou hast proven thyself unworthy of the high confidence which I have given thee; unworthy of the love which I have freely bestowed upon thee; unworthy—"

"Stay, I beseech thee!" cried Saul, raising his hand. He had grown deathly pale, and trembled visibly. "It is true, I have forgotten myself. I am well nigh mad because of the failure of all that I had confidently hoped for. Day after day have I gone forth to do battle for Israel, and day after day have I been worsted. I am of all men most unworthy, in that I have failed—miserably failed. I will return to Tarsus, and thou shalt see my face no more."

"Nay, my son," said Annas softly, "because thou hast acknowledged thy fault, it is forgiven. And dost think that I have not watched thee in this thy struggle against iniquity; that my heart has not bled for thee? Possess now thy soul in patience, trust in the Lord—and in me— and it shall assuredly come to pass. Thou shalt see the confusion of thine enemies; for the honor of Israel shall this day be vindicated right gloriously. As for the thing that thou hast spoken of, it shall be even as thou hast said. There is no lack of them that can witness against this man. Ay! and that will witness right gladly for the glory of Jehovah. Surely there is no need for us to say, 'Who will come up to the help of the Lord?—to the help of the Lord against the mighty?' Israel shall arise in her might, and shall gird herself against them that would do her violence, that would plague her with idolatrous and blasphemous practices. Too long have we held our peace in the presence of this devouring evil; the very stones of the Temple will cry out if we longer submit to them that profane its sanctity."

"As in the case of the Nazarene, it will be possible to do nothing of ourselves," said Saul bitterly. "And the Romans—they care for none of these things."

"Ah—there we have gained a signal victory over our enemies," said Annas triumphantly. "Herod is with us this time, though not openly. I have taken good care that reports should reach his ear from time to time how that these fellows continually proclaim the return of the crucified one to reign over Israel. He loves his paltry throne, and actually fears that the thing may come to pass. Not many days since he sent for me. He was lying at full length among his purple cushions.

" 'Hast thou heard what these Galileans are saying,' he said, scarcely tarrying for the accustomed greetings.

" 'They are saying many things that are unlawful,' I answered him, 'but nothing more dangerous to the peace and prosperity of the nation than that the dead malefactor—whom they claim is alive—will shortly return to rule over Israel.'

" 'Dost thou believe that the man is alive?' he asked, fixing his eyes upon me.

" 'If he be not alive,' I said, 'the sedition is none the less to be feared, for these fellows are capable of forcing the people to believe what they will. Wilt thou not then take measures against them who alone art in power?'

" 'I cannot,' he whined fretfully, 'I fear the people—I fear the man—the—the dead man. I am not well. Hast thou not a law which will stop their prating?'

" 'We have a law—yes,' I made him answer; 'but we cannot enforce it since—'

" 'The law—the law,' he interrupted.

" 'The law is this—He that blasphemeth the name of the Lord shall surely be put to death, and all the congregation shall certainly stone him. The stranger, as well as he that is born in the land, when he blasphemeth the name of the Lord shall be put to death.'

" 'Carry out your law upon these men,' he cried, throwing himself back upon the cushions.

" 'Not so,' I answered, 'lest we fall upon evil times afterward. We be law-abiding in all points—civil as well as religious—and it is not lawful for us to put any man to death.'

" 'There shall no harm come to thee,' he cried, 'I swear it. There is now no governor in Jerusalem. I am a Roman. I am the law.'

" 'Give me a warrant sealed with thy seal,' I said. And he gave it straightway."

"Hast thou this writing with thee?" said Saul.

Annas drew a parchment from his bosom and gave it into the outstretched hand of the young man without a word.

"Inasmuch," he read aloud, "as the peace of Jerusalem and all Judaea is endangered by malicious persons, who proclaim that a crucified malefactor, to wit, one Jesus of Nazareth, is alive, and will shortly overturn the present government that he may himself rule; and as these persons moreover blasphemously affirm that said malefactor is the Jehovah-sent Messiah, I, Herod, do empower the Senate of the people of Israel, called also the Sanhedrim, to deal with such seditious persons according to their judgment and after their laws, which do fully provide for the scourging, imprisonment, and putting to death of all persons whether Hebrew or alien, who believe, affirm, and declare mischievous doctrines of the like. Signed and sealed, to the glory of Jehovah and the peace of the nation, this fifth day of Nisan, in the Asmonean Palace."

"God hath given them into our hand, my son," said Annus solemnly. "We must deal with them even as Elijah dealt with the prophets of Baal, and 'let not one of them escape.' "

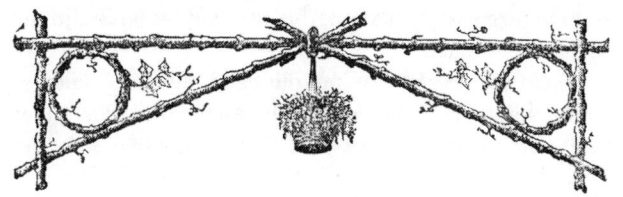

CHAPTER XXVI.

UNTIL THE DAY BREAK.

N the morning of that same day, before it was yet dawn, Stephen arose and went away out of the city. After the supreme renunciation of the night before, he had experienced a strange, a wonderful peace: the world had vanished from out his sight; he felt that he had already entered upon the life beyond. And while he yet marvelled and rejoiced because of this, he slept. How many hours had elapsed before he awoke he did not know; it was dark in the house-place, and the darkness lay heavily upon him like a pall. With the darkness there had also fallen the icy shadow of his approaching doom; before the shrouded face of this awful impalpable presence peace and joy fled away in affright. He strove to pray, but his tongue clave to the roof of his mouth. Near by he could hear the regular, peaceful breathing of John and Andrew; somehow the sound added an intolerable poignancy to his anguish. For the first time he realized to the full the utter loneliness of the soul. "They love me," he said within himself bitterly,— "but they sleep."

After a time he arose, and wrapping his cloak about him, stole out into the courtyard. The fresh wind as it smote him brought with it a sense of relief. The stars glittered keenly overhead against the dark blue of the heavens; the fragrance of a tall white lily abloom beside the little cistern hung heavy upon the air. An irresistible impulse to go swiftly—somewhere—anywhere—came upon him. Undoing the fastening of the outer door, he slipped out, feeling a quick thrill of satisfaction in the fact that he had accomplished this noiselessly. The cocks were crowing as he started swiftly down the street, first one, then another, then half a dozen at once, dying away into silence only to break forth again as some faint challenge from a distance rang out triumphantly.

As yet there was little token of day, but the keeper was drowsily undoing the fastenings of the city gate, in due anticipation of the market-men, who would soon be coming from every quarter. Stephen hesitated for an instant, then slipped through the opening without being observed. Before him lay the Roman road, hard and white, stretching dimly away into the darkness. All the young life in him leapt up at the sight.

"I have but to follow this road," he thought, "it will bring me to safety. And why, after all, should I remain? Wicked men have laid a snare for me, and it hath been made known to me in the mercy of God. It must needs be that I escape; I am young, I can and will do good service to them that believe for many years. What shall it profit any man if I perish now?"

He was walking the more swiftly as he communed thus with himself, and hearing, or fancying that he heard, a sound as of pursuit behind him, he thrust his fingers into his ears and ran, the road still dimly unrolling itself out of the darkness before him like a dusky ribbon from the loom of night. After he had gone thus for a long distance — his breath being well-nigh spent and his laboring heart knocking loudly for relief— he paused, and withdrawing his fingers from his ears, listened. There was no sound save the soughing of the wind in the gnarled branches of the trees and the shrilling of insects in the lush grass. He sank down for a moment to rest.

"If I go away now—as indeed those older and wiser than myself have advised—I can remain till the present danger be passed, afterward I can return, and—there is Anat. The world is wide, there is no need that we remain at Jerusalem. We two will go away into far countries and among strange peoples, that we may spread the Gospel among all nations, even as the Master commanded. It is right that this should be, else why do these thoughts come to me. As for means for my journey, I have here in my pouch the money with which I was to buy provisions to-day, this would the apostles gladly give me for my present needs—ay, and more. Yes, I will go—I must go." And he arose and girding himself resolutely, started once more upon his journey.

"I will go," he repeated to himself more than once. "I must go." But after a time he ceased to walk swiftly; at length he stopped altogether and turned his face toward the East. Faint rosy flushes—momently brightening—merged finally into long tremulous beams of pure unearthly light, which shot up as if in an ecstasy of triumph over the conquered gloom. Stephen's heart expanded at the sight. He sank upon his knees.

" 'Blessed art thou, O Lord our God, King of the universe,' " he murmured aloud. " 'Who createst light and formest darkness, who makest peace and createst all things! He in mercy causes the light to shine upon the earth and the inhabitants thereof, and in goodness renews every day the work of creation. Blessed art thou, the Creator of Light!"

Something in the familiar and well-loved words spoken in that dewy solitude seemed to sweep away the paralyzing and unworthy fear from out his soul. He looked at the Roman road, showing hard, white and dusty in the morning light, it no longer appeared alluring. He thought again of his resolve to use the money from the almoner's fund to make good his escape, and the honest crimson rose to his cheek.

"I am no better than a thief," he cried aloud, "I will go back; and if it needs be that I suffer, God help me, for the flesh is weak."

As he arose to his feet he saw with a shock of surprise that he had paused near to the little rocky knoll, called, from its strange resemblance to a human skull, Golgotha. Upon the bald summit of this place of death stood a cross, and upon the cross hung the figure of a man—naked save for his scanty rags which fluttered fitfully in the light breeze, the clear light of the dawn revealing with ghastly insistency his drawn features, and the purple wounds in his hands and feet. At the foot of the cross lay two Roman soldiers, evidently detailed to watch the dying man; they were snoring loudly, a half-emptied wine-skin upon the grass between them revealing the manner in which they had beguiled the night watches.

As Stephen gazed at this horrible sight, the figure on the cross writhed feebly, the blue lips parted. "God! daylight again, and I live—live" were the words which gushed out from them in a quavering shriek.

Sick with a fear that he could not control, Stephen approached the cross, treading carefully lest he should awaken the brutal sleepers at its foot.

"Water!" cried the sufferer. "Yes, I see it—a brown stream running over its pebbles—a lake deep and cool. I will hide in it, my hands are burning—no, no, they are dead."

"Here is water," said Stephen in a trembling voice, holding his flask to the lips of the dying wretch—for he hung low, his feet almost touching the ground.

But the man could not drink; he opened his glazing eyes, apparently not seeing the face of angelic pity at his side, for he fell to babbling disconnectedly of many things, mingling frightful curses on his tormentors with prayers to the pagan gods.

Stephen sent up a swift prayer for help; he could pray now. "Listen!" he cried, not heeding the fact that a group of wayfarers had stopped and were regarding him with open-mouthed amazement. "Listen—thou mayest yet be saved. Jesus of Nazareth can save thee! Master, hear—I beseech thee—and save!"

The dim eyes were turned upon him now; there was a gleam of understanding in them. "Art thou—Jesus—of Nazareth?"

"Nay, I am but his servant. Call upon him quickly to forgive—to save."

"Jesus—forgive—save!" gasped the failing voice, then all was still.

Stephen looked once into the quiet face of the man on the cross, then down at the soldiers, who were beginning to stir a little. One of them sat up and threw his arms above his head and yawned.

"By Bacchus!" he exclaimed. "I must have slept,—a murrain on these night watches, the fellow could not have gotten away." Then his eye fell upon Stephen, "Who art thou?" he cried, springing to his feet; "and what art thou doing here? If now thou hast meddled with the malefactor—ha! the fellow is gone. Didst thou give him aught to help him to his death?"

'No, friend," answered Stephen quietly. "I but spoke to him of Jesus, the Redeemer; and if God will, that word hath helped him to eternal life."

The man to whom he had spoken made a motion as if to seize him, but the other, who had also awakened, held him back.

"Let be," he said in a low voice; "he hath done no harm; 'tis Stephen, the Nazarene."

The soldier dropped his arm. "Go," he commanded briefly; "we had orders to allow no one near the cross of this man."

Stephen bowed his head and passed on. He walked swiftly—as he had done before the dawn—but this time his face was steadfastly set towards Jerusalem, and upon it shone the light of a peace which the world had not given, and which from henceforth it was powerless to take away. Verily, when the day breaks, the shadows flee away.

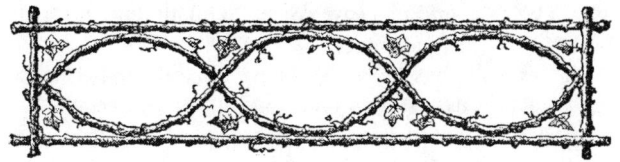

CHAPTER XXVII.

IN THE VALLEY OF THE SHADOW.

O thou, Ben Obed, watch the man till such time as I shall send thee word. Then—thou art known unto him? A fortunate chance—say this to him, 'There is one ailing at my house, who desireth thy immediate presence.' He will at once follow thee, and thou shalt fetch him without delay into the Council Chamber.

"Suppose that he will not follow me?" said the young man, fixing his black eyes upon the floor with a somewhat sullen expression.

Caleb looked at him keenly for a moment before replying. "If thou art zealous to secure for thyself the position whereof I have spoken, and the sum of silver which shall also be the reward of thy diligence, thou wilt not lack means to bring the man away from the multitude without exciting any tumult. It is not expedient for me to appear in this matter, else would I undertake it. But thou art not the only one, there is Malluch, or—"

"I will fetch him," said Ben Obed looking up hastily; "have I not said that I would do it?"

"The reward is sure," pursued Caleb. "And thou wilt have moreover the approval of thine own conscience in the matter, in that thou art, in serving thine own interests, also serving God—and doubt not that thine obedience will be as a sweet savor before him."

"What will they do with the—with Stephen?" asked the young man shifting uneasily about in his place. "He is—that is—I think—" and he stopped short, his eyes fixed eagerly on the face of his superior.

Caleb straightened himself, and his face hardened. "I have not asked the question of them above me in authority. To receive an order and to obey it without question, comment, or opinion hath ever been my way. It should also be thy way if thou hast a desire to advance thyself in life. As also it is written, 'Seest thou a man diligent in his business, he shall stand before kings.' This have I done; not once, but many times," and the speaker drew himself up to his full height, and passed his beard through his hand with the same impressive gesture that he had observed many times—and admired—in the lordly Annas. "Go now, young man, " he continued, "and acquit thyself well, as becometh the son of a wise and diligent man. So shall thy mother rejoice in the day of thy birth."

"They will imprison him," muttered Iddo Ben Obed to himself as he turned away. "He hath assuredly spoken contrary to the law; and why should I not witness to the truth? A man must faithfully perform the duties whereunto he is called without partiality. This Stephen is a Greek—at least by his father—and is it lawful to set the son of a malefactor in a place of authority? I say not. If he were once out of the way I could win the maid Anat. I know that I could. I can give her a home and abundance of all that she hath need of. I will do this thing. He hath brought it upon himself, for I have thrice warned him to leave Jerusalem. He will not leave, and why?—he thinks forsooth that I am blind."

And having come to the place where the daily distributions were wont to be made, he mingled with the multitude and waited for the appearance of the seven, as the deacons were now commonly called. They appeared at last, laden with the day's alms, and began to make distribution among the waiting poor. Iddo noticed that Stephen's face was very pale, and that blue shadows lay beneath his dark eyes. He smiled evilly. "He is afraid," he sneered. And being now determined upon the course which he meant to follow, he allowed his jealous hatred of the man to spring up unchecked, and because hatred is a plant of quick and easy growth, especially when nourished by envy, it came to pass that within the half hour Ben Obed had seen every trace of love, justice and pity in his soul quite destroyed. "I hate him," he whispered to himself, clenching his fists. "I care not what they do with him. I hate him."

The distribution took an unusually long time that morning, and Iddo noticed with a scowl how that all the poor widows and little children lingered for a word with the youngest of the seven—Stephen, the well-loved of the poor, as he was often called.

"Hypocrite!" said Iddo beneath his breath. As he uttered the word he was startled to feel a light touch on his shoulder; turning quickly, his eye fell upon the messenger appointed by Caleb.

" 'Tis the time," said the man with a wink. "Bring him outside now; I will be at hand should you need help."

Ben Obed nodded. He could not trust himself to speak, the hatred had grown so mighty that it struggled to cry out. He approached Stephen cautiously, and laid his hand upon him.

"There is one—who is ailing—at my house," he said with difficulty. "Wilt thou come with me?"

Stephen looked up with a smile. "Peace be with thee, Ben Obed, and to all that are within thy house; yes, I will come with thee, but let me first speak with this woman, who hath patiently waited for me since the beginning of the distribution. What is it that thou wouldst ask of me, woman?"

"I have brought hither my babe," answered the woman in a low, anxious voice. "He doth not wake and smile on me as formerly, but only sleeps. Surely it is not well with him."

"If he sleep he shall do well," said Stephen, unconsciously quoting the words of his Master when told of the sickness of Lazarus. "And if God will that he wake in heaven, then wouldst thou have a child growing to manhood among the angels. Dost thou not covet this for thy child?"

"Nay, for I love him too much to wish him out of my arms," said the mother, dashing the bright drops from her eyes; "and I have not seen heaven."

"My business with thee is urgent," whispered Ben Obed imperatively. Stephen did not seem to have heard. He laid his hand on the child's head, "Thy will concerning this little one be done, O Father, in the name of Jesus."

"But thou hast not asked for his healing!" cried the mother.

"I have asked for the best that heaven holds for him, or for any one of us," said Stephen gently. "But see, thy child hath awakened, "then he turned to Ben Obed. "I will go with thee," he said simply, but there was that in his eyes that caused Iddo to drop his own to the earth.

Once on the street Stephen walked swiftly, so swiftly that Ben Obed had some difficulty in keeping up with him. He exchanged glances with the messenger of Caleb who was following at a discreet distance, and the man rapidly over took them.

"We will go this way," said Ben Obed in a hard voice. But Stephen was silent. Something in his still face angered the young man at his side beyond control. "Why dost thou not speak?" he cried in a choked voice, scarce knowing what he said.

"There are times when silence is more excellent than speech," said Stephen.

Ben Obed cursed the temple under his breath, then he grasped his companion by the arm. "At least I am not a hypocrite," he said violently. "I have been commanded to fetch thee before the Council of Sanhedrim that thou mayest answer for thy heresies. And I am going to do my duty. Lay not the consequences of thine own despicable folly at my door."

"I had not expected this at thy hands," said Stephen with a look of full understanding. "I had rather that it had been another—but it matters not." There was a slight tremor in his voice as he spoke the last words.

Ben Obed laughed aloud. "Thou wouldst rather that it were another, for then mightest thou hope to escape; but it is not another, it is I, Ben Obed, and because thou hast cheated me out of the woman I love, I—hate thee."

Stephen was silent. The twain, followed by the ill-omened messenger, presently came to the temple enclosure. Without a word Ben Obed hurried his companion through the crowded courts, neither heeding the curious looks with which they were regarded, till at length they stood before the closed door of the great Chamber of Council, called also the "Hall of Squares."

Caleb with a detachment of temple police stood on guard. He was looking anxious and worn, but his eye brightened as it fell upon Stephen. Motioning to the guard to close in around the prisoner, he himself listened at the closed door; presently he laid a cautious hand upon the fastening and with an air of deep solemnity introduced his head into the sacred apartment. Apparently receiving some signal from within, he immediately withdrew it. "Pass in," he said briskly, laying a compelling hand upon Stephen's shoulder.

There was an awful stillness in the great room as the two entered, followed by the lesser officers, who ranged themselves on either side of the accused man. Then a murmur ran about the circle. At the sound Stephen raised his eyes and looked calmly about him. These were the men who had slain his Lord; they would also slay him—he knew it—and yet the knowledge brought with it only a singular joy. "They hate me, because I am like him," he said within himself, and the glory of that thought became visible upon his face.

Jonathan, the High Priest, was speaking now; with an effort the prisoner compelled himself to listen. "Thou art arraigned before this sacred assembly and Senate of Israel on the charge of blasphemously speaking against Jehovah; against this most Holy Temple; and against the laws and institutions of Moses and of the Prophets, ordained by Jehovah to speak his pleasure to the children of men. We shall hear these charges confirmed by witnesses, according to our laws which thou hast despised, but which thou shalt tread under foot no longer with impunity. Fetch the first witness.—Dost thou, Ezek, recognize this man Stephen who hath blasphemed God, the temple, and the law?"

"I do, most worshipful and High Priest of Jehovah. This is the man."

"Tell us now what thou hast heard him say."

"I have heard him say that the malefactor, Jesus of Nazareth, who of late died the accursed death, after having been duly and righteously convicted of his crimes before the most sacred Council—I have heard him declare, that this man was Jehovah made manifest in the flesh. And that therefore his precepts and commands are more binding than the precepts of Moses, who was a sinful man like unto ourselves."

"Hast thou heard him say aught concerning the temple?"

'I have heard him say that the Nazarene shall shortly return to destroy this place, so that no one stone shall remain upon another, and that all things which Moses commanded shall be done away. The Gentiles moreover and them that are alien shall see these things and rejoice, for that this Jesus shall hereafter come in the clouds of heaven and gather his elect from the uttermost parts of the earth. The Nazarenes have the intent moreover to possess the earth, and to overthrow all powers and governments and all gods that have ever ruled among men, to the end that they may establish the man Jesus upon the throne of power."

"Didst thou hear the man declare these things?"

"I did, most sacred High Priest."

"Enough!—Iddo Ben Obed, thou mayest stand forth. Dost thou know this man?"

"I do, my lord."

Stephen looked up at the sound of his voice, and a keen spasm of pain swept across his face.

"Look at him!" whispered Issachar to his neighbor. "He evidently fears this witness more than the other—though his testimony was sufficiently damning."

"And what hast thou to say concerning him?" continued the monotonous voice of the High Priest.

"He hath spoken blasphemously against Moses and against this holy place, even as hath already been said in your hearing, declaring that God regardeth neither temple nor the holy city of Jerusalem, inasmuch as the Lord

Jesus did in his lifetime pronounce against them anathema; he also—"

"Hold! How is it that thou dost call the Nazarene Lord? Art thou also one of them?"

The witness turned pale. He cast a murderous look at Stephen. "No," he said fiercely. "I but repeat the word which these men make use of in their blasphemous harangues to the people; the words slipped from me unawares."

"Proceed."

"He hath declared that neither by laws of man's devising nor by temples of man's building can Jehovah be pleased. That all these things shall be brought to naught; but that the words of the Nazarene shall remain."

"Enough! There is no need for further testimony. Let the accused stand forth."

Stephen obeyed. And all that sat in the Council, looking steadfastly on him, saw his face as it had been the face of an angel.

CHAPTER XXVIII.

THE LIFTED VEIL.

THEN said the High Priest, after the manner of the formal procedure, "Are these things so?"

And Stephen, looking about on the seventy men before whom he stood, the heads and leaders of that forlorn remnant of the chosen people, desolate because of their rebellion against the God who had borne with them so long and patiently, was moved to bring again the wonderful promises of Jehovah to their minds. So plain did it all appear to him, filled as he was with that spirit of light which the Lord had vouchsafed according to his word, and which he had also promised to pour out freely upon all men. A glorious hope was stirring in his breast as he looked from one to the other of the stern faces before him. Hatred indeed and stubborn self-satisfaction he saw written thereon, but what could stand before the all-powerful spirit of truth? What if it should be granted him to mightily convince these men; to see, perchance, some such glorious exhibition of God's grace as had been manifested at Pentecost.

"Men, brethren and fathers, hearken!" he began, and at the sound of that inspired voice every eye was fastened upon him. "The God of glory appeared unto our father Abraham and said unto him: 'Get thee out of thy land and from thy kindred, and come into the land which I shall show thee.' Then came he out of the land of the Chaldaeans and dwelt in Haran; and from thence, when his father was dead, God removed him into this land, wherein ye now dwell. He gave him no inheritance in it, not even so much as to set his foot upon; but he promised that he would give it to him and to the generations after him, when as yet he had no child.

"And God spake thus unto him, 'Thy children shall sojourn in a strange land, and they shall be enslaved and evil entreated for the space of four hundred years. But the nation which hath persecuted them I will judge; I, Jehovah, have declared it. And after that shall thy children come forth out of bondage and they shall serve me in this place.' And he gave him the covenant of circumcision. And so Abraham after that Isaac was born, circumcised him on the eighth day. And to Isaac in due time was born Jacob; Jacob also had twelve sons, whom we call the patriarchs. And the patriarchs, moved with jealousy against Joseph their brother, sold him into Egypt. Nevertheless God was with him, and delivered him out of his afflictions, and gave him favor and wisdom before Pharaoh, King of Egypt, insomuch that Pharaoh made him governor over all the land.

"Now there came a mighty famine, which extended throughout all Egypt and Canaan, and the people were wasted by it. Our fathers also had no food, but Jacob, hearing that there was corn in Egypt, sent forth his sons to fetch some. And when that was consumed which they brought, they went again the second time; and Joseph made himself known unto his brethren, and he brought them into the presence of Pharaoh. After that, Joseph sent for Jacob his father, and for all his kindred, numbering in all three score and fifteen souls. They went therefore into the land of Egypt, and Jacob died there and in due time the patriarchs, our fathers, also; and they were buried in Shechem, in the land which Abraham had bought for a burial place.

"But as the time of the promise drew nigh, which God had given unto Abraham, the people grew and multiplied, till there arose another king over Egypt which knew not Joseph.

"The new king dealt deceitfully with our nation, wickedly compelling our fathers that they should cast out their babes to die. At this time Moses was born, and he was beautiful in the sight of God. Three months he was nourished in his father's house, and when he was cast out, Pharaoh's daughter rescued him and brought him up as her own son. So Moses was instructed in all the wisdom of the Egyptians, and he became mighty in word and deed.

"Now when he was well nigh forty years of age, it came into his heart to visit his brethren, the children of Israel. And seeing one of them suffer wrong, he defended him, and avenged him that was oppressed, smiting the Egyptian that he died—supposing that his brethren would understand how that God by his hand was giving them deliverance; but they understood not. And the day following he came again upon two of them at strife, and urged them to be at peace, saying;--

" 'Sirs, ye are brethren; why do ye wrong one another?'

"But he that did his neighbor wrong thrust him away, saying, 'Who made thee a ruler and a judge over us? Wouldst thou kill me, as thou didst kill the Egyptian yesterday?'

"And Moses fled at this saying, and became an exile in the land of Midian. Here he took to himself a wife, and two sons were born to him. And when forty years had passed, an angel appeared to him as he wandered one day in the wilderness of Sinai; and the angel was a burning flame of fire in a bush of the mountain—the bush burned, yet was not consumed. When Moses saw it, he wondered at the sight; and as he drew near to behold, there came a voice of the Lord, saying:

" 'I am the God of thy fathers, the God of Abraham, and of Isaac, and of Jacob.'

"Then Moses trembled, and hid his face, and the Lord said unto him:

" 'Loose the shoes from thy feet, for the place whereon thou standest is holy ground. I have surely seen the affliction of my people which are in Egypt, and have heard their groaning, and I am come down to deliver them. Now come, I will send thee into Egypt.'

"So it came to pass that this very Moses, whom the people of Israel had refused, saying, 'Who made thee a ruler and a judge?' God sent to be both a ruler and a deliverer, by the hand of the angel which appeared to him in the bush. And this man, Moses, led the Israelites forth, working great signs and wonders in Egypt, and in the Red Sea, and in the wilderness, for the space of forty years.

"This is that Moses which said unto the children of Israel, 'A prophet shall God raise up unto you from among your brethren like unto me.' This is that Moses that was with the people in the wilderness, with the angel which spake to him in the Mount of Sinai, who also received the law at the hands of the living God to give unto us. But our fathers refused him their obedience, and thrust him away from them, turning back in their hearts unto Egypt and saying unto Aaron:

" 'Make us gods which shall go before us, for as for this Moses, which led us forth out of the land of Egypt, we wot not what is become of him.' Then made they for themselves a golden calf, and brought a sacrifice unto the idol, rejoicing in the works of their hands.

"But God turned, and gave them up to serve the host of heaven; as it is written in the book of the prophets:

" 'Did ye offer unto me slain beasts and sacrifices forty years in the wilderness, O house of Israel? And afterward ye took up the tabernacle of Moloch, and the star of the god Rephan, the figures which ye made to worship them. I will carry you away beyond Babylon.'

"Our fathers had the tabernacle of the testimony in the wilderness, according to the covenant of God unto Moses, who fashioned it like unto the figure that was revealed unto him. This tabernacle also our fathers brought into the promised land, when they entered it with Joshua, God thrusting out the heathen nations from before their faces, and in it they worshipped unto the days of David, who, finding favor in the sight of God, asked that he might build a habitation for the God of Jacob. And Solomon, his son, built a temple. Howbeit the Most High dwelleth not in houses made with hands; as saith the prophet—

> " 'The heaven is my throne,
> And the earth the footstool of my feet;
> What manner of house will ye build me? saith the Lord,
> Or what is the place of my rest?
> Did not my hands make all things?' "

Here the speaker paused and looked about upon the faces of his audience; some were sneering outright, others whispering to their neighbors, while others still regarded him with looks of malignant hatred. Not one of all the seventy had apprehended his meaning. Not one cared for his words. Of what use to continue the sublime retrospect. A wave of fiery indignation swept away the last remnant of fear, and in a voice ringing with inspired passion, he burst out:

"Ye stiff-necked and uncircumcised in heart and ears! Ye do always resist the Holy Spirit; as your fathers did, so do ye. Which of the prophets did not your fathers persecute? And they killed them which showed before of the coming of the Righteous One, of whom ye have now become the betrayers and murderers. Ye who received the law as it was ordained by angels and kept it not!"

For an instant there was a breathless silence, that mighty arrow tipped with a living fire had found lodgment in every heart. Then a low, murderous hiss ran about the circle. With one accord the assembly rose to their feet, but some invisible power held them back.

Stephen, the despised follower of the crucified Nazarene, was looking up steadfastly. Angels had lifted for him the dark veil of mortality; the hall of judgment and the faces of his infuriated judges faded from before his eyes; he saw instead the unspeakable glories of the New Jerusalem, God enthroned amid innumerable companies of angels, and Jesus standing with outstretched hands to receive him. In an ecstasy of joy he cried out:

"Behold, I see the heavens opened, and the Son of Man standing on the right hand of God!"

Only a glimpse, but what mattered it now to him that the dark flood of hatred had broken loose and was sweeping him away with wild tumult towards certain death. He did not see the infuriated mob of his executioners; he scarce realized that he was being dragged through the streets followed by a yelling multitude, roused from their apathy by the familiar scent of blood.

"Beyond the gates—it is the law!"

"This is the place—here are stones in abundance! Quick! or the Nazarenes will be to the rescue."

"Let the witnesses cast the first stones—it is the law!"

"Well thrown, Esek! Again—here is a larger one! Now the other, quickly!"

But the other witness, with face as white as that of the dying man, had broken through the circle and fled away shrieking towards the city—"My God! my God! they are killing him!"

"Let be, the law is fulfilled. Quick, or he will yet be rescued—the mob is increasing. What is that he is saying?" For the victim, blood-stained, faltering, had dragged himself to his knees.

"Lord Jesus, receive my spirit."

A shower of stones and fierce yells; he is sinking but again he speaks. Saul can hear it, for he stands near, guarding the garments of them that are fulfilling the law. They can all hear, for he cries in a loud voice, that his murderers may remember it afterward for the comfort of their guilty souls:

"Lord, lay not this sin to their charge." And when he had said this, he fell asleep.

CHAPTER XXIX.

THE WATCHFUL LOVE.

NAT was spinning in the cool shadow of the house; the stones of the little court had been newly washed, and a refreshing odor of cleanliness mingled with the fragrance which poured out from the snowy bells of the lilies beside the cistern. Close to her feet snuggled the three small brown children, listening while she sang. After a time the singer faltered a little; she was chanting the Psalm of the Watchful Love:

> "Jehovah is thy keeper,
> Jehovah thy abode on thy right hand;
> The sun shall not hurt thee by day,
> Neither the moon by night."

She paused. What was that deep, dull roar? Her face paled a little.

"Sing!" cried the boy imperatively, pulling at her robe.

"Sing!" echoed the baby, looking up at her with his soft, starry eyes.

As for the little maiden, she contented herself with softly stroking the girl's sandaled foot.

> "Jehovah keep thee from all evil."

THE WATCHFUL LOVE.

Yes she could surely hear a sound of tumult—what could it be?

> "He will keep thy life,

—"O my God! Keep him—keep him!—

> "Jehovah keep thy coming and thy going
> Henceforth and forever!"

The singer started to her feet with a cry. The street door had burst open violently, a man rushed in, ghastly, breathless, with wild staring eyes; she at first failed to recognize Ben Obed.

"My God! they are killing him!"

"Where?"

"Outside the Damascus Gate—they are stoning him!"

Anat stood for an instant like some beautiful soulless statue of despair. Then a wild fire leapt to her eyes.

"Tell them!" she said, and fled away out of the open door, away—away toward the Damascus Gate.

Women stared after her, men stretched forth their hands to grasp her, but she heeded them not; her feet seemed leaden, the minutes hours. The Damascus Gate—would she ever reach it? Again and again Ben Obed's awful cry sounded in her ears:

"My God! they are killing him!"

The gate—the gate at last; but it is choked with people coming in. Men, she dimly saw, men with long robes and broad phylacteries; men to whom the gate-keepers did reverence while they shrank back with involuntary fear. Men who drew away from her white robe and whiter face muttering, "A mad woman—a mad dog!"

At last she has struggled through them, outside the Damascus Gate at last. Where—where? Yes, yonder is a crowd, it must be there.

"Let me through, for God's sake! Let me through!"

Staring stupidly at her, the crowd separated. There upon the ground, half-hidden under a pile of stones, lay—something. She threw herself upon her knees, pulling madly at the rough, broken rock with her delicate fingers. Then she gave a long, broken-heart scream and fell forward in merciful unconsciousness.

. . . .

"My daughter." There was no answer, though the black eyes were wide open. Mary hesitated an instant, her sad lips moved in prayer. "Anat, my child," she said, softly. "Wilt thou not look once more upon his face before they bear him hence. I would that thou see for thy comfort that God hath set upon him the visible seal of his love, in that the peace that passeth understanding is writ thereon."

The girl rose feebly. "Take me to him," she said, putting out her hand.

And Mary led her into the peaceful chamber where they had laid him. The afternoon sun shot long rays of splendor across the face on the pillow, beautiful with the beauty of youth and of holiness, and touched with the sublimer beauty of death. The look that he had worn when he cried out at sight of Jesus waiting to receive him yet lingered there, his face was as the face of an angel who slept.

"For so he giveth his beloved sleep," murmured Mary, who stood at her side. At that word the maiden turned and the pent-up fountain of her tears broke forth. And the two wept together—but not as those without hope.

And so as the sad hours crept by, devout men carried forth the dead Stephen to his burial, making great lamentation over him. And the poor to whom he had daily ministered, and them that he had healed and comforted from all the city and the country round about

THE WATCHFUL LOVE. 219

followed him to the tomb; and the streets of the city were filled with the sound of the wailing and loud crying.

As for the men which had done this thing, they hid themselves; and some of them exulted because that an enemy was dead, and some were ashamed, while others still—amongst them Saul of Tarsus—listened to the sound of the wailing, and shook their fists.

"It is the beginning of lamentations for such as blaspheme the law," said these. "To-morrow they will forget this dead man in the multitude of their own distresses."

In the house of John, the family sat that evening on the house-top as was their wont, and they talked together of him that had gone; and while they mourned indeed they also rejoiced, for they knew that he had fought a good fight, and that while the earth-clouds hung dark and threatening above their heads, this beloved one had passed through and beyond and was safe forever more.

John remembered the words of Jesus how on that last night he said to them, "Let not your hearts be troubled; ye believe in God, believe also in me. In my Father's house are many mansions; if it were not so, I would have told you. I go to prepare a place for you, and I will come again, and receive you unto myself; that where I am, there ye may be also."

While he yet spake, another came suddenly into their midst, a ghastly, despairing figure, his garments hanging in rags about him, his face torn and bleeding. And as they looked in amazement and affright, the man spoke and his voice was hoarse and weak, as of one who had wept many hours.

"I am a dying man," he said, "for I will expiate my guilt before to-morrow's sun rise upon the earth. But first I must confess before you what I have done, then if thou wilt slay me for it I shall rejoice, in that I shall be spared the further guilt of taking my own wretched life!"

"Ben Obed!" cried Anat, with a sudden premonition of what he was about to confess.

"Yes, Ben Obed, apostate—false witness—false friend—murderer." And he poured out in rapid disjointed sentences the story of his part in that awful day's work. There was silence when he had finished, and the wretched man turned blindly as if to go away, but John laid a detaining hand upon his arm.

"Stay," he said, and there was the boundless love and forgiveness of Jesus in his voice. "Thou hast indeed sinned, and grievously, but he forgave thee at the last, even as did Christ when he prayed for them that slew him. And thinkest thou not that he would bid thee live—live to carry on the task which he has left unfinished?"

"I am unworthy," groaned Ben Obed.

"Which of us is worthy?" said Peter. "Behold, I denied the Lord himself with curses, yet he bade me care for the church, saying unto me, 'Simon, Simon, behold Satan hath desired to have you, that he may sift you as wheat; but I have prayed for thee, that thy faith fail not. And when thou art converted strengthen thy brethren.' I wot that this word was not for me only, but for all them that have been tempted beyond that they can bear."

And when Ben Obed heard this, he fell on his knees weeping, and they all prayed with him that he might yet be restored and his sins forgiven. When presently he rose up, his face was full of hope. "Behold," he cried, "the Lord hath forgiven me, for the burden hath been eased from off my soul. Yet must I go away from this place whither the spirit shall lead me." Then he turned to Anat. "Canst thou also forgive?" he asked, and his voice trembled.

THE WATCHFUL LOVE. 221

The maiden was silent, but only for a moment. She rose in her place, and stretched out her hand toward the young man. "I forgive thee," she said slowly, "as I know you would have me forgive."

Ben Obed kissed the extended hand humbly, then he went away whither the Spirit led him, and no one of them saw his face more while they lived. But in after years John heard of one who preached Christ among the slaves of Alexandria, suffering many things for Christ's sake, and at the last dying beneath the scourge. The name of this man was Ben Obed, so said the pilgrim who told the thing.

CHAPTER XXX.

A FLASK OF CRYSTAL.

HE beasts are gone, and there is an end of it; but I care not."

"Thou wouldst have told a different tale not many years since." And the speaker laughed. "Poof! I am cold," he continued, stooping to stir the fire. "We might as well have gone back before the sun set; there is no fuel here."

The other man shrugged his shoulders indifferently, and spread his lean fingers over the scanty fire. But he said nothing; after a time his companion spoke again in a slow, meditative way, as if to himself:

"My lord will say this: 'A poorer than I hath need of the beasts, therefore he hath taken them. Would that he had asked me, and I would have given him freely; nevertheless if he hath need, it is in itself sufficient to excuse the deed.'"

"Verily," broke in the other with a sneer, "and because of this senile madness the tribe waxes poorer day by day. Abu Ben Hesed is a fool! I, Ben Kish, say so. What inheritance will my sons have that is worth the having if these things continue?

"Senile madness, dost thou call it? And what says Ben Abu, who succeeds as chief when the old man shall be gathered to his fathers?"

"I have no dealings with him," answered Ben Kish sullenly. "He harps continually on the same string. 'Do this because the Nazarene commanded it. Forbear the other because the Nazarene declared that it was wrong.' What do I care for this dead Nazarene or his sayings? Moreover I do not believe the tales that they tell of him, nor do any believe in Judaea, save them that be poor and have nothing to lose thereby. I asked concerning the thing when I went up to Jerusalem of a great Rabbi, whom I saw in the temple. I had paid my vows and offered my sacrifice according to the law, and I heard the man speaking to the people concerning this new doctrine of the Nazarene. 'Blasphemous,' he called it; 'a cunning device of Satan to entrap the foolish of heart, and above all, contrary to the law of Moses.' Moreover, them that practise these unlawful sayings in Jerusalem are shortly to be dealt with."

"Said he so indeed?' exclaimed the other man, who was called Simeon. "Then it is something more than senile madness that doth ail our worshipful lord; the devil himself hath a hand in it."

"Listen," said Ben Kish, leaning toward his companion, "I am minded to tell thee what he further said to me in private. Swear to me that thou wilt not reveal it?"

"By the temple!" cried Simeon readily.

Ben Kish looked behind him and on either side as if he feared that some one might be lurking near. The glimmering wastes of desert showed vast and empty, stretching away beneath the keen sparkle of countless stars; the night wind wandering in the hollow darkness cried aloud for loneliness; the crouching camels stared at the meagre fire and chewed their cuds in drowsy contentment. "I have a feeling that some one is near—and listening," he said, shivering a little, and throwing a fresh handful of fuel on the dying fire.

The other man laughed, but he also shivered. "There is always that feeling in the desert at night," he said. "It must be the stars, that look down like large eyes out of heaven; or the wind, that hath in it the sound of a woman wailing for her dead. But what hast thou to say to me?"

"Thou hast sworn?"

"I have sworn—and by the temple; what more wouldst thou?"

"I spoke with him concerning our chief," said Ben Kish, "of how he came up to Jerusalem and fell in with them that told him of the Nazarene, and how that since that time he doth continually exhort and preach to us concerning the man, calling him the Messiah, the Holy and Righteous One foretold by the prophets and by Moses.

" 'Alas,' said the Rabbi, 'he hath been snared by evil counsels, and he will also lead away after him all that hear.'

" 'He hath not so led me,' I said, 'for I believe not on a man who commands that if an enemy smite thee on one cheek, thou immediately turn to him the other that he may smite again; and if a thief take away thy camel let him have thy horse also; it is unjust!'

" 'It is not only unjust; it is unlawful,' said this wise Rabbi. 'An eye for an eye, a tooth for a tooth is the law—a good law and wise.' "

"Yet must we submit to the chief of our tribe," said the man who listened, "that is also the law."

"Nay, friend," cried Ben Kish triumphantly, "listen sitill further. I said something of the like to the wise Rabbi, and he made me answer thus: 'The unbeliever and the blasphemer shall be given to them which are faithful, for thus is it written in the law. If, therefore, there be them amongst you which are able, rise up and overcome this man who hath spoken thus blasphemously, and cast him forth that the inheritance be thine; so may the Lord ever prevail against false prophets and workers of iniquity.' "

"Holy Jerusalem!" exlaimed Simeon under his breath. "Smite Ben Hesed? Cast Ben Hesed forth from his own tribe? The man wot not of whom he was speaking."

"One must use discretion with such a one," admitted Ben Kish. "I have already spoken of the matter with the father of my wife. He is a wise man, as thou knowest, and he hath moreover a bitterness against Ben Hesed because that he spake severely to him of his dealings with the two Egyptian brats, whom we found half dead in the desert some years ago. The man was ready to believe the word of strangers rather than the word of his sister's son, which was unjust; Pagiel moreover hath not forgotten the matter—nor will he forget."

"If Ben Hesed be cast forth, who would then be chief?" said Simeon, drawing his beard thoughtfully through his hand and looking intently into the coals.

Ben Kish studied the face opposite him in silence for a moment before replying. "Who else should it be but Pagiel, the next of kin?" he said at length.

"And after him?"

"After him, the husband of his daughter, since his sons are both dead." And Ben Kish drew himself up proudly and looked about him as if he were already chief.

"Ah!"

"Hast thou aught to say against it?" demanded the son of Kish sharply, half involuntarily laying his hand upon the knife in his girdle. "Dost thou then prefer a chief who sends for his enemy when he hath been despoiled of him, and reasons with him forsooth, and gives him a present and soft words, instead of rising up and smiting him, as is the fashion of men since the world began? ay, and will be, despite the driveling commands of any number of false prophets. Betray me if thou wilt. Go to Ben Hesed and say: 'The son of Kish hath devised evil against thee in his heart, therefore smite him.' Would he smite me, the doting greybeard? Pah, I spit in his face!" And he leaned forward and spat venomously into the fire.

The other man laughed silently at the sight of his rage. "I will not go to Ben Hesed with this tale," he said at length; "have I not sworn—and by the temple? Say on, friend, how wilt thou bring this thing to pass?"

Ben Kish looked at him suspiciously. "I will say no more," he said sullenly. "If thou wilt side with the follower of the Nazarene, who is become a fit prey for the vultures because of his blasphemous folly, well. But I tell thee that strange things will come to pass. Thou wilt see it."

"I have not said that I believe in the Nazarene," said his companion. "The old law is good; as for Ben Hesed, I—" he stopped short and stared fixedly at a certain red coal which winked sleepily at him from the midst of the fire, and from which he seemed presently to have gotten some further inward light, for he went on more briskly. "I also have an account to square with Ben Hesed, therefore thou mayest speak freely with me; I promise thee that I will help on the lawful issue in this matter, and that right diligently."

"Dost thou swear this?"

"By the soul of my father; by the God of the Covenant, and by the stars of heaven."

"Well then, to-morrow Ben Hesed will set forth for Jerusalem — never mind how I know, thou wilt see—he will set forth, he and certain chosen ones of his who also believe on the Nazarene; and we will remain behind in charge of the stuff—of the women, of the children, the young men, the maidens, the tents and the furniture thereof, the herds and the flocks."

"But he will return."

"He will not return, he nor any that go forth with him, nor shall any know what hath befallen him."

"And how canst thou accomplish this?"

Ben Kish looked about him once more; the stars were very bright over-head now, and the lonely wind wailed loudly in his ear; it swept away with a moan into the empty desert, the loose sand leaping up beneath the trail of its unseen garments.

"There be many things under the sun," he said at length, his face whitening a little—"of which thou hast not heard, and of which I have heard only a moon since. This is one of them." And he drew from his breast a tiny flask of crystal, filled with a colorless liquid. "I have but to drop the contents of this flask into water," he whispered, leaning forward, and laying his hand upon his companion's breast, "and they that drink thereof will sleep—sleep sound and long."

"What meanest thou?" exclaimed the other, drawing back into the friendly darkness.

"They will wake no more who drink, either for war or peace; the desert shall work its will upon them who have trodden under foot the law."

CHAPTER XXXI.

A SCARLET THREAD.

HESE matters whereof thou hast spoken to us are good, my lord; of the truth of them am I well convinced, because of thy wisdom in showing forth the prophecies which are writ by the hand of holy and righteous men in the scriptures," and Pagiel bowed himself before Ben Hesed with a solemn countenance.

Ben Hesed laid aside the parchment roll from which he had been reading, and a smile of exceeding sweetness dawned in his keen eyes. "My heart is rejoiced, son of my sister," he said gently, "because thou hast believed these wondrous tidings. It shall be well with thee, both in this present world and in the world to come; even as our glorified Lord hath declared, 'Blessed is he that hath not seen and yet hath believed.' Would that every one in this company of ours could also find the light."

" 'In the mouth of two or three witnesses shall every word be established,' as is it written, my lord. If now of those holy men who consorted with the Nazarene in his life-time, one could come into the desert and preach to us of him that was crucified there would remain not one of us all who should not believe."

"I have thought of that—many times," said Ben Hesed, drawing his heavy brows together. "Surely I ought to do this thing, that all they that dwell in this land may hear the good tidings of this exceeding great joy. To my enemy also could be preached the words of love and good will, then would peace reign in the desert. His will should be done on earth even as in heaven, no more shedding of blood, no more strife, no more hatred. And why indeed should not these things be?" and the speaker's face glowed. "It is most simple—most easy. We have but to obey—obey exactly the words of the holy Jesus."

"Most easy—most simple," murmured Pagiel, rolling up his eyes sanctimoniously. "It will doubtless soon come to pass; then will the lion lie down with the lamb, even as it is written."

"I will do it," cried Ben Hesed, "and I will set forth without delay. Some one of them can surely be spared, if not of the apostles, the young man Stephen, a most learned, most holy one. I will also fetch the two Egyptians, who will by this time have grown wise in the faith. Thou wilt love them now, my Pagiel, because of the love of Christ in thy heart. Love is the fulfilling of the law."

"Assuredly!" cried the other, with a venomous gleam in his eye, "the fulfilling of the law; very good—very true. We must all think of the law."

"We need think of but two laws now, God be praised," said Ben Hesed. "Even as it was declared by the Crucified One, 'Thou shalt love the Lord thy God with all thy heart, and with all thy soul, and with all thy mind. This is the first and great commandment. And the second is like unto it, Thou shalt love thy neighbor as thyself. On these two commandments hang all the law and the prophets.'"

"Wilt thou that I command the beasts to be made ready for the start?" suggested Pagiel with an impatient glance at Ben Hesed's abstracted face. "On such an errand there can scarce be too great speed."

"Thou art right. Make ready, and at once; I will take thee with me, also my sons, and ten men which are skilled with the bow, since it may be that we fall in with evil company by the way."

"Resist not evil, as saith the Nazarene," quoth Pagiel piously. "Will it not be better, my lord, to leave me in charge of the women and little ones, since I am next of kin to my lord?"

Ben Hesed looked sharply into the meek face of Pagiel. "I will leave thee in charge," he said; but he looked thoughtfully at the man more than once within the hour.

As for Pagiel, he was glad because that the eye of man is not able to read the heart. He laughed within himself as, with the help of Ben Kish, he made ready the beasts of burden and the provisions, for he thought that his day was come. And he laughed yet again aloud when Ben Hesed set forth on his journey, taking with him his two sons together with ten men who were skillful with the bow.

His wife heard him laugh as he stood in the door of the tent, and she asked him, "What is it that hath pleased the heart of my lord?"

"To every man cometh a time to rejoice," he made answer, "and long enough have I eaten out my heart in bitterness. Make ready now a supper, for we will feast this night." Then he turned to his son-in-law. "Where is Simeon?"

"Nay, I know not," answered Ben Kish. "He is perhaps with the herds."

"Go and fetch him," commanded Pagiel.

A SCARLET THREAD.

Ben Kish made search for the man Simeon; but he found him not, neither with the herds nor anywhere about the encampment. "The man is gathering fuel," he said scowling, "or he hath gone perchance after some wild beast to slay it." But at the setting of the sun Simeon had not returned. Nor did he come that night.

"I hope," said Ben Kish, "that a wild beast hath slain him."

All that day Ben Hesed, with his two sons and the ten men who were skillful with the bow, made haste on their journey and stayed not. "For," said Ben Hesed, "I should have done this thing many moons since; I alone am not sufficient for the work."

At evening an encampment was made so that they might rest and be refreshed. As the servants were gathering fuel for the fires, one of them saw a man running toward the place where they were, and he went and told Ben Hesed, saying, "Behold, we have seen an appearance as of a man running. How can this be, seeing that we are already a day's journey in the wilderness?"

But even as he told the thing, the runner approached the encampment, and he fell on his face before Ben Hesed.

"It is Simeon," said Ben Hesed. "Raise him up and give him water that he may speak. He hath perchance evil tidings."

So they raised him up and offered him water, but he would not drink until he had seen the skin from which the water was taken; then he drank deep and long.

"What doth this mean?" said Ben Hesed, "art thou then smitten with madness, or hast thou tidings of evil?"

"Tidings of evil, alas, my lord," said Simeon, bowing himself before his chief. And he told Ben Hesed all that the son of Kish had said; also how that he had showed him the crystal flask in the desert by night. "The water-skin wherein the portion was mingled is marked," he said. "I went away by stealth into the desert that I might meet thee as thou camest out, but it chanced that thou camest out by another way, and I was not able to overtake thee till now." He showed them, moreover, the water-skin bound with a scarlet thread about its nozzle.

Ben Hesed rose up after that Simeon had told him all, and he went away into the desert alone for the space of three hours, that he might take counsel with the Almighty concerning the thing. When he returned he called four of the strong men unto him, and he said to them, "The moon is full to-night, therefore get ye up and make haste to return to the encampment. And when thou art returned seek out Pagiel and the son of Kish and say to them: 'My lord hath commanded the presence of you both that he may speak unto you concerning a matter of importance.' Say no more than this to the men, and if they come with you willingly, well, but if they will not come, then fetch them straightway. We will remain in this place until thou shalt return."

So the four men made haste all that night to return, and in the morning they stood before the tent of Pagiel and called for him to come out—for he slept late because of the feasting.

Pagiel came forth after a space and heard what the men had to say. And he bowed his head before the messengers of Ben Hesed. "I will arouse my son," he said, "that we may obey the commands of my lord. He would doubtless give to us some further directions concerning the herds."

"Awake!" he cried in the ear of Ben Kish. "Awake to see an evil day, for my heart mistrusts me concerning the man Simeon. Thou shouldst not have told him."

"I told him at thy bidding," cried Ben Kish; "and thinkest thou that we could carry out this thing without adherents? If thou fearest Ben Hesed, why not refuse to go? Tell the men that thy wife is ailing and that I am with the herds. When they shall search for me I will flee in the opposite direction."

Pagiel shook his head gloomily. "Thy counsel is evil, son of a herdsman," he replied. "My wife is already at the fountain, and for thee would they make instant search. We had best go peaceably, for if we refuse they will suspect evil of us—It may be after all that he hath heard nothing; and at the worst, Ben Hesed is a merciful man."

So the two came forth with great show of willingness, and they went with the messengers of Ben Hesed into the wilderness a day's journey.

At evening they stood in the presence of Ben Hesed, and he spoke to them of the crystal flask straightway. "Thus wouldst thou have slain more than a half-score of souls of thine own kindred," he said, his eyes burning with a fire that was terrible to see. "And that without warning and without mercy. What hast thou to say in thy defense?"

The face of Pagiel became the color of death when he heard these words, and he would have fallen had not Ben Kish held him up. "Thou art unjust," cried the son of the herdsman, boldly. "Prate not of mercy to righteous men. An enemy hath told thee this lie concerning us. Twice hast thou believed the word of a stranger before the word of thy near kinsman. Thou art unjust!"

"Is the thing not true then?" said Ben Hesed, mildly, though his eye yet burned with that still and terrible light.

"It is not true," cried Ben Kish. "I swear it by—"

"Hold!" said Ben Hesed, sternly. Then he turned to Pagiel. "Is this tale of the poisoned water true, or is it a lie?"

"It is a lie—a foul lie—a blasphemous lie," cried Pagiel stoutly, the color stealing back to his livid face. "Would I, thinkest thou, lift up my hand against my next of kin? An enemy hath dealt deceitfully with thee—may God requite him!"

"God will requite him," said Ben Hesed solemnly; "and he will also requite thee. Hear now what I shall say. We are by swift dromedaries a day's march from the encampment; this distance ye can accomplish on foot without undo fatigue to yourselves within the space of three days. Return, therefore, in peace, and we will proceed on our journey."

Pagiel bowed himself before his lord. "Thou art a just man," he cried. But in his heart he called Ben Hesed a fool.

"Wilt thou give us provisions that we faint not by the way?" asked the son of Kish, looking suspiciously into the calm face of his chief.

"Assuredly," answered Ben Hesed, "both of food and of water." "And he arose and gave command to his servants that provision should be made for the sustenance of the two men, during a three day's journey, of the best of the corn, of the dates, and of the cheeses of goat's milk which they had provided. A skin of water also commanded he to give them. And so they presently set forth, Ben Hesed and his company upon their swift dromedaries, their faces turned toward Judaea, Pagiel and the son of Kish walking slowly in the opposite direction, bearing upon their backs the provision which Ben Hesed had given them.

No sooner was the caravan out of sight and hearing than Pagiel threw down his burden and burst into a loud laugh; and he kissed Ben Kish on both his cheeks. "Verily," he cried, "thou art a son worth the having; for this day thou didst save me from the incredible folly of confessing to yonder hoary knave all that was in my heart—the words were even upon my lips. Ha, ha! The wisdom of Ben Hesed is very foolishness compared with the wisdom of the son of Kish. Give me to drink, son, for I thirst already because of my laughter."

Ben Kish let down the water-skin from his shoulder. Then he stared at it, his eyes bulging from his head in terror. About the nozzle was bound a scarlet thread.

CHAPTER XXXII.

BEN HESED IN JERUSALEM.

N the fifth day of his journey Ben Hesed reached Jerusalem. And he encamped without the city, saying to his servants, "Bide ye here while I offer a sacrifice in the temple; afterward I will seek out the men with whom I have business.

So he went his way into the city, he and his two sons, leaving the men in the encampment. And he went straightway into the temple and offered a burnt offering for his tribe by the hand of the priest, casting also a goodly sum into the treasury for a thank-offering, as he came out, because that he had completed his journey in safety. "We will go now to the house of John the Apostle," he said to his sons, his face shining with peace.

But as the three of them went their way through the streets, they came suddenly upon a great concourse of people gathered about the doors of a synagogue. They could see that the synagogue also was crowded, the doors standing open because of the pressure of the multitude.

Ben Hesed paused for a moment, and it seemed to him that he could hear the sound of heavy blows and of groaning from within. The multitude also heard, and they cried aloud and gnashed their teeth at the sound.

"Fetch the blasphemers forth!" cried one.

"Stone them!" howled another.

"What is this that is taking place within the synagogue?" asked Ben Hesed of one who stood next him the crowd.

The man glanced carelessly at his questioner. "They are scourging two of the Nazarenes," he replied. "There is no use to try to get in, friend," he added. "One must come early to secure a good place for seeing the sport. Fetch the blasphemers forth and stone them," he yelled, putting his hand to his mouth. "Ha! they will fetch them forth; we shall see them after all!" And he struggled through the crowd toward the steps of the synagogue.

"What is the meaning of this tumult?" said Ben Hesed again, and this time he put his question to a respectable-looking man in the garb of a carpenter, who stood eyeing the scene with an inscrutable expression upon his face.

The man turned at the sound of his voice, and looked at him suspiciously. "Whence dost thou come that thou shouldst ask?" he said coldly. Then with another searching glance he added, "They are merely torturing some of the followers of the Nazarene under the scourge. It is lawful."

"Lawful!" cried Ben Hesed. "Who is it that dares call such an outrage lawful? Room here! that I may look further into this matter."

But the carpenter laid a warning upon his arm. "Hist, man," he whispered. "If thou art indeed a friend of the Nazarenes, hold thy peace; else wilt thou shortly find thyself where thou canst advantage neither thyself nor them that believe."

His last words were drowned in the savage yell with which the multitude greeted the appearance of a detachment of temple police armed with drawn swords. These marched rapidly down the steps of the synagogue—the crowd opening to let them pass—half dragging, half carrying the limp figures of two men, whose blood-stained garments and drawn, ghastly faces betrayed what they had suffered within. After them poured out the congregation, gesticulating and talking excitedly.

"Stubborn fools," Ben Hesed heard one man say. "They have but to confess the crucified Nazarene accursed, to escape all. If they will not do that, let them die."

"Where are they taking these man?" said Ben Hesed to the carpenter, who still stood at his elbow.

"To the prison, to recover from this scourging, when they will receive another—or worse—if they repent not of their blasphemous folly," answered the man in a hard voice. "Let us get out of this crowd, for our sake," he whispered in the next breath, "or we shall both be seized."

The upper end of the street was comparatively clear of people, and here they presently found themselves.

"Thou art then a stranger in Jerusalem?" queried the carpenter, wiping the great drops from his forehead. "And a follower of the man Jesus? Ay, I thought so. Verily, thou must needs know that it were best to get thee back into thine own country—and as speedily as possible; Jerusalem is no place for them that believe. I myself am going this very day with my wife and little ones; only this morning I saw the spies of Saul in our street."

"Thou blowest both hot and cold, friend," said Ben Hesed severely; "but a moment since—"

"Yes, yes, I know what thou wouldst say. I spoke of their blasphemous folly, but" –and he lowered his voice to a whisper and looked anxiously about—" one of the temple police stood at my elbow; I have a family to feed, therefore I must needs be cautious."

"'Trust in the Lord and do good, so shalt thou dwell in the land, and verily thou shalt be fed.' Why didst thou not hold thy peace altogether rather than speak deceitfully?"

The man shrugged his shoulders. "I have no mind to be either scourged or stoned for the faith," he said; "I saw the stoning of Stephen and—"

"What is it that thou art saying?" cried Ben Hesed aghast.

"The stoning of Stephen—hast thou not heard of it? The very day after his death this persecution broke out. Saul of Tarsus and the Sanhedrim—"

"Where is John?" interrupted Ben Hesed. "And the other apostles—what of the women?"

"Some of the apostles are in prison," answered the man; "others are in hiding. Many of the disciples are fled from the city. Some are in their graves; they alone are safe," and the speaker shivered with apprehension, and again looked furtively about him.

"'Verily, they build up Zion with blood, and Jerusalem with iniquity," said Ben Hesed solemnly. "'Therefore shall Zion for your sakes be plowed as a field, and Jerusalem shall become as heaps; and the mountain of the house as the high places of the forest.'"

"I cannot tarry longer," said the carpenter impatiently. "If thou art a discreet man thou wilt leave Jerusalem before nightfall. For my part I would that I have never heard of the Nazarene. Farewell."

Ben Hesed looked after his retreating figure thoughtfully. "What shall be the end of these things, O Lord?" he murmured. "'Behold many shall be purified, and made white, and tried; but the wicked shall do wickedly and shall not understand; the wise shall understand.'"

"Wilt thou that we return unto the encampment?" said his younger son. "We shall not be able to find them that we would; and we are not sufficient in number to succor the distressed."

The eyes of Ben Hesed flashed. "Return if thou wilt, son, and hide beneath the robe of thy mother; but as for me, the Lord hath brought me up to Jerusalem at this time that I might smite the destroyer."

"I am no coward, and that thou knowest right well, my father," answered the young man haughtily; "but remember, I pray thee, that we have left the tribe with no lead—now that Pagiel hath been proven false. If we should all three fall, what of our wives, our little ones, our flocks and our herds? Verily they would come upon evil days, and shall not a man set them of his own household before them which are strangers? Return thou, my father, we will remain."

"Thou hast spoken not unwisely, son," admitted Ben Hesed. "We must even go cautiously about this matter; and if presently it appear that there is a likelihood of bloodshed, thou, Ben Abu, shalt return with two of the strong men. As for me I am already old; if I fall, it matters not. Come, let us be going."

So they went their way towards the house of John; past the market-places where excited groups were discussing the reign of blood which had begun in Jerusalem; past the synagogues crowded with people—for the scourging of the Nazarenes was going forward briskly in many places at once; through dark alleys and beneath covered archways, where men garbed as temple police lurked to entrap the unwary; till at length they had come to the street which they sought. It was choked with people from end to end; but a singular and almost breathless silence prevailed.

"What hath befallen here?" asked Ben Hesed of a woman who stood holding a baby in her arms. The woman turned upon him a white frightened face. "Alas," she cried. "They refused to fly when they were warned, declaring that God would take care of them. And now it hath come to pass that Saul himself hath entered into their dwelling. God help them!"

"Dost thou speak of the household of John?" asked Ben Hesed.

"Yes, yes.—My God, he has seized them!" and the woman burst into a hysterical shriek as a deep low murmur arose from the multitude.

"Shame! Shame!" cried several voices at once. "Leave the women in peace!"

"Room there! Silence!" cried a harsh voice. "Use your swords, men, to clear the way!"

There was an instant scattering amongst the crowd, mostly composed of women and children—two or three of the more timid ones bursting into loud screams at sight of the glittering weapons.

"Forward!" commanded the leader, a swarthy undersized man, from whose scowling face and fiery eyes the frightened children hid their faces.

So this was the dreaded Saul of Tarsus. Ben Hesed looked at him with undisguised contempt. "Murderous coward!" he muttered beneath his breath.

But now the prisoners, bound with heavy chains, were filing past. Three women, their faces wrapped in their mantles, in whom he nevertheless recognized Mary, the mother of Jesus, Anna, the wife of Caiaphas, and Anat the Egyptian girl. Behind these walked a young man, also bound, whose bleeding face and torn garments betrayed the fact that he had not failed to defend those committed to his charge.

"If we had but come an hour earlier we might have held the place," exclaimed Ben Hesed, clenching his fists. "Let us follow and see whither they will take them. It is useless to attempt a rescue now."

"To the Temple," came the second command. "Close up there, and march more rapidly. Save thy tears, woman; thou wilt have a further need for them."

"Coward!" cried Ben Hesed again.

And this time it was evident that the quick ear of Saul had caught the sound, for he turned and fixed a murderous look upon the speaker. "Dog of an apostate!" he hissed, "thy day is coming."

"Callest thou me dog?" cried Ben Hesed in a fury, and would have closed with the Pharisee on the spot, had not his two sons held him.

"Let be," whispered the younger of the twain, "or we shall not be able to save them."

Ben Hesed drew back, muttering fiercely. "I will slay him for that word," he said. "Let us follow them in."

But this it presently appeared was impossible; for the prisoners being now arrived at the Temple, were conducted by way of the Court of the Women into the lesser chamber of judgment. And immediately the doors were shut.

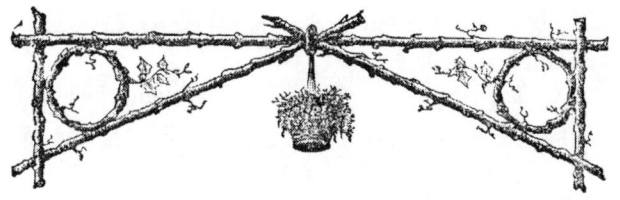

CHAPTER XXXIII.

THE MERCY OF ISRAEL.

HE light which streamed in from the single window high up in the massive wall revealed a square room, ceiled and paved with stone. It was empty save for an oaken table, behind which in a high-backed chair sat an old man of severe and reverend aspect. On either side of him stood two officers of the temple police, motionless as statues and armed with long spear-pointed staves. All this Anat, who was the first of the women to pass into the chamber, saw with a single timid glance. She shrank back before the stern eyes of the man in the chair, and reaching out one manacled hand touched the robe of Mary, who was just behind her. The mother of Jesus took the little trembling hand and held it firmly.

Saul advanced to the table and laid upon it a slip of parchment, at the same time whispering a few words into the ear of the old man, who frowned slightly and nodded once or twice as his eye passed slowly from one to the other of the four prisoners.

"Where is the man John?" he demanded suddenly.

No one answered.

"Can ye not speak?" he cried, striking the table with his clenched fist, "or hath it come to pass that your scurrilous tongues are already withered in your mouths?"

"If thou art questioning me," said Seth calmly, "I wot not where the apostle is; he went on some errand of mercy early this morning, leaving me in charge of the house. We be law-abiding citizens, dwelling in a law-abiding city, wherefore hath it come to pass that we are thus dragged through the streets in chains?"

"That shalt thou shortly hear," replied Annas grimly. "Hast thou examined these prisoners?" he asked, turning to Saul.

"I examined them briefly before making the arrests, according to my custom," answered Saul. "For I would not that I transgress the law in this work of purging the holy city of them that blaspheme. I found all of the prisoners obstinate and stiff-necked, unwilling to renounce their sins and to make confession of their unrighteousness, therefore I have brought them before thee for further examination and sentence."

"This being so, the law must take its course with them," said Annas sternly. "Do thou, Mary of Nazareth, stand forth. Remove the veil from off thy face."

With a firm step the mother of Jesus advanced and stood before the table; she threw back the shrouding mantle, her beautiful, pallid face shining forth as if illumined with a strange inward radiance. Annas looked at her for an instant, then he dropped his eyes and fell to turning over the parchments which lay before him.

"Art thou the mother of the Man of Nazareth?"

"I am."

"Thou didst teach him to believe unholy and blasphemous things regarding himself when he was a child," said Annas, still looking down at the table; "therefore did he continue to delude himself and others when he was grown, and at the last perished miserably on the accursed tree. Hath not God punished thee sufficiently for thy presumptuous sin that thou dost still persist in pretending that thy son is the Messiah of Israel?"

"He is the Messiah of Israel," said Mary, her deep eyes shining. "Wherefore my soul doth magnify the Lord, for he hath regarded the low estate of his hand-maiden; behold from henceforth all generations shall call me blessed. He is the Messiah of Israel, but he is also much more, he is the Prince of Peace, the Saviour of the world. For the Lord hath shewed strength with his arm, he hath scattered the proud in the imaginations of their hearts. He hath put down the mighty from their seat, and exalted them of low degree. And God hath delivered his holy child Jesus from death and from the power of the grave, and hath set him down at the right hand of power of ever more."

"Daughter of Abraham," said Annas, lifting his shaking hand, "thou hast blasphemed. Thou knowest the penalty."

"Father," cried an agonized voice, "forbar this last awful sin, lest God smite thee in his wrath and consume thee to ashes!"

At the sound of this voice the face of Annas changed. He rose to his feet and stared for a moment at the shrouded figure which knelt before him.

"Who—who is it that speaks to me?" he said, and his voice trembled.

"It is I—thine own daughter, Anna; dost thou not know me? I beseech thee by the mercies of Jehovah that thou raise not thy hand against the mother of Christ."

"Woman, I know thee not. Get thee up and stand back. Out of thine own mouth art thou already condemned."

"I care not for myself—death were welcome. But take heed to thyself, I beseech thee, before thou layest violent hands upon this holy woman."

Annas laughed contemptuously. "Have we not crucified the carpenter?" he said, "and are unscathed; is the mother of the carpenter more exalted? Nay we shall deal with her after the law; the law is just."

At this Seth started forward. "Prate not of the law who art a murderer!" he said in a choked voice. "The man Jesus was guiltless and ye did condemn him. Guiltless also are these women; release them, but do with me as thou wilt—the servant is not greater than his lord."

Annas trembled with rage. He essayed to speak, but the words died on his lips.

"Now seest thou what manner of perverse and pestilent apostates there are," said Saul. "Furthermore, the man is an alien. There is no need that we continue to argue this matter with them. Israel is ever merciful and just, according to the commands of Jehovah, therefore let them be publicly scourged without the gates; if the stripes be wholesome to bring them back to their right minds and to a knowledge of the truth, well. They will then confess right gladly that the man of Nazareth and all his works are of the devil. After this shall a blood offering be made for them; so shall they be cleansed from their iniquities. But and if they will not so confess, let their sin abide upon them; let them die the death appointed in the law of Moses for such as are blasphemers."

"Justice and mercy are in the words of thy mouth," said Annas slowly. Then he turned to the prisoners: "Forty stripes save one shall be laid upon each and every one of you to-morrow at about this hour, according to the magnitude of your offences and the law of Moses, who thus appointed it for the peace of Israel. Afterward—if ye will not confess—ye shall die the appointed death."

"Mercy—have mercy!" cried Anna, laying hold of his robe. "We cannot but believe the things which we have

THE MERCY OF ISRAEL.

seen and heard. Nay, thou wouldst thyself believe if the Lord should reveal himself to thee."

Annas drew away with a gesture of abhorrence. "Unhand me, woman," he said sternly. "Satan hath blinded thee to the truth; I will pray for thee that thou be undeceived at the last. Take them away."

"Thrust these blasphemers into the inner prison," commanded Saul a half-hour later, "and remember that thou answerest for them with thine own life. Come not to me on the morrow with any whining tale of angel or devil, and think thus to excuse thyself for their escape. Let them be missing at the third hour to-morrow, and thou thyself shalt suffer in thine own body the penalty to which these are condemned. Thou hast heard."

The chief jailer shrugged his shoulders. "I have heard, my lord. This night at every watch will I inspect the prisoners. But I pray thee send also additional guards, for life is precious to me, and I have not forgotten what hath happened more than once when these Nazarenes have been imprisoned; peradventure the man himself might appear."

"Coward!" growled Saul. "The man hath perished off the face of the earth, so likewise shall perish all who believe on him. If thou art one of these, room shall be made for thee within."

"Nay, my lord, nay," cried the jailer trembling. "I do not believe—I swear it; but there have been strange things of late, and the devil himself hath powers—"

"I will send a guard," interrupted Saul shortly. "Hold thy peace and do thy duty, and all shall be well with thee. Admit no one."

The chief jailer bowed himself almost to the ground before the Pharisee, whose renown had by this time spread throughout Jerusalem, and in whose presence the temple officials from the highest unto the lowest trembled. "I will admit no one," he said, and he again made obeisance as Saul strode through the prison gate.

"Lock the gate and double bar it," he cried irritably to the guard. "Then stand there for your lives; if these prisoners get away, and I have to die for it, be sure that not one of you shall escape. Thrust the man into the stocks," he added to the turnkey, who stood at his elbow; "as for the women, chain them to the floor. I will come after a little and look to them. Food? No; let them fast. Give them water."

In the inner prison, where the darkness seemed only the more intense because of the feeble rays of daylight which struggled through the little square of grating above the door, were the four who were condemned to death. The young man Seth made fast in the stocks, the three women chained to heavy rings which were riveted into the stone floor.

"Dost thou think that He will deliver us?" whispered Anat, laying hold of the robe of Mary and pressing it to her lips.

"He will deliver us, beloved, in his own best way," answered Mary tenderly. "If the way lie through the dark valley, then will the end thereof be only the more glorious."

"But the scourging—the shame, how—how shall we endure it?" wailed Anat piteously.

"He also endured—being divine," said Mary, her voice trembling; "and shall we who are but mortal shrink back? Think not of the morrow, save as thou dost think that to-morrow we shall stand before Him in clothing of immortality."

"But if we fail, deny him?" faltered Anat. "I know not my own heart—whether I can endure unto the end."

"He will give thee grace when the need comes. Wouldst thou at this moment deny him?"

"No—ah, no."

"Neither wilt thou deny him on the morrow. He giveth his strength in due season, and to-morrow is in his hand."

As for Anna, the wife of Caiaphas, she sat silent, her head bowed upon her knees. Mary thought that perhaps she slept, and in her tender heart she hoped that this was so.

Every hour the chief jailer flashed the light of his torch into their prison. "Where now is he that delivereth?" he cried tauntingly. And again, "If angels visit thee during the night watches cry aloud, for I have sworn by my life to deliver thy bodies to judgment on the morrow." Being insensible—as indeed are most mortals to celestial sights and sounds—he did not perceive that the whole place was filled with the airs of heaven and with the rustling of angelic pinions.

At midnight the drowsy guards were awakened by a loud knocking upon the outer gate of the prison.

"Open!" cried a voice. "Open at once, in the name of the Sanhedrim." The governor of the prison looked out, and beholding by the light of the lantern that it was Caleb himself who knocked, he opened cautiously and admitted him.

"I have orders," said Caleb, "to speak a word in private with one of the women who are in ward here; this is the token of my authority," and he displayed before the eyes of the chief jailer the signet ring of Annas.

"But the Pharisee Saul—"

Caleb waved his hand impatiently. "Fetch the woman out to me and at once," he said.

"They are chained to the floor," grumbled the jailer, "and I will not fetch out any one of them, were it by the order of Herod himself. Go thou in."

So Caleb went into the prison, the jailer following close upon his heels. "Which is the woman called Anna?" he said. "I have here a message for her."

And when the daughter of Annas had been pointed out to him, he thrust into her hand a packet. "Use what is within to save the honor of thy house," he whispered. "It is sent thee in mercy by the hand of Annas." Then he turned and went swiftly out.

Anna opened the packet, a vague hope stirring at her heart; but she shrank back with a shiver as the flash of the departing light fell upon the blade of a dagger.

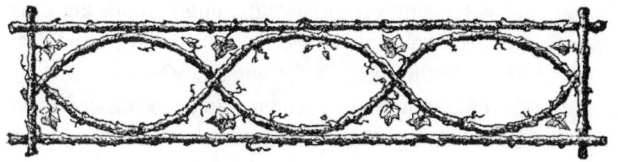

CHAPTER XXXIV.

AT THE THIRD HOUR.

N the morrow a great crowd had assembled about the prison which held the four who were condemned to public scourging and to death; for evil tidings travel fast, and there is ever an ignoble multitude who reckon as high holiday a spectacle of human agony.

Yet there were those who looked in one another's faces with sombre and despairing eyes. "The last days are at hand," they murmured, "the days of wrath and burning. For shall not God avenge his own elect which cry day and night unto him? Yeah, he will avenge them, and that right speedily." But still the sun poured down with impartial splendor, gilding alike the gloomy walls of the blood-stained prison, and the yellow curls of the year-old babe. And the placid heaven gave no sign of invisible hosts of glory behind its azure wall.

Exactly at the third hour, Saul accompanied by a strong guard approached the prison. His face was pale and haggard, but upon it was stamped a look of savage determination before which the mob fell back with a dull low murmur.

The governor of the prison greeted him with manifest joy. "The prisoners which thou didst commit to my charge are safe—quite safe, my lord," he said, rubbing his hands. "We had no visions; neither angels, earthquakes, nor demons. We are—"

"Fetch them forth," said Saul, with a peremptory gesture and a fierce look at the jailer, before which that functionary drew back with an apologetic obeisance.

"Yes, certainly, at once, my worshipful lord; just as soon as we shall be able to undo the chains. Here you," he roared, addressing the turnkey, "fetch the four from the inner prison."

So presently the condemned came forth into the prison yard, and stood before Saul. Their faces were calm, even joyful, and the Pharisee ground his teeth as he looked at them.

"Hast thou counted the cost of thy perverseness?" he said abruptly.

"We have counted the cost," replied Mary of Nazareth in a firm voice, "and the reward is exceeding glorious above all that it hath entered into the heart of man to imagine."

"Thinkest thou so?" answered Saul. "Those of thy company may be of a better mind. Take heed to what I shall say," he added, turning to the other three. "The Sanhedrim is full of mercy and compassion; and while it will without faltering carry on the work which it hath undertaken of cleansing and purifying Israel of this monstrous and blasphemous belief in a perished malefactor, it also offers pardon freely to all who confess and forsake the error of their ways. If now at this last hour ye will acknowledge that the Nazarene was an impostor inspired by the father of lies; that he justly died the accursed death; that his body moreover was stolen by his followers from out the tomb in which it was buried, for the express purpose of confirming this accursed blasphemy; if ye shall now make confession of these things, it is the merciful mandate of them which are in authority that ye be immediately released without further scathe or punishment. Ye have heard. Wilt thou, maiden, so confess, thereby securing to thyself bodily safety and the blessing of the Almighty?"

There was a breathless silence for an instant, then Anat raised her large dark eyes to the face of the Pharisee. "Sir, I have heard thy offer of safety, and this is my answer. I believe on the Lord Jesus Christ, because I who was once blind now see; I believe that he was put to death upon the cross that he might draw all men unto him and heal them from their sins, even as Moses lifted up the serpent in the wilderness that the stricken Israelites might look and be saved; I believe that he arose from among the dead on the third day, and is set down forever at the right hand of God. These things I do affirm and believe in this the last hour of my mortal life."

"Thou art condemned," said Saul slowly, but his face was more white than the face of the maiden.

"Young man," he said, turning to Seth, "Wilt thou confess to the things which I have already enumerated, that thou mayest live out thy days in peace?"

"I cannot deny him on whom I have believed, even for the sake of life — and life is sweet," faltered Seth, on whom the shadow had lain very heavily all the night.

"Thou art condemned," repeated Saul in a hollow voice.

"Woman, who by reason of thine exalted birth shouldst have remained a mother in Israel, wilt thou renounce these vile errors after which thou hast strayed? In so renouncing thou shalt find again a father's, a husband's forgiveness and favor. For so I am bidden to say unto thee."

Anna trembled and was silent.

"Dost thou so acknowledge thy sin?" said Saul; and it seemed to them that listened that there was a note of entreaty in his stern voice.

"God of my fathers!" cried the wife of Caiaphas, looking up into the dazzling blue of the sky. "Help me to know without shadow of doubt what is truth; and enable me to witness to it without faltering." Then she turned to Saul. "Tell my husband and my father, that the forgiveness and favor of God is rather to be desired than the forgiveness and favor of any mortal, however beloved. I believe that Jesus of Nazareth is the Messiah of Israel; and if I must now die for that belief, I die willingly."

Saul bowed his head without speaking. "Close up about the prisoners," he commanded the guard, who had stood silent witnesses of the scene, "and conduct them to the place of punishment."

. . . .

Abu Ben Hesed had not been idle during the hours which had passed since he had seen the prisoners disappear behind the closed door of the judgment hall. He had followed them to the prison; and from a temple underling who was not insensible to the glitter of gold as seen through the fingers of the desert chief, he had made shift to find out the number of guards, the strength of the walls and the general plan of the prison.

"A safe prison, truly," he said to his informant, as the gold changed hands—neither apparently being aware of the transaction.

"Safe as the tomb," assented the temple official, slyly rubbing the coin with a corner of his robe. "Once within yonder walls, a man is seen no more till he is fetched out." Then he fell to eyeing the hand of Ben Hesed, fancying that he again saw there a gleam of something yellow. He was not mistaken; and his face grew proportionately genial as a second coin joined the first in his own greedy palm.

"I am but lately arrived in Jerusalem," said Ben Hesed, "and have as yet not witnessed the punishment of any of these apostates. 'Twere a goodly sight to see a blasphemer suffer?"

"Ay, a goodly sight. I have seen many. Man, but they be obstinate! Wouldst thou witness a grand spectacle, then be without the Damascus Gate to-morrow. 'Twill be in the very place where they stoned the pestilent Gentile, Stephen."

"They will stone only the man, I suppose?" said Ben Hesed with apparent unconcern.

"They will scourge all four—forty stripes save one," and the fellow smacked his lips in anticipation. "I myself am to handle one of the scourges, and I understand the business as none other in Jerusalem. I can fetch the blood every time; thou wilt see." And he winked at Ben Hesed, and cautiously clinked the gold pieces with the air of a man who is at peace with himself and all the world.

Ben Hesed could with difficulty keep his hands from the throat of the wretch.

"After the scourging, the Sanhedrim will give them one more chance to renounce their evil beliefs," continued the official, "a mere form, for they are all as stubborn as the father of lies himself. A few stones will suffice to finish them. So perish all who blaspheme the law!"

"I shall be there," declared Ben Hesed. "Ah, stay, should they change the hour and place bring me word, and I will recompense thee with as much again as thou hast already in thy hand. I am not minded to lose the sight. Thou wilt find me encamped just without the Damascus Gate."

"I will bring thee word, son of Abraham, I swear it by the veil of the Temple. Peace be with thee."

An hour later Ben Hesed held a council of war in his camp. "We cannot take the prison," he said, drawing his heavy brows together. "For they would straightway rouse the Romans at the citadel, which is but a stone's throw from the outer wall of the place. We must wait till they fetch them out to-morrow, and may the Almighty give us the wisdom and the strength which we need. Ay, and he will give it," he added, his eye flashing fire. "It is ever the pleasure of Jehovah to show forth his power by the hand of the few, even as by the hand of Gideon with three hundred men he overthrew the hosts of the Midianites and Amalekites, which were as the grasshoppers for multitude."

Then directed he the twelve men who were with him after what manner they should do on the morrow, and every man of them lay down and slept. But Ben Hesed slept not all the night, for he prayed mightily unto God that he would deliver them which were persecuted out of the hand of the destroyer; and he prayed also for him that was wasting the church, that his eyes might be opened. At the coming of the dawn he also laid down for a space, for he said, "I will both lay me down in peace and sleep; for thou Lord only makest me to dwell in safety. The Lord will save the afflicted people, he will give me the necks of his enemies, for God is a God of great deliverances."

Very early the people began to pour out from the Damascus Gate, that they might secure good places for the seeing. They brought them food and drink also, that they might make merry. Ben Hesed looked at them and he waxed exceeding angry.

"Behold!" he said, "these dwellers in the holy city are come out as to a holiday, with laughing and feasting.

They are become as the dwellers in Sodom, and as the inhabitants of the earth before the flood, for they delight themselves in blood and violence. They make merry and eat and drink to-day, but the days shall come wherein they shall mourn and cry aloud, and their tears shall be their meat day and night."

As the third hour drew nigh, the people began to crane their necks toward the gate through which the condemned were to come forth, and they grew impatient and murmured as the moments dragged by.

"What now if they have already confessed?" said one woman. "We shall have put ourselves to this trouble for naught. Nay, but I believe that they have confessed."

"Mayhap," said her neighbor, "but I shall not give up the matter before noon, now that I am here. Verily," she added with a shrug, "I am glad now that I did not go over to their number; I came near it once when the man Peter preached in our street that their Messiah would come back and that right speedily. If what they tell about the Nazarene being alive were true, he would certainly come in these days." Then they fell to gossiping in neighborly fashion about their husbands, the linen that they had spun, and the preparations for the approaching feast-day, stopping suddenly to listen as a loud and ever growing murmur of sound arose from within the gates.

"They are coming!" cried the multitude as with one voice.

"They are coming!" said Ben Hesed, tightening his grasp on the strong bow upon which he was leaning. The little band of fourteen men had established themselves on a rocky eminence directly above the spot where the scourging was to take place, well screened from observation by a tangle of low-growing shrubs.

The procession, headed by a strong detachment of temple guards, soon came in sight, the prisoners heavily chained walking two by two. Behind them followed a number of Sanhedrists, among whom the women pointed out to one another the famous Saul of Tarsus, as second only in interest to the condemned prisoners.

"They do say," whispered one, "that he enters without ceremony into the houses wherein dwell them that believe on the Nazarene, and that he drags them forth to prison and to death without mercy."

"That is true," returned her neighbor. "I chanced to be in the house of Mary when he came there—for as thou knowest, she was a kind soul, whatever her sins, and ready always to lend from her store for the convenience of them that lacked—indeed one might say as much of them all."

"And how didst thou escape?"

"I simply repeated what the man bade me, without ado; but I had like to have fainted. How I reached my home afterward I scarce know; my husband hath forbidden me to speak with any of them hereafter—though God knows the command was needless. But see! They are about to bind them to the posts for the scourging." At the next breath the speaker screamed aloud in terror, grasping her neighbor by the arm. A swift something had smitten the man who was advancing to lay hold on Mary of Nazareth, and with a wild yell of agony he leapt high into the air, falling stone dead at his victim's feet.

Before the startled multitude had time to recover themselves, a very whirlwind of destruction, savage, swift, merciless, had swept down upon them from the rocky eminence above their heads, the wild battle-cry of the desert sounding in their guilty ears like the trumpet call of the last day. And the people fled from before it in a frenzy of mad fear, running, stumbling, falling, the strong trampling the weak under foot, amid a wild tumult of shrieks, curses, and entreaties to God to spare them.

The temple guard, encouraged by the ringing voice of Saul of Tarsus, made at the first some faint show of resistance, then they too turned and fled for their lives.

"Cowards!" shouted Saul angrily; "there are but a handful of them."

But his voice was drowned in the general uproar. Seizing a spear from the hand of one of the flying guards, he flung himself into the thickest of the fight, striking out right and left in a sort of blind fury. Then something struck him full in the forehead, a wave as of fire flashed before his eyes, the spear dropped from his nerveless fingers, and he fell—down—down into darkness and silence.

CHAPTER XXXV.

ON THE ROAD TO DAMASCUS.

EIGHBOR, dost thou think it is safe for us to come down? Verily, for myself, I shall take the risk, if risk there be, for my limbs are as stiff as those of yonder dead man."

By way of answer, the other man shook a warning finger at the speaker, and proceeded to clamber up still further into the branches of the tree in which these two spectators of the stirring scene which had just transpired were hidden. "Wait a little," he whispered, "till I shall make sure that the fellows have gone. By the thunderbolts of Jove!" he exclaimed with a laugh, as he presently descended to a level with his companion, "that was a greater sight than the stoning which we came out to see; I would not have missed it— no, not for ten shekels of silver!"

"Have they gone?" said the first querulously. "I tell thee that my limbs have lost all feeling, so long have I sat here without moving."

"Thou mayest thank the gods that thou art alive to complain, friend. But come down, come down; there is naught to hurt thee now, and we must look to these dead men."

"Who were the rescuers, thinkest thou?"

"Nay, I know not. There were thirteen of them, for I counted; verily, I believe that the multitude thought them the twelve apostles headed by the Nazarene himself." And the speaker threw back his head and laughed again.

"Nay, there were fourteen," said the other, with an obstinate shake of the head. "I also counted, and I never make a mistake. They were wild men out of the desert, I opine," he added sagely. "I have seen the like many times when crossing to Egypt, for I have traveled in my day." Then he looked anxiously about him. "There is no one dead here save the man yonder," he said, "and he was smitten at the first. We had best make haste and return to the city; this affair is nothing to us."

"Hold, dost thou not see a body yonder in the shadow of the bush? By the rod of Moses, I think I saw him move; let us look to it."

"We had best leave the whole matter alone, I tell thee," insisted his companion with irritation. "Thanks be to Jehovah, I have had nothing to do with it so far—save to look on; and I tell thee that I will not lay a finger to yonder body, be it dead or alive. Come, I am going to the city." And without stopping for further parley, the speaker began to run toward the city gate, apparently not hearing the loud cries to stop which his companion sent after him.

"Coward!" muttered the one who was left; then he walked over to the body, which lay face downward in the shadow of the bushes, and deliberately turned it over, starting back with a cry of surprise as the identity of the unconscious man became apparent.

"'Tis Saul of Tarsus! So the wolf is himself bitten for once; but not unto death, I am thinking." He sprinkled the face of the wounded man with water, and forced a little wine between his clenched teeth. "Only a bruise," he continued reflectively, as he examined the body with care. "I suspect that the Nazarenes would thank me should I thrust him through as he lies. He is a hard man—a hard man. Yet that is nothing to me. Ha! he is reviving already. Another sip of the wine, friend; thou hadst a sharp blow, and it hath confused thy senses somewhat; but thou wilt shortly—"

"Did the blasphemers escape me?" said Saul in a hollow voice, sitting up and looking about him. Then his eye fell upon the four empty posts which had been set up for the scourging, and he groaned aloud.

"Be thankful rather that thou hast thyself escaped with so slight an injury," said the man who still stood at his side, flask in hand. "Another sup of—"

"Hold thy peace, fellow," said Saul savagely, springing to his feet. "The cowardly knaves!—to flee from their duty before a dozen peasants,—where are they? Which way did they go?" And he fixed his angry eyes on his rescuer, who was calmly girding himself.

"Thou hast bidden me hold my peace, Pharisee; and I am not the man to be bidden twice. Farewell, and a good recovery to thee." And the man turned resolutely away.

"Stay, friend. I should not have spoken thus to one who had done me a kindness," said Saul. "Grant me thy pardon, and tell me, I beseech thee, what thou canst of this affair—if thou wast witness to it. God knows that it was untimely; another hour might have seen four penitent ones restored to the fold of Israel."

"Thinkest thou so, Pharisee?" said the other carelessly. "Now for myself I think otherwise. Another hour would have seen four corpses yonder, where now we see but one. The affair was timely enough for the Nazarenes."

"Thy name, man?"

"My name, Pharisee, is Festus; I am a freeborn Roman, resident of Jerusalem yonder for a score of years back, but answerable to no man for my beliefs or practices. If it pleaseth me to believe on a crucified man instead of on Jove or Jehovah, thou canst neither scourge nor stone me for it. And now, most courteous rabbi, let me advise thee to return with all haste into Jerusalem, and in future to moderate thy zeal, lest thou come to an untimely end." With which bit of advice, received by Saul in contemptuous silence, the man strode away toward Jerusalem.

Left to himself the baffled Pharisee examined the ground carefully, pausing at length to question several peasants who had left their work in the neighboring fields to gather at the scene of the disaster.

"Didst thou see which way the knaves fled?" he asked of one.

The man looked at him stupidly. "They be fled along the road yonder," he said, pointing with his finger to the highway.

"Which way, north or south?"

"They went that way, master," said the peasant, pointing toward the north, which was indeed the opposite direction from that which Ben Hesed and his company had taken.

"He asked me which way the knaves were fled," said the man to his companions, as they stood staring after the departing figure of Saul. "Assuredly the knaves who came out to look upon the death of the just went that way, since it took them back to Jerusalem. As for the Nazarenes and those that saved them this day, God be with them, I did not look to see which way they fled. Jehovah grant them a swift journey and a safe abiding-place from the hand of that pestilent Pharisee."

"Thou hast spoken!" cried the others with an air of enjoyment, after which they went peacefully back to their labors.

In the meantime Saul was hastening back to Jerusalem with rage in his heart; bruised, baffled, humiliated as he was, he lost no time in seeking Annas that he might acquaint him with the untoward occurrence of the morning.

"I will pursue them," he said, "even unto strange cities. Within this hour will I set forth."

Annas looked thoughtful. "Thou sayest," he said, "that they be fled towards the north. It hath come to my ears of late that there be many of these accursed apostates who have taken refuge in Damascus. So that there is now a goodly company of them dwelling in fancied security in that city, waxing fat and flourishing, as doth this pestilent weed of evil wherever it taketh root. The men who have this day interfered with the just sentence of the law, have doubtless accomplished the mischief through the connivance of some person who hath played traitor to the cause, and are now fled to Damascus, thinking to find there a refuge from the wrath of Israel."

"Who is the traitor?"

Annas hesitated for an instant. "There be foes among them of a man's own household in these days," he said in a half whisper. "Caiaphas hath disappeared, I know not whither; but I fear—I fear."

"Damascus is under Aretas, Emir of Petra, now," said Saul after a pause. "With him thy house hath friendly relations. Give me therefore letters that I may carry fire and the sword into the camp of Jehovah's enemies. I will not let so much as one of them escape me," and he ground his teeth savagely. "I will fetch them chained to Jerusalem, that they may perish in sight of the walls which they have dishonored."

"Thou hast spoken wisely and well, my son. I will procure the letters for thee at once, so that thou mayest start without delay. As for matters in this city, there shall be no sparing of pains nor effort to carry on to its completion the good work which we have begun. Jehovah hath prospered us mightily so far. We hear of no more blasphemous gatherings in Solomon's Porch; no more preaching of a false Messiah in the synagogues; no more healing of vile beggars in the name of the accursed one; no further prating about apostles or disciples Men walk soberly in these days as they have not since the days of the malefactor. Let us continue in this good cause, my son, and we shall have triumphed gloriously. This disgraceful heresy, which is even as a spot of foul leprosy on the fair body of Israel, shall be utterly purged away. Then indeed may we hope once more for the coming of the Anointed One!"

The eyes of the young man flashed fire. "Amen and Amen!" he cried. "May Jehovah hasten the day!" But his brow was gloomy and forbidding as ever, when an hour later he had finished the visitation of the prisons wherein groaned many that believed.

"Neither scourgings, threatenings, revilings, nor torture of any degree hath the power to move these Nazarenes," declared the chief-jailers; "and the women yield no whit easier than the men."

"A spot of leprosy indeed," muttered Saul to himself, "it hath by stealth crept into the very life-blood of the nation; and how hardly shall the deadly leprosy be cleansed."

Another hour and he was in the saddle pressing forward with all haste towards Damascus, for he hoped to overtake the fugitives before night. With him traveled a well-armed escort of tried and experienced men, to whom had been promised large rewards should the mission be successful. The journey to Damascus was a long one; the roads were rough and ill-made moreover, so that progress was necesarily slow. Hasten as he might, Saul could not hope to reach Damascus before the better part of a week. As for them that had escaped, it was impossible for him to decide whether or not they were still before him. Now and again he heard from the khans along his route, of a troop of horsemen with whom were traveling also women, but when on the third day he actually overtook such a company of wayfarers it turned out to be merely a caravan of wine merchants, traveling with their wives and little ones.

"I will at all events press on to Damascus," he decided, "for even should I not immediately lay hand upon the ones I seek, there are in that city other lost sheep of the house of Israel which I must needs bring back into the fold."

On this journey for the first time in many months Saul found time to think. Habitually taciturn and forbidding, his subordinates did not venture to address the haughty Pharisee save when it became necessary; so for long hours the man sat silent, while his beast picked its slow and difficult way along the rocky roads.

Strangely enough his thoughts wandered again and again from the object of his journey; in these vernal solitudes the wily words of Annas faded from his mind. Something in the pure-eyed flowers that leaned in shy welcome from the roadside grass put him in mind of Stephen, the dead apostate, as he bitterly termed him. Before his mental vision there arose again that never-to-be-forgotten face; now radiant with the fire of youth and enthusiasm, as he remembered it in many a heated debate over law and prophecy; now stern and unrelenting as he pronounced the terrible arraignment which yet echoed in the ears of the Pharisee: "Ye stiff-necked and uncircumcised in heart and ears; ye do always resist the Holy Ghost; as your fathers did, so do ye. Which of the prophets have not your fathers persecuted? And they have slain them which shewed before the coming of the Just One; of whom ye have now become the betrayers and murderers!" Then pallid beneath the icy shadow of approaching death, yet shining with a mysterious glory as he cried out, "Behold, I see the heavens opened, and the Son of Man standing on the right hand of power." And yet again, touched with the mystic seal of the great deliverer as he had lain "asleep" on the stony ground beyond the Damascus Gate.

In vain did he endeavor to shake off these haunting visions, resolutely repeating aloud commands, prohibitions and long passages of the law, rigorously observing the ceremonial washings and cleansings whenever the company halted beside a running stream. All was in vain, "Ye who received the law as it was ordained by angels, and kept it not!" sounded the inexorable voice. And with and through it, mingled the wail of women bereft of their little ones, the groanings of strong men beneath the scourge, the sullen clang of prison doors, and the clank of chains.

On the fifth night of his journey the agony became so intolerable that he left his tent and wandered out beneath the open heavens. "My God!" he groaned aloud, "have I not kept thy law, and loved thy statutes? Yet have I no peace: my days are consumed with anguish. Surely thou hast hated iniquity and thou hast loved righteousness; behold now I have done all these things that thy name might be exalted before the people, that blasphemy and deceit might cease from out the land." And he vowed a great sacrifice before the Lord of fat sheep and oxen. But again came the haunting voice, "O ye house of Israel, have ye offered to me slain beasts and sacrifices for the space of forty years. But behold, I will carry you away beyond Babylon—who have received the law ordained of angels and have kept it not."

"I have kept the law!" he cried aloud, and the hills replied in melancholy echoes, "the law—the law."

Then there crowded into his thought the faces of the four who had escaped out of his hand, and he remembered the look in the eyes of the maiden as she said, "I believe that he was put to death upon the cross that he might draw all men unto him and heal them from their sins, even as Moses lifted up the serpent in the wilderness that the stricken Israelites might look and be saved," and with these words there mingled the solemn voices of prophecy, "Surely he hath borne our griefs and carried our sorrows; yet we did esteem him stricken, smitten of God, and afflicted. But he was wounded for our transgressions, he was bruised for our iniquities; the chastisement of our peace was upon him; and with his stripes we are healed. All we like sheep have gone astray; we have turned every one to his own way; and the Lord hath laid upon him the iniquity of us all."

"God, if it be true," he murmured; and for a moment the soft radiance of that ever-brooding presence of love had well nigh penetrated his dark soul, then he lifted his head stubbornly. "I cannot believe," he cried. "I will not believe.—Shall I, a Pharisee of the Pharisees, accept a Messiah who hath died the accursed death? I am mad. I will not believe—unless I too can see the heavens opened."

He laughed aloud as he spoke the words, and the sound of his laughter fled away through the silent night to the dark hills which caught it and tossed it back upon him in mocking echoes.

On the morrow they journeyed in the plains of Antilibanus, a vast arid burning desert, wherein was neither water nor verdure, and the men and the beasts were parched by reason of the great heat. Certain ones of the company therefore besought Saul that they might tarry by the way. "Let us rest till the heat of the day be past," they said, "then shall we with ease reach the village of Kaukab; there will we abide till morning, that we may enter Damascus before the hour of the great heat."

"We will not tarry," replied Saul, "until we reach Damascus." And there was that in his eye which forbade remonstrance. So they toiled on silently beneath the burning Syrian sky. The village of Kaukab—which was being interpreted the village of the Star—was reached, and passed; and now before them lay the city of Damascus in all its beauty. "The City of the Paradise of God," for so has it been called in every age, embowered in gardens of palm and roses, its walls and towers of snowy whiteness shining like "a handful of pearls in a goblet of emerald." A land of flowing streams, a city of cool fountains, set like a bit of heaven in the midst of a barren and thirsty land.

The exhausted wayfarers paused for a moment that they might feast their eyes upon the beauty of the scene, but Saul, with an imperative gesture, bade them hasten.

"We are not come to Damascus as one who journeyeth for his pleasure," he cried savagely; "we seek the blood of them that confess the accursed Jesus."

But even as he spoke the sacred name, some invisible power smote him to the earth; and a great light, brighter even than the fierce shining of the noonday sun, blazed round about him. In the midst of this terrible light he beheld a form upon which he gazed appalled; then was there the sound of a voice, and the words were these:

"Saul, Saul, why persecutest thou me?"

True to the utter fearlessness of his soul, the man also has a question to ask, "Who art thou, Lord?"

And the answer came clear and decisive, "I am Jesus whom thou persecutest; it is hard for thee to kick against the pricks."

Then indeed did the strong man tremble, and he made answer from out the depths of his soul, "Lord, what wilt thou have me to do?"

"Arise, and go into the city, and it shall be told thee what thou must do."

The majestic presence was gone; the light faded to the light of an earthly noontide. Yet Saul still lay upon his face in the the dust of the Damascus road. The men that journeyed with him stood speechless, staring at one another with livid faces. They had seen the blazing light, they had heard the strange and awful sound of a voice, but their eyes had been holden to the vision of the glorified Jesus.

Presently Saul arose from the earth, the first command of his newly-acknowleged Lord ringing in his ears, "Arise, go into the city." But when he opened his eyes that he might obey the words, he opened them upon darkness. He was blind.

And they led him by the hand and brought him into Damascus.

CHAPTER XXXVI.

THE AMULET.

T was high noon in the desert encampment. The shadows of the palms, which had boldly displayed themselves in the early cool of the morning, had gradually retreated before the triumphant progress of the sun, till now they lay a shrunken heap about the slender stems of the trees, which in their turn scarcely dared murmur to their children of the coming hours, when the burning tyrant overhead should again be brought low and the shadows reign triumphant. Through the shimmering air came the insistent voice of dropping water, telling over and over again of great depths of refreshing hid away in the secret places of the rock, safe from the thirsty ball of fire above, safe from the hungry sands which crept uneasily to and fro about the rocky margin of the fountain.

The camels crouched in the meagre shade, their large, heavy-lidded eyes half closed; they heard and understood both the faint murmur of the palms and the voice of the water; therefore were they silent, being satisfied. But from within the tent of goat's hair close at hand there came the sound of voices. "These men," grunted an old camel, "they be forever making a noise with their mouths; why cannot they be silent, and look and listen as do we?"

This is what the voices were saying:

"God is good, my husband, and as yet I have scarce had room in my soul for more than the sense of that goodness which hath snatched me from the jaws of death, and with life hath also restored to me the more precious treasure of thy love. Tell me how it chanced that thou hadst a hand in our rescue?"

"It is not unknown to thee, beloved, how that for many months my soul was a very hell of fear and remorse. I was blood-guilty; I knew that upon my head rested the blood of an innocent man; nay more, I knew in my inmost soul that my crime was yet more deadly—that I, even I, had condemned to an accursed death the very Son of God. Yes, I believed; but alas, it was even as the devils, who believe and tremble and yet—are devils still. I cast thee forth because thou didst also believe, I, black-hearted wretch that I was, did pronounce upon thee a curse, then my angel fled and the curse recoiled upon mine own head. I will not tell thee—I cannot—how I tried to strangle the ever-growing misery in my soul; how I flung myself, heart and strength, into the deadly persecutions against them that believed; all the while with the mean hope that the fire would drive thee back from the heavenly path which thou wast climbing into the black road down which I was plunging alone. I saw and gloried in the death of Stephen; I gloated over the agonies of them that suffered beneath the scourge; I outdid Saul of Tarsus in the work of denouncing men and women whose only crime it was to believe on God manifest in the flesh. There is a hell, for I have sojourned there.

"One day I was told that thou wast in prison; that on the morrow thou wouldst be scourged—stoned. Issachar himself told me, with an air of mock sympathy.

" 'She is less to me,' I declared to him coldly, 'than the stones beneath my feet.' But I lied when I said it. That night I begged Annas on my knees to have mercy.

" ' I will have mercy,' he said. 'I will send a message to the woman within the hour,' and he called Caleb. I waylaid the man, and offered him gold to show me the message; he showed it me.

"That night I went to my chamber resolved to die before the light of another day, but each time that I lifted the dagger to my breast something seemed to hold my hand. At last I flung it from me and sank upon my knees, crying aloud, 'God be merciful to me a sinner! God be merciful to me a sinner!' Again and again I repeated the words till at last there came into my soul a great peace. God was merciful—I knew, I felt it; and then and there I made confession of all my guilt before him. 'I am guilty of the blood of him whom thou didst send to save me,' I cried, 'yet he prayed in his last agony, saying, Father, forgive them, for they know not what they do.'

"I rose up forgiven, and the morning dawned. 'I will go,' I said, 'to the place where she is to suffer, and there before them all I will make confession of my guilt and my belief; then shall I die also.'

"But when I had come to the place outside the Damascus Gate—very early, for I could not wait—I fell in with the man Ben Hesed, and because my soul was full even to overflowing, I told him all. 'I will die,' I said, 'with them.'

" 'Nay,' he cried, 'rather must thou live, that thou mayest overlay the wickedness of the past with the pure gold of righteousness.'

"Thou knowest the rest, beloved."

Then the voices ceased for a space, and the sound of the falling water again filled the stillness.

That evening when the shadows were displaying themselves once more in triumph, and the voice of the fountain had sunken to a low murmur because of the more insistent voices of the women who were filling their jars at its cool brim, Ben Hesed held converse with them whom he had snatched from death.

Their talk was sweet and comforting, as of those whose feet had trod the margin of the river of death, from whose hither bank the traveler can hear faint echoes of the heavenly melodies of the redeemed, and where every breeze wafts the perfume of the blossoming tree of life.

"It is good to have been near death," said Mary of Nazareth, "because it is good to have touched the boundary of the life more abundant. There is no terror to them that believe on him that hath conquered death; 'he that believeth *hath* everlasting life.'"

Afterward, while the day merged slowly into the night, they told Ben Hesed of all that happened to them since he had left them in Jerusalem; of the last days of Stephen, of his death and burial; of that stern enemy, Saul of Tarsus, and his unrelenting hatred of them that believed.

"Nay," said Anat, after a pause, "I know that he would have rejoiced truly had we but confessed as he bade us; there was a look in his eyes that was not all hatred; perchance God is leading him into peace by some sure way of his own, even as he led the Egyptian, Amu. Surely, God's ways are unsearchable."

"That is a true word," said Ben Hesed musingly. "But tell me of the Egyptian, Amu."

So Anat told him how that he had rescued Stephen from death by the sacrifice of his life, together with all the story of their own wrong at his hands. "I would that God had given him one more breath," said the girl sighing, "for then would he have told us the name of our mother's kindred."

Ben Hesed looked at the clear profile of the girl as she sat looking away into the afterglow which still burned dully at the horizon, and a haunting memory of the past suddenly awakened in his breast. "Hast thou aught that belonged to thy mother, maiden?" he said, and there was a strange thrill in his voice.

"I had anklets of wrought silver when I came out of Egypt," said Anat slowly, without turning her head; "also a necklace of coins; but when I was healed of my blindness I made an offering of these baubles to the Lord's poor. It was all that I had to give." Then she was silent for a moment. "I kept but one piece from the necklace; I thought that I should like that one small bit of my mother's past. It is a strange coin."

"Show it to me," said Ben Hesed.

Without a word Anat took from off her neck the slender chain of wrought silver, from which hung the one token that bound her to an unknown past.

Ben Hesed took it, his iron fingers trembling like those of a woman. In that simple amulet lay a strange power, for no sooner had he examined it in the fading light, than all else before his bodily eyes vanished. It was a bright morning now, and the sun was shining merrily on a caravan of strangers out of Egypt. He was trading with them, horses and sheep and cheeses of goat's milk, receiving in exchange bales of cloth and divers weapons of war, together with utensils of wrought brass and jars of pottery.

"Give me also the horse," said the chief merchant, pointing to the animal which Ben Hesed himself bestrode. "I will give thee for it a bale of scarlet and another of fine linen for thy women."

"Women of the desert do not wear scarlet nor fine linen," he answered. "Dekar is the prince of all the herd; I will not sell."

"Nay then, I will give thee gold—fifty pieces," persisted the merchant.

"Give me a hundred," he had said, "and the beast is thine."

So the merchant gave him a hundred pieces of gold for the horse—which was truly a great price, but he paid it without murmuring for he knew that he could again sell for a greater to the king of Egypt.

Of the gold pieces there was one of strange device, and this Ben Hesed gave to his eldest-born, that she might hang it upon her necklace. The maid was beautiful to look upon, and Ben Hesed felt for her a great tenderness, which was a thing quite by itself and apart from the pride which filled his breast when he looked upon his mighty sons. The name of this maid was Zarah, which signifies the Dawn; and truly she was fair and pure as the first beams of the new day, ere yet mortals have sullied it with sin.

It came to pass—Ben Hesed saw it all once more because of the wonderful amulet which he held in his hand—that one day a stranger came to the encampment alone. He was sick and exhausted because of the hardness of his journey, and he begged of Ben Hesed that he might sojourn for a space with his tribe till he should recover himself. And Ben Hesed made him welcome, as was ever his custom, and the stranger tarried many days; the women also ministered unto him, for he was both comely and young.

And when he was recovered, he came to Ben Hesed and said to him, "Behold, I have received kindness at thy hand, and the springs of life are again strong within me.

Now, I pray thee, give thy servant further of thy bounty; for there is yet one thing that I would ask of thee."

And Ben Hesed said, "Speak, my son, for my hand is open to satisfy the utmost wish of him that is an honored guest within my borders."

Then the young man bowed himself and said, "If I have found favor in the sight of my lord, give to me thy daughter Zarah for my wife; for I love her with my soul."

Ben Hesed looked at the young man long and earnestly, and his heart went out to him.

"Tell me," he said, "all of thy past; for thou hast asked of me the most precious thing that I possess, the maiden who is called the Dawn. Speak freely, for as my soul liveth, if thou dost keep back aught that I should know, thou shalt die accursed!"

At this the young man groaned aloud; but he told him how that he had disputed with his brother over the inheritance, and had smitten him that he died—for so he believed at the time.

And when Ben Hesed heard all he rose up and his voice was cold and stern. "Go," he said, "that I see thy face no more. Thinkest thou that I will give my daughter to one that is a murderer? Go, lest I fall upon thee in wrath."

And he went straightway without a word, but he found the maiden, Zarah, beside the fountain, and he told her all that had passed. That night when all were sleeping, the two rose up and fled away from the encampment and were seen no more.

When Ben Hesed found that they were gone, he said only one word: "My daughter is dead." And from that time no one durst speak to him of the matter. But he did not forget, though long years were passed. And now as he held the coin of strange device once more in his hand, he knew it for the token which he had given the maiden,

Zarah, so long ago. And as he looked into the face of Anat, he saw that the Dawn was again risen.

Then he called the two, and he told them all the story, and when he had finished, he said, "Long ago hath the bitterness passed from my soul; but there hath remained ever an aching wound which the years have not healed. God hath given me many wonderful mercies, but none more wonderful than this, that the children of my daughter have returned to her father's house."

Then they fell on his neck and kissed him; and all that were in the encampment rejoiced, and the rejoicing continued many days.

Afterward, by the word of messengers which Ben Hesed sent to Jerusalem, they learned that the great persecution was at an end, because that Annas was now dead, and the others of his family were too much taken up with disputing over the inheritance of lands and houses, to trouble themselves further about the religious beliefs of any man. As for Saul of Tarsus, strange tales were told of him; some said that he was dead; others that he was blind; while others still declared that he had been rebuked of the Lord in a vision, and that he now believed. But this tale was not credited of many.

"Let us return to Jerusalem," said Mary of Nazareth, "for I would fain know whether my son John be safe; then there is also the house to be looked to."

So they went back to Jerusalem for a space. Ben Hesed and his grandchildren also.

But Anna and her husband went not all the way. "Jerusalem is hateful to me," said Caiaphas, "and, moreover, we should be in peril of our lives at the hand of our kindred. We will go away into Galilee, for I would fain behold all the places where the Lord lived and taught, and where also he passed his childhood."

So the two parted from the others after that they had passed the wilderness, and they traveled humbly as pilgrims; sojourning long in all the places where Jesus had been in his life-time; and this did they for many years, till that Caiaphas was grown to be an old man.

"I am not worthy," he said humbly, "to write of all that he taught and suffered, that should be writ by the hand of one that loved him while he yet lived; but I can gather up the tales that are told of his sinless childhood."

And so as they journeyed he made inquiry everywhere concerning the child Jesus; insomuch that after a time the children would point him out and whisper, "Yonder old man is the prophet of the Child Jesus."

And after many years he made a book of these tales. He took great pleasure and comfort in the work, and it occupied all the closing years of his life.

"One thing only do I regret," he said to his wife many times, "and that is that I did not begin this work while the mother of our Lord yet lived; for she could have told me whether it be truly set forth; but now I shall never know."

"Thou wilt know, beloved, afterward," said Anna, her eyes shining with a wise and tender light. "For it must needs be that angels watched with awe each moment of that earth-life; be sure that it is all writ in heaven."

~ The End. ~

Lamplighter Rare Collector's Series

The Basket of Flowers. CHRISTOPH VON SCHMID

First written in the late seventeen hundreds, this book is the first in the **Lamplighter Collector's Series** which gave birth to Lamplighter Publishing. Come to the garden with the godly gardener, James, and his lovely daughter, Mary, and you will see why Elisabeth Elliot and Dr. Tedd Tripp so highly recommend this rare treasure.

Titus: A Comrade of The Cross. F. M. KINGSLEY

In 1894, the publisher of this book gave a $1,000 reward to any person who could write a manuscript that would set a child's heart on fire for Jesus Christ. In six weeks, the demand was so great for this book that they printed 200,000 additional copies! You will fall in love with the Savior as you read this masterpiece.

A Peep Behind The Scenes. O. F. WALTON

Behind most lives, there are masks that hide our hurts and fears. As you read, or more likely cry, through this delicate work, you will understand why there is so much joy in the presence of angels when one repents. Once you read it, you will know why two-and-a-half-million copies were printed in the 1800s.

Jessica's First Prayer. H. STRETTON

What does a coffee maker have in common with a barefoot little girl? You will want to read this classic over and over again to your children as they gain new insights into compassion and mercy as never before.

Stepping Heavenward. ELIZABETH PRENTISS

Recommended by Elisabeth Elliot, Kay Arthur, and Joni Eareckson Tada, this book is for women who are seeking an intimate walk with Christ. This book will reach deeply into your heart and soul with fresh spiritual insights and honest answers to questions that most women and even men would love to have settled.

Joel: A Boy of Galilee. ANNIE FELLOWS JOHNSTON

If you read *Titus: A Comrade of the Cross* and loved it, let me introduce you to Joel. This is a story about a handicapped boy who has to make a decision to follow the healer of Nazareth or the traditions of the day. You will talk about this treasure for years.

Christie's Old Organ. O.F. WALTON

This is a child's story for all ages. Join a little boy named Christie and an old organ grinder as they search for the path that leads to heaven. This dramatic story has already led children to the saving knowledge of Jesus Christ. Be prepared to cry.

Jessica's Mother. H. STRETTON AND M. HAMBY
(sequel to Jessica's First Prayer)
Rewritten by Mark Hamby, this sequel will take you through the emotions of the greatest of all sacrifices. Embittered against God and anyone who bears the name of Christ, Jessica's mother is determined to take her daughter back regardless of the consequences. This is a story of human tragedy and divine love that will inspire families to take a second look at the real meaning of the gospel of Jesus Christ.

The Inheritance. CHRISTOPH VON SCHMID
This is another classic by the author of *The Basket of Flowers*. Seeking first the Kingdom of God and His righteousness will be a theme that parents and children will see through the eyes of a faithful grandson and his blind grandfather.

The Lamplighter. MARIA S. CUMMINS
Written in the 1800's when lamplighters lit the street lights of the village, this story will take you on a spiritual journey depicting godly character that will inspire and attract you to live your life with a higher level of integrity and excellence. Mystery, suspense, and plenty of appealing examples of integrity and honor will grip the heart of anyone who reads this masterpiece.

The Hedge of Thorns. ANONYMOUS
Based on a true story about a little boy who will do almost anything to find out what is on the other side of a hedge of thorns. Enticed and frustrated, a child is about to learn why boundaries are a necessary part of God's plan for his life.

The White Dove. CHRISTOPH VON SCHMID
This is another classic by the author of *The Basket of Flowers* that will once again lay a beautiful pattern of godliness for all to follow. Surrounded by knights and nobles, thieves and robbers, this story will take parent and child to the precipice of honor, nobility, sacrifice, and the meaning of true friendship. If you enjoyed *The Basket of Flowers*, you will not want to miss *The White Dove*.

Mary Jones and Her Bible. ANONYMOUS
Another true story of a little girl whose strongest desire in life is to possess her very own Bible. Through hard work, determination, prayer, faith, and even a twenty-five mile walk, Mary Jones will do whatever it takes to obtain a copy of the Word of God. This true story will not only kindle a fire in children's hearts but give them a role model to follow that exemplifies hard work, faithfulness, and the reward of patient obedience.

Mothers of Famous Men. ARCHER WALLACE

Take a step back in time and visit with the great mothers of great men. Join Mrs. Washington, Mrs. Wesley, Mrs. Franklin, Mrs. Adams, Mrs. Lincoln, Mrs. Carnegie and many others and see what type of motherhood shaped such unusual greatness. You will enter their homes as well as their hearts, as you learn for the first time, portions of history rarely revealed. This is a book every parent and young person needs to read.

Clean Your Boots, Sir? ANONYMOUS

Finally, a book for boys that I would say equals *The Basket of Flowers*! In this captivating story you will meet a brave little boy who cares for his ailing father and two baby brothers. As a shoeshine boy, the little savings that he makes each day is just enough to meet their basic needs until a small act of honesty changes his life forever. Join the shoeshine boy as he introduces your children to integrity, honesty, faith, and sacrifice, in a way that they will never forget!

Melody, The Story of A Child. LAURA E. RICHARDS

An inspiring and beautifully written story that invites the reader to see life through the eyes of a most unusual child. Each chapter is filled with charming freshness as a blind child weaves her gift of "seeing" into the hearts of friend and foe alike. .

The Lost Ruby. CHRISTOPH VON SCHMID

Another classic that will teach children the important lesson of honesty regardless of the cost. Also included is one of Von Schmid's finest short stories, **The Lost Child**. This is a story of mystery and intrigue as the reader learns that God allows hardships for our good.

The Little Lamb. CHRISTOPH VON SCHMID

This story will teach our readers that all things do work together for good to them who love God. Parents and children will be filled with captivating suspense as they taste and see that the Lord is the God of the impossible.

True Stories of Great Americans for Young Americans.

Written for young readers, this edition of American history will inspire and reveal the character qualities and difficult circumstances that led these Americans to greatness. The seldom heard stories of George Washington, Robert E. Lee, Patrick Henry and many more will inspire and challenge young readers to value the past and guard the present as they themselves become agents of change for the future.

Boys of Grit Vol. 1 & 2. ARCHER WALLACE

Children and adults will be inspired when they read about boys who overcame great misfortunes, trials, and overwhelming circumstances to become great and godly men. When so many others saw only difficulties, they saw possibilities.

The Three Weavers. ANNIE FELLOWS JOHNSTON

Fathers and daughters will take a journey back to Camelot and learn the unforgettable lessons of virtue and vice.

The Stolen Child. CHRISTOPH VON SCHMID

Another Von Schmid classic that captures the beauty of God's creation as seen through the eyes of a child who lived in darkness most of his childhood. Lessons of responsibility and forgiveness are among the many virtues taught in this classic.

Always in His Keeping. ANONYMOUS

Based on a true story during the time of John Wesley, a brother and sister who are stolen as infants struggle to find their true identity and the faith to rest in a God who sometimes allows the righteous to suffer.

Rosa of Linden Castle. CHRISTOPH VON SCHMID

In this unique Von Schmid classic, a daughter's love for her condemned father will inspire children of all ages to see that though it was meant for evil, God always intends it for good.

The Pillar of Fire. J.H. Ingraham

This is the most eloquently written, filled with the most illustrative accounts of the Prince of Tyre during his visit to Egypt over 3500 years ago. The author brings full color and inspiration to every page, while weaving his most suspenseful dramas in connection with the Scriptures. Truly, a fresh breath of literary air.

Teddy's Button. AMY LEFEUVRE

Here's a story that will warm your heart, make you laugh, and above all, will help children to understand the spiritual battle that rages in their souls. Join Teddy as he demonstrates that even a child can enlist in God's army and carry the banner of love and victory high.

Christie, the King's Servant. O.F. WALTON

In the sequel to Christies Old Organ, we find Christie pastoring a small parish in New England, where a forgotten acquaintance steps back into his life. Here in this quaint village where fisherman take to their boats for a living, there is intense drama each time the clouds and winds begin to blow.

Stick to the Raft. Mrs. George Gladstone
This is a story that children will never forget. Young and old will enjoy taking a journey with a poor young boy who is honored for his hard work and honesty. However, when misfortune entered his life, he became the target for mischief among jealous peers. In dramatic style, the lesson that there is no fear in love will be forever etched on the heart and soul of all who read this classic.

Probable Sons. Amy LeFeuvre
Etched into the heart issues of unforgiveness and reconciliation, Probable Sons is a delightful book that will keep you smiling throughout. In a world of broken relationships, our little heroine Milly will help us tear away the layers of stubbornness and pride to provide a path that can help restore the injured from the most hurtful pain of the past. May the truths found in this little story find a resting place in many hearts that have strayed so far from home.

The Wide, Wide World. Susan Warner
The first book by an American author to sell one million copies, *The Wide, Wide World* is an endearing novel about a little girl who faces unrelenting affliction, only to be reminded of the One who has charge over her. On a blustery winter day, this is the book to reach for!

Shipwrecked, But Not Lost. Hon. Mrs. Dundas
Impulsive, impatient young boys find themselves reaping the dreadful consequences of following foolish counsel. But there *is* a God of mercy who wants to spare his children from shipwreck!

Tom Gillies. Mrs. George Gladstone
Tom Gillies and Dick Potter secretly meet at their favorite cave to plot the mischievous schemes which have given them so bad a name. The townspeople complain that the island is too small to hold such troublesome boys. Tom is sent away to work, where he learns that his bad habits have fastened strong chains around him, and sin has tied binding knots, making him a prisoner. He discovers the One who can untie those dreadful knots and free him to live a productive life among the people of Norton Island.

The White Knights. W.E. Cule
It all started that lonely night in the chapel. Those few dreadful moments when he not only *heard* the silence, he could *feel* it. That night Horace passed the test—his life as a knight had begun. The motto of The White Knights, following that of King Arthur, *"To ride abroad redressing human wrongs,"* was a high order to fill. Little did they know what different shapes that would take, and what adventures and challenges lie ahead. But none of that mattered, for they all agreed, *"The spirit's the thing!"*

Amy and Her Brothers. ANONYMOUS
In every world-worn man there is a human heart that craves a God to trust, a Christ to lean upon—an unsatisfied heart. In *Amy and Her Brothers* the heartache and innocent faith of an orphan child paints a real-life picture of the hidden suffering all around us, challenging us to be more attentive to the hurts of those nearby.

Sir Knight of the Splendid Way. W.E. CULE
Sir Knight of the Splendid Way is a captivating allegory—a rich literary masterpiece that will encourage any weary traveler. This beautifully-bound work depicts life as a journey, reaching toward a beacon of hope in the City of the Great King. In the midst of conflict, *Sir Knight* will inspire you to press on.

The Stranger At Home VARIOUS AUTHORS
The Stranger at Home, along with its accompanying stories, *The Coveted Bonnet* and *The Cords of Sin* might seem a little "hard-edged," but it is, without a doubt, provocative. The folly of permissive parenting, and the inevitable consequences of obstinacy, disobedience, lying, and vanity are brought forth with "not-so-subtle" clarity.

Me and Nobbles. AMY LEFEUVRE
An enchanting story about imaginative Master Bobby and his beloved "friend," Nobbles. With great expectation, Bobby daily awaits his absent father's return, knowing he hasn't been forgotten. In the meantime, Bobby strives to find the secret to obtaining his very own clean white robe so that he can enter the golden gates that lead to the splendid golden city.

The Wrestler of Philippi. FANNIE NEWBERRY
Here is a story of Rome's staggering contrasts—extreme poverty amidst the wildest extravagance; treacherous dungeon life in darkness and chains amidst the splendors and amusements of luxurious court life. This dramatic unfolding of *The Wrestler of Philippi* will grip your heart as you experience the true test of loyalty and the triumph of faith!

The Boy Who Never Lost A Chance. ANNETTE LYSTER
Roger Read has learned from his grandfather never to miss a "chance." His hard work, honesty, and diligence are richly rewarded. But having become self-absorbed in his own pursuits, Roger finally realizes something is missing in his life, and he can't seem to find it—until his true friend Jack Sparling helps him to see the best "chance" of all! If you want to inspire your children with an entrepreneurial spirit, balanced with service for God, this is a must-read!

The Bird's Nest. CHRISTOPH VON SCHMID
Strength of character lies in the determination to hold on to truth regardless of circumstances or consequences. The hero in this story proves to us that every seemingly insignificant deed is noticed by God.

Buried in the Snow. FRANZ HOFFMAN
You will be blessed by the gentle wisdom of an old grandfather and the unconditional love of his grandson as they come face to face with one of the most difficult decisions of their lives. From the depths of despair to the pinnacle of blessing, this dramatic encounter will surely elicit a full spectrum of emotional responses.

A Puzzling Pair. AMY LEFEUVRE
Inseparable twins, Guy and Berry are bursting with creativity and spunk. They are on a mission...to fill Guy's very big picture of the second coming of Jesus with all the people who are ready to meet Him! But his picture must be true, and time is running out! This rather unique approach to evangelism is as pure, bold, and simple as it gets!

The Hidden Hand E.D.E.N. SOUTHWORTH
Reader BEWARE—this is NOT your typical Rare Collector book! Strewn with mystery and suspense that never lets up, *The Hidden Hand* will keep you on the edge of your seat! There are not too many books that cause me to laugh aloud (even when I'm alone!) Truly laughter is like medicine, giving health to the bones! But please don't let the feisty, mischievous character of 17-year-old Capitola and the cantankerous personality of Old Hurricane derail you from seeing the gracious providence of an all-wise God. (For ages 16 and up.)

Little Sir Galahad. LILLIAN HOLMES
Since the "sad thing" happened, young David spends his days sitting beside the window, watching the children and working people of Alverton pass by. But he is so rich in sunny smiles and imaginative play that they have no reason to call him "Poor David." Young David's greatest desire is to become strong again, but he learns that real strength comes in fighting his own temper and choosing to do what is right, especially when it is so difficult! Because of his pure heart, inner strength, and noble deeds, he is donned "Sir Galahad," an honorable title for one "whose strength is as the strength of ten because his heart is pure."

The Cross Triumphant. FLORENCE KINGSLEY

This extraordinary sequel to Titus and Stephen will take the reader on an unforgettable journey seventeen years after the crucifixion. Rich in biblical history, Mrs. Kingsley is able to weave several dramatic themes that climax at the devastating destruction of Jerusalem. Eleven hundred thousand persons are said to have perished during the siege, while nearly a hundred thousand were made prisoners. It was in the midst of this deep tribulation that Mrs. Kingsley births hope during one of the most tragic events in history. If you enjoyed Titus, you will not want to miss this classic!

Winter's Folly. O.F. WALTON

Winter's Folly is a tender story of lonely Old Man Winter, who demonstrates the epitome of selfless love. In the meantime, young Myrtle is determined to bring comfort and cheer to this misunderstood, desolate old man. This true-to-life story reminds us once again that when life seems to hold more than we can bear, we can rest assured that we have a loving God who is orchestrating events for our good.

The House of Love. ELIZABETH CHENEY

Aurelia Wilde is cruelly selfish and downright miserable—a victim of her mother's desperate attempts to place her delicate, "prized possession" on an unreachable pedestal. But her glory is only surface deep. Aurelia's ungrateful, complaining spirit is a stark contrast to that of her servant-girl, Doris. She knows that God is Love, and the "house of the Lord" must be the House of Love. Her many talents and her cheerful disposition cause her to be loved and appreciated, even by the notable residents of Waverly Manor. How jealousy swells within Aurelia's vengeful mother! She'll get even yet...

Tales of the Kingdom. MAINS

Back in print by popular demand, this allegorical children's classic will take you on a journey to the enchanted city as you relive the wonderful experiences of God's great deliverance. I would place this treasure on an equal with *Chronicles of Narnia and Pilgrim's Progress.*

Fireside Readings Vol. 2. VARIOUS AUTHORS

In our day of situation ethics and relativism, it is refreshing to read a story like *Annie, the Flower Girl* who, in spite of the fact that she'd be helping her poor grandmother, decides to do the right thing, simply because it is right to do right! In this second volume, the consequences of covetousness, jealousy, and disobedience ring loud and clear, while the rewards of honesty, obedience and contentment bring forth a sense of inner satisfaction.

LAMPLIGHTER
Publishing
MAKING READY A PEOPLE PREPARED FOR THE LORD

P.O. Box 777
Waverly, PA 18471
1-888-A-Gospel

e-mail: lamplighter@agospel.com
www.lamplighterpublishing.com

Making ready a people prepared for the Lord.
Luke 1:17